A Book of
Angels

Also by Sophy Burnham

The Art of Intuition

The Art Crowd

The Landed Gentry

The President's Angel

Revelations

For Writers Only

The Ecstatic Journey: Walking the Mystical Path in Everyday Life

The Treasure of Montségur

The Path of Prayer

PLAYS

Penelope: The Odyssey Retold

Snowstorms

Prometheus: A New Conclusion

WORKS FOR CHILDREN

Buccaneer

The Dogwalker

The Witch's Tale

Beauty & the Beast

The Emperor's Nightingale

AUDIOTAPES

Piercing the Veil

When You're Hurting and in Need

A Book of
Angels

REFLECTIONS ON ANGELS
PAST AND PRESENT,
AND TRUE STORIES OF
HOW THEY TOUCH
OUR LIVES

· · · ·

Sophy Burnham

Jeremy P. Tarcher/Penguin
member of Penguin Group (USA) Inc.
New York

JEREMY P. TARCHER/PENGUIN
Published by the Penguin Group
Penguin Group (USA) Inc., 375 Hudson Street, New York, New York 10014, USA ·
Penguin Group (Canada), 90 Eglinton Avenue East, Suite 700, Toronto, Ontario, M4P 2Y3 Canada
(a division of Pearson Penguin Canada Inc.) · Penguin Books Ltd, 80 Strand, London
WC2R 0RL, England · Penguin Ireland, 25 St Stephen's Green, Dublin 2, Ireland (a division of
Penguin Books Ltd) · Penguin Group (Australia), 250 Camberwell Road, Camberwell,
Victoria 3124, Australia (a division of Pearson Australia Group Pty Ltd) · Penguin Books India Pvt Ltd,
11 Community Centre, Panchsheel Park, New Delhi–110 017, India · Penguin Group (NZ),
67 Apollo Drive, Rosedale, North Shore 0632, New Zealand (a division of Pearson New
Zealand Ltd) · Penguin Books (South Africa) (Pty) Ltd, 24 Sturdee Avenue, Rosebank,
Johannesburg 2196, South Africa

Penguin Books Ltd, Registered Offices: 80 Strand, London WC2R 0RL, England

Originally published in 1990 by Ballantine Books
Copyright © 1990, 2004 by Sophy Burnham

Most Tarcher/Penguin books are available at special quantity discounts for bulk purchases for
sales promotions, premiums, fund-raising, and educational needs. Special books or book
excerpts also can be created to fit specific needs. For details, write Penguin Group (USA) Inc.
Special Markets, 375 Hudson Street, New York, NY 10014.

Library of Congress Cataloging-in-Publication Data

Burnham, Sophy.
A book of angels : reflections on angels past and present, and true stories of how they touch our lives / Sophy Burnham.
p.   cm.
ISBN 978-1-58542-877-9
1. Angels.   I. Title.
BL477.B87   2011   2010051797
202'.15—dc22

Printed in the United States of America
1   3   5   7   9   10   8   6   4   2

Book design by BTD NYC

IN MEMORY OF
Jane Vonnegut Yarmolinsky

Contents

PREFACE TO THE 2011 EDITION   XI

PREFACE TO THE 1990 EDITION   XV

ACKNOWLEDGMENTS   XIX

INTRODUCTION   XXI

• PART I •
Angels & Ghosts I Have Known

Chapter 1 Angels & Ghosts I Have Known   3

Chapter 2 Angels Unawares   27

Chapter 3 Turn a Stone/Start a Wing   52

• PART II •
Angelology, or the Knowledge of Angels

Chapter 4 The Sons of God   83

Chapter 5 A Thunder Like Drumming   113

Chapter 6 The Battle of Heaven & Princes of Hell   135

Chapter 7 The Angelic Doctors   162

• PART III •

Images & Dreams

Chapter 8 Wings of Silence   199

Chapter 9 My Black Angel & Other Friendly Spirits   231

• PART IV •

Letters on Angels   257

Preface
to the 2011 Edition

*T*wenty years ago, when *A Book of Angels* was first published in the United States, no one had any idea what a sensation it would create. Even today I marvel at its effect, as people bought ten and twelve copies and gave them to friends, who in turn bought ten and twelve copies to give to theirs. A friend of mine saw copies in a Hong Kong bookstore, and the book has sold in something like twenty-four languages, including Croatian, Finnish, Polish, Latvian, Japanese, Russian, Korean, and most recently Chinese. *Chinese?* It leaves me humbled.

Now I have the privilege of speaking and giving workshops all over the United States and in many countries abroad. And all because of this one book. I have seen the book influence people and reshape their image of the world; and to participate in that with my workshops and talks, offering hope and strength, is no small thing when the media bombard us daily with hysterical reports of disasters everywhere.

Many compliments have been given to *A Book of Angels*. I remember two in particular. The first came from a priest, who told his congregation in a sermon that everyone should have two books beside their bed: the Bible and *A Book of Angels*. The second came from a stranger who informed me that her mother while dying held this book in her hands.

It is therefore with deep appreciation and gratitude that I mark this new edition of *A Book of Angels*. May it act as a blessing to its readers. May it serve as a catalyst for your own stories of inexplicable coincidences and intervention, those moments when a dream or voice, a serendipitous confluence of actions, or perhaps the simple nudge of intuition, shows that Something Out There is watching over us.

How do we know the angels are real and not the product of an overwrought imagination? This is the huge question. I can only tell you that all the events described in the book you hold in your hand are true. They happened either to me or to someone so close that I know they weren't lying. I have no explanation for them. Often I'm left baffled—disbelieving in the face of evidence. But when you hear of some inexplicable event—invisible hands, an external voice; when you see the face of a man light up as he recounts the improbable series of coincidences that saved his life, or that of his child; when you feel yourself uplifted and inspired by the Divine, mantled in light, warmth, safety, joy, your heart bows down before a reality that cannot be explained.

Many years have passed since I wrote this book, and I have written others since—novels, plays, nonfiction—on a range of subjects. None has had the effect of *A Book of Angels*. I'm amused (and a little disconcerted) at being called "the Angel Lady," not certain if it's a designation I quite know how to handle. But this I tell you. We humans are also expressions of the Divine. We are formed of the spark of Divinity. We have within us the Kingdom of God. Divinity. Angel-dust. Whatever you wish to call it. And when our spiritual eyes open, and we see from the center of our being, with the innocence of our inner hearts, we reach that spacious arena in which for rare and dramatic moments an angel may appear in all its own glory, radiant, supernal illumined momentarily to our mortal eyes.

And what of all the horrible moments when no angel comes to save a life? Or help in crisis, or ease you loneliness? Oh, darling! That's the sorrow, isn't it? Unspeakable things happen in this life. But we are not promised that nothing bad will happen in our lives. We're promised that when it does, we're not alone. I hope this book moves you. I hope it reminds you of those times when you have felt the brush of an angel's wing, your heart lifting even in difficult times, your soul surprised by joy. And (purely selfishly) if you have a story you would like to share, I welcome it. I'd love to hear it. Please contact me at www.sophyburnham.com.

> I dedicate these pages to you
> and to the angels that surround you
>
> always with love,
>
> Sophy Burnham

Preface
to the 1990 Edition

*T*his book began as a kind of personal history, written for myself and for my friends, because it occurred to me around the age of forty-three that many curious and mysterious things had happened that could not be passed off anymore or explained away as logical. I just wanted to set them down, all in one place, where I could look at them, turn them like stones in my hands, and see what truth they made.

Because the fact is this: I did not grow up believing in the paranormal, and by the time I reached midlife, I felt confused. How could I ignore the fact that my own life had been saved in a miraculous fashion? Or that strange coincidences and meetings seemed constantly to occur?

This book began, then, as a series of stories strung like pearls on a necklace—stories of things that had either happened to me personally or to friends so close that I could attest to their sanity. Each encounter is true.

The book has grown now, and changed, as I have, and includes encounters with angels from all over the world. Some of these encounters involve famous people, prophets, and seers, but most happen to ordinary people. Right now. Today. As I heard these stories and became more immersed in my research, I wanted to know more. Are angels real? What do they look like? Why is it that every culture seems to have myths of angels, believes in guardian spirits that take care of us, sometimes even by interfering with the physical laws of the universe? Do angels have feet? Have sex? Are those of one culture the same as those in another? To whom do the angels appear, and why do children seem to see them more than anyone else?

Therefore, woven into the text is what you might call "grounding" information about angels, which places belief in angels in a historical context, and recounts the angel visitations of various cultures. Implicit throughout are the more fundamental questions that this whole book raises: Who am I? Why am I here? Is there life after death? And are there really forces that dive, invisible, into our petty affairs?

Each question leads to another, for if I answer yes to any one, then I must also ask: What is my responsibility to myself, to you, to God?

I cannot answer any of them. I can only record what I have seen. I offer this book in joy, in hope, in gratitude for what I've been shown and what I want to share. I offer it as a hymn of praise—to living life alive. And I offer it as a prayer of thanks, that we need not be afraid to die: that we do not die! This I have learned. This much I have seen with my own eyes. I know it, and if even one person's anguish and fear of dying can be relieved by reading these true tales, then this book will have done what it's supposed to do.

If not, then this: Strange things happen in this world. I don't pretend to understand them, but I put them down in case other people have had such experiences and want to know they're not alone.

．　．　．

William Blake saw angels in the trees. He was merely a ten-year-old boy who one day looked up and saw angels and afterward could not stop drawing them and writing his ecstatic poetry in homage of them . . . Jacob wrestled with an angel . . . And an angel came to Abraham . . . and Joseph Smith founded the Mormon Church after a meeting with the angel Moroni . . . And today a little child will see an angel, or an angel will unexpectedly swoop in to save an adult's life, as happened once with me.

It seems extraordinary: I cannot forget it. Once an angel saved my life. I saw him the way you see the words on this page: the colors, the magnificent leap of my heart on seeing him—*Home!* cried my soul as he scooped me out of the path of death. But I'm not sure he was more miraculous than the Jamaican charlady who entered my mother's hospital room at exactly the right moment to bring me an insight a few days before my mother died. We are told that angels appear as voices, dreams, signs, visions. They carry messages. The mystery is why they appear at all, much less in one form or another, changing their spots with such engaging charm.

Of course, some people insist that angels don't exist, never having seen one. And other people ask why they appear only to certain humans, though others still say that angels come to

Miracles do not happen in contradiction to nature, but only in contradiction to that which is known to us of nature.

—SAINT AUGUSTINE

•　•　•　•

everyone. The question to ask is: Who will recognize them when they come?

> Be not afraid to have
> strangers in your house,
> for some thereby have
> entertained angels unawares.
> —HEB. 13:2

Acknowledgments

This book is the product of many people, and attention must be paid: first to my dear friend Jane Vonnegut, now dead, in whose barn on Cape Cod much of it was written and whose luminous enthusiasm carried me over its initial conception; to Elinor Fuchs and Tom Kelly, who read it in its early stages; to Anne van Rennslaeur, who picked it up when I had dropped it in discouragement and made me play with it again; to my agent Anne Edelstein, whose infectious delight found it a publisher; to my editors Stephanie von Hirschberg and Elizabeth Rapoport, whose grace and sensitivity to the work is evident on every page; to Alain Cornec, Elizabeth Puccini, Elizabeth Miller, and Marie Monique Steckel, and to countless others who passed me encouragement or an illustration, a fragment of verse or a dim historical nugget, or who narrated so humbly their own encounters with the divine. Many of these stories I have been unable to use in this book, but those people know what they have seen and the fact that their tales were not included in no way diminishes their truth.

To all who helped this book, then, I give my thanks.

Introduction

*F*ifteen years have passed since *A Book of Angels* first came out, and I am not the same as when I wrote it.

I read it now and am impressed: there's little I would change. The difference lies in my higher certainty—not an advantage necessarily. Because once you think you've found the truth, that's when the real danger begins. Carl Jung was once asked in an interview by the BBC: "Do you believe in God, Dr. Jung?"

"I don't believe. I know," he answered. The next morning he saw himself misquoted in the *Times* of London, which had left out that all-important period: "I don't believe I know." It's wise to keep in mind the distinction between opinion and knowledge, to remember how little we know.

Here is what I know: that we live in a spiritual medium, like fish in water, and most of the time we aren't thinking about it, aren't aware—*Awake!*, in the Buddha's words. But somewhere at the shadow of consciousness, we remember, and I think that's why we love angels and love to hear about angels; because we love to be loved, and we love to love; and even to think about angels is to remember moments of un-fathomable love.

There are hindrances. We live in stressful times. Every generation lives in stressful times, but ours allows little time for solitude, silence, reflection. Our days are jammed with Things to Do—and if we forget, then others are always ready to remind us how much must be done and *now!* Bills to be paid in fifteen days (when the mail may take twenty) lest you're hit with interest charges, children and animals to feed, furnaces breaking, pipes bursting, electricity gone, the computer down—so that we run panting for breath just to stay, like Alice on her chessboard, in the same place. (This doesn't even take into account the real disasters of mudslides, earthquakes, tornadoes, and twisters that kill thousands and leave a wake of devastation.)

How can we expect to see the angels around us or feel the swell and humming movement of the universe, when we leave ourselves no empty time? It takes purposeful practice, a discipline, to build into my days those periods of silence and solitude.

These days I see angels easily. I see auras. I engage as a Reiki master in giving healing touch to those in pain. I give psychic or intuitive readings. No big deal. As a seer, I can hold an object belonging to someone, go into a slightly altered state, and know a lot about that person's past and present and, to some degree, the choices they face in the future.

But it's taken a while for me to accept these gifts as normal—or as coming from God instead of being delusions of my imagination or, worse, the distortions of a hungry ego looking for grandiosity. It's a journey of stumbling, doubt, despair, sometimes anguish, when the laws of God and nations conflict (as they will), or as you outgrow the social and cultural conditioning that no longer serves to help history.

. . .

When *A Book of Angels* came out years ago, it took everyone by surprise. Suddenly total strangers were phoning and writing me, wanting to tell their stories. I would come home after being out of the house for an hour to find twenty-seven phone messages, all from strangers, needing to talk to me. The mail came in stacks (this was before e-mail). It was sudden and disturbing, and in just a couple of weeks I went from the life of a quiet mole, scribbling by myself (and apparently to myself, given my narrow readership), to that of a public figure.

The publishers, too, were caught off guard. Not thinking the book terribly important, they had ordered a modest printing of five thousand copies, and now they found people buying ten and twelve copies to give to their friends, who in turn would buy ten and twelve copies to give to theirs. What was going on? The bookstores faced another difficulty: where to shelve the book? It was like no other. Some catalogued it under Philosophy and some under Religion and others under New Age or Self-Help—because they didn't have (as they would a year later) an entire section devoted to Angels.

As for me, I staggered into therapy, stunned by my new role and the projections people laid on me. There I discovered that success always carries within it the pain of loss—loss of tranquility, equilibrium, identity, self-image. In the years since then, I've accepted my role as teacher, public speaker, spiritual guide, the Angel Lady, and "expert." But at first it was confusing. I didn't know what had happened or how to deal with it.

Certainly this publicity had nothing to do with me. Great books die and ghastly ones leap to the bestseller lists in quite arbitrary ways. Success belongs to God, to the angels, as happened in this case. Look, for example, at how it developed.

One day early on, a reporter called me from *The Washington Post.* He wanted to interview me about angels. We sat at my kitchen table, he and his girlfriend, and talked for something like two hours. When I asked how he had heard of the book, he said his girlfriend had given it to him, and that he had been so interested that he'd persuaded his editor to do a piece on this local Washington author. The editor reluctantly allotted him six inches—two or three paragraphs at most.

When the article came out, however, with photos, it covered the top half-page of the Style section and another full page inside. After that other papers fell on the story: the *Los Angeles Times,* the *Chicago Tribune, The Wall Street Journal.* Then the magazines: *Newsweek, Time, People* magazine, *McCall's,* the *Ladies Home Journal,* not to mention radio and TV shows. An acrostic in *The New York Times* gave a quotation from the book. Mind you, the publishing house had not budgeted any publicity. All of this just came, by the grace of The Holy Spirit.

Gradually I learned to give a talk, to teach a weekend workshop. Today my papers are kept at Georgetown University, and every now and again I pause to marvel: goodness gracious! I have "papers" that someone wants to keep. I'm pleased about this, don't get me wrong—just bemused. How did it happen?

Then too, as others have jumped on the bandwagon, waving their angel books, or hustling bric-a-brac, selling angel mugs and T-shirts and angel dolls, I find myself both amused and annoyed at the trivialization of these magnificent and majestic beings. I'm ashamed sometimes, humiliated by our crass commercialization—the greedy exploitation of the sacred. Then I shrug and smile, and remind myself that each person approaches God from the place where she or he is right at that moment; that it's okay; angels are big enough to take our capitalism, and these items are the expression of our love for them.

I said above that I no longer question the angels in our lives. I've written other spiritual books now, and having admitted my embarrassment at commercialization, I'll shamelessly ask you to read or look at them, because each one delves deeper into the mysteries or takes up other questions of the Divine: *The Ecstatic Journey* is about what happens when you have a spiritual or mystical experience, and what happens to you afterwards; *The Path of Prayer* is about prayer and how best to pray, and what actually happens (scientifically) when you send out an intention, for prayer is a powerful tool, the gift by which we pull down spiritual power—call angels to our aid. In addition, I've written eight plays and three novels in my attempt to touch the full gamut of human experience. They all have a spiritual bent, exploring the dark side and this contradiction of who we are and what we are called to be. I've gone back to the church of my childhood. I serve as a spiritual director or guide to people searching for deeper meaning in their lives.

But mostly I'm different because I feel that an angel—Christ—a sacred Presence moves beside me now (does it sound boastful? schizophrenic?); and all the time I am seeing with two sets of eyes, the physical and the spiritual, simultaneously. Seeing auras, seeing angels, foreseeing, processeeing. And yet—don't get me wrong—I doubt. I get afraid, anxious, depressed, troubled, lost. I too wander in the darkness; that's part of being human.

Extraordinary things have come to me, and I still *forget!* I forget all the time, overcome by doubt or fear. The function of the mind after all is to analyze, criticize, examine, compare, doubt, test, experiment; in other words, to use our God-given faculties of intellect. But angel sightings come from the interior silent spaces, the dreams of poets, those meanderings of wonder, acceptance, release. So we vacillate between the two poles: intellect and imagination.

Are angels the product of our imagination, then? The answer is yes, and also no. When you hear of a woman pulled by invisible hands out of a burning car, you know there is something out there helping us; and yet imagination plays its part. In the play *St. Joan,* by George Bernard Shaw, a nobleman sneers at the voices of the maid. "They're your imagination," he insists, to which Joan answers yes! That's how the messages of God come to us, she says: in joy, in memory, in longing, in sorrow, and in our imaginations.

So what about the angels?

*A*ngels are messengers of God. The very word *angel* means messenger, and they come in the form in which they can be received: as dreams, accidents, coincidence, intuition—that tap on the shoulder that says "go there" and "don't go there." We've all had that. We've all said, "I *knew* I should have taken that road, and I didn't *listen!*" They come in books that we read or as animals (especially dogs, it seems) or as humans. Someone will come up to you and say exactly the words you need to hear at that moment, or you will act as an angel for someone, being spoken through. You may not even know that you were acting as an angel, but sometimes the hairs on your arm will lift or you'll get goose bumps or you'll feel enveloped in warmth and light. I know a woman who asked a spiritual teacher an important question—important to her, since she had a difficult decision to make. As the teacher answered, the woman felt the two of them enclosed in a globe of silence; all noise of traffic and the crowd around them ceased. She was aware only of the teacher's voice, her eyes turned to her, and the answer delivered in a furry silence that broke into her heart.

Afterwards, she turned excitedly to her friend. "Did you hear what she said?" she asked, only to receive the reply, "No. I was standing right beside you, but I couldn't hear a word."

Ah, but sometimes—rarely—the angels come in their own form: radiant, luminous, and beautiful beyond words. They may have wings—or not (because surely they don't need wings for locomotion, moving quick as thought). They may be male or female, old or young, adult or child, brown haired or blond. However they are seen, they bring comfort, joy. They are formed of light, and some people report this as being golden while others as purest white; still others see them clad in a myriad of colors, pinks or blue and green. One woman reported that she saw an angel robed in purple with stars showering off its shoulders and glittering down its back.

At one large conference in Boston, a courtly and handsome African American stood up and asked me a question so important that his voice shook.

"Why do you never hear of black angels?" he asked. "Why are they always white?"

At the time I didn't answer well, and his concern has sat on my heart.

I said that angels can take any form, including of black or brown-skinned humans, and I referred him to one account found in *Angel Letters,* of a young man who during the Depression was forced to live a hobo life, riding the rails. He had jumped onto a moving train and was hanging halfway out of the baggage car, about to fall and slide under the wheels, when a black man, a tramp like himself, pulled him into the empty box car. The man collapsed in exhaustion. It took a moment for him to catch his breath, and when he looked up, safe now in the swiftly moving train, to thank the hobo, no one else was in the car. . . . "My guardian angel," he wrote, "is a black man."

It wasn't a bad answer, but I wish I'd said this: that angels appear when in their own form as white because they are pure spirit—as the human soul is likewise white, no matter the color of the person's skin.

Angels have feet. This is of interest only because ghosts or spirits don't. I don't talk much in this book about ghosts. Enough to say I've never met an evil ghost. The ones I've seen are loving ones, attached to this earthly plane by concerns or love for those still left behind. They come back to tell us they're okay, or because of an attachment here on earth; and having less shape-shifting abilities than angels, they form a wispy, white ectoplasm visible to the human eye, but it's hard to do and they don't bother going down below the knees.

Sometimes they don't even appear in their own form, but, like angels, they come in dreams or signs. One guest at a party not long ago was telling of his mother's death.

"Did she come back?" I asked, to his surprise. He said no, that he had had no "communication" from her . . . except that a few nights earlier he'd dreamt about her, a dream so real it startled him, and she was smiling and telling him how happy she was. "Does that count?" he asked in sudden confusion, not having considered the possibility before. Yes, that counts.

Water holds special meaning to ghosts, and often they will use that medium to send a message. The daughter of a dear friend died in a horrible accident—or possibly murder or suicide—by falling off a balcony. Afterwards the broom in my friend's dust closet kept filling up with water. Good house-keeper that she was, she always stood the broom on its handle to protect the straw, but for months whenever she took out the broom, a cup or two of water would pour out on the floor, always accompanied by the image of her daughter in her mind, and since there were no pipes in the broom closet and no way that water could fill up the broom, she took it as a message from the girl. There are other water tales, but it's of angels we're speaking now.

I write in this book of the three marks of an angel, but let me repeat them here. First, they always say the same things. They always say, "Don't be afraid. Fear not. Leave everything to us." They never say, "Look at the mess you've made of things now!" They never scold or criticize. I'll come back to this in a moment.

Second, you are filled with joy. With warmth, light, a sense of safety. Of *home.* Or *Mother*—the mother of your heart. Indeed, so many people report this feeling and always in the same words that it's worth noting.

Third, you may not believe it happened—that an angel came to you—but you cannot forget it. And here's another curious thing. The memory not only does not fade but it gets stronger with the passage of time, and this is unlike normal memory, or dreams, which fade with time. But when an angel comes you don't forget it. The memory does not fade.

. . .

Once, years ago, I was in New Mexico and feeling despondent, depressed, discouraged, full of doubt and unknown yearnings, I prayed, "Oh, help me, God." It did no good. I had an urgent feeling there was someplace I was supposed to be, something I was supposed to be doing. I didn't know what. Restlessly I paced my room and finally went out to the car.

"Where do you want me to go?" I asked the Unknown silently. Listening. At the time I was not so certain about angels as I am now, but I was willing to wait and listen for a nudge. The tap of intuition.

I began to drive, pausing at each corner for direction. The car wound up in the mountains, on unfamiliar dirt roads, climbing finally onto a lumber road that turned into a rutted track almost too rough to pass; and then I made a sharp left and the car dipped down onto a grassy meadow beside a stream. It was lovely. Marveling, I got out and began to walk, my feet following upstream, and I climbed over fallen trees and branches, until, to my surprise, I came out onto a green grove, a circle of thick rich grass.

How beautiful.

I lay down on the grass in the warm sunlight, eyes closed, thinking of nothing, when suddenly my heart burst wide with joy! The feeling was so intense that I opened my eyes, and there in the sky immediately overhead hung an angel formed by a thin white cloud, and it was lying on top of me, looking down at me—head, wings, arms, body. Was that why my heart had cracked with joy? I could hear the birds calling to one another—songs I hadn't noticed before; they were trilling hymns of praise and flashing yellow, blue, green like jewels, flitting and flying in the trees. I thought of them as gemstones scooped out of the earth by God and tossed into the air to fly. The trees themselves were waving their tiny paws in joy; and at that moment the beauty was so intense, I could taste it. Overwhelmed, I shut my eyes. A few minutes later when I opened them again, the angel-cloud was gone; the sky displayed a flawless, cloudless blue. The birds had returned to being birds, but I had been given a message of joy and hope beyond my dreams, and I have never been able to forget that moment when the veil was pierced and with spiritual eyes I could see the world as it really is.

That angel came as a cloud, but it was no less real for that. Driving back home I remembered that I had prayed for help.

Do you think I remember that moment when I go into a trough? Not a chance. I have to be reminded, and therein lies the strength of this and other books that repeat our tales and reinforce our hope and love, reminding us of the love of God, whether in the birth of a baby or the mysterious dog that barked to save a child.

Sometimes the angels come merely with a sign. More than one person has written me of hearing a choir of angels, the most beautiful music. Did they make it up? Others told of praying the novena to St. Theresa, nine days of prayers, and how the eighth day always brings a rose. Someone will send a notecard with a rose design, or gift candy shaped like a rose, or else a real rose will be dropped at your door. It always happens before the last day, and the more sincere the prayer, the more definite the sign will be. Still others wrote of the special scent that accompanies the answer to their longing.

I said that sometimes we are used by angels to deliver a message. In addition, spiritual beings also walk the earth with us. Rarely are we allowed to see them. They enter our lives, perform a deed, and are never seen again. The flat-tire angels are like that. I have an entire file of flat-tire angels, who form the quintessential angel story. Here is how it goes.

A woman is driving along when she has a flat tire. These interventions seem only to occur to women, and she may or may not necessarily be in trouble. Maybe she can call AAA or maybe there's a gas station only a mile up the road. But sometimes she's elderly or out in a wilderness far from help. Suddenly a car pulls up and one or more young men get out. If it is just one man, he doesn't speak but sets to work quickly and efficiently changing the tire. If it is more than one, they may talk to each other but in tones so low that the woman can't catch any of their words. They are dressed in something light colored, a T-shirt or a yellow blazer, and usually there's something quirky and typical about their dress such as a baseball cap turned backwards. If there is oil on the road they may lie down in it, but when they get up they aren't dirty.

In one story the young man turned to the woman at a certain moment and murmured, "You'd better step back. The jack may fall." She took two steps back, and sure enough the jack fell. If they speak, their voices are gentle and soft.

When the tire is changed the young man or men accept no money. They get in their car and drive off, turn the corner and disappear. Or if the road is flat and straight, the woman may glance away for a fraction of a second and when she turns back . . . the car's not there! It's vanished. Quick-change artists.

Here is a story witnessed by four people not long ago in West Virginia.

*I*t was winter. Nan, her husband, his brother, and his brother's wife were at their second home, an old family place built in the 1800s. It was 10:30 at night and it had begun to snow. This town of Moorefield is a tiny place, population 3,000, and their house sits on the main street. The snow was so deep and the hour so late that the town was totally deserted. No cars, no tracks, no people moving. They were all four sweeping the sidewalk "to get ahead of the snow," when suddenly a man appeared carrying a sack on his back and walking toward them from the right-hand side of the house. They said hello and he answered hello back to them.

"Where did you come from?" they asked, but he evaded the question.

"Well, I'm not from around here."

They thought it strange, his just appearing: "How did you get here?" they asked, trying to engage him in conversation, but again he didn't answer.

"I just arrived."

"Well, where are you going?" They wanted to know, since he was just walking in the snow through the dark town.

"I don't know," he said, and walked on past them and off to their left. The four then kept on sweeping, and when they looked up next, he'd "literally gone." They were astonished. Where had he disappeared? They put down their brooms and followed his footprints, which came to a dead stop in the middle of the snow. The trail of footprints simply ended.

What are we to make of such reports?

Is it any more impossible than the numerous accidents that are prevented by a voice, an apparition, an angel?

One night last summer, my friend Marie-Monique Steckle, the most pragmatic of women, was visiting a friend in Italy. After dinner she walked into the black night around the back of her friend's house to her car, crossing the unlit grass, when she was suddenly stopped cold by a pressure on her chest so strong it thrust her backwards . . . and then discovered that had she taken one more step forward, she would have pitched down the cement hole of a cellar stairwell. She phoned me from abroad to tell the frightening tale. "It was my guardian angel!" she exclaimed horrified, astonished, glad. "It saved me."

I've heard similar stories. One is of a woman about to cross F Street in Washington, D.C., just near Old Ebbitt's Grill, who felt a hand push her chest so hard that she was forced back onto the sidewalk. At that very moment a car careened around the corner. It would have hit her.

But *Why?*, we ask. Why do angels come at some moments and not at others? Why to some people and not to others? To children more than to adults, to women more than to men? We have to ask, because people are killed every day falling down the stairs, or burning up in buildings, or being hit by cars, and no angelic interventions save their lives. Are there ways to attract the aid of angels? Or was it simply their time to go?

I don't know the answers. But I think I know what draws these beings to us. It's love. It's as simple as that. It's our need. It's our longing and prayer. Earlier I spoke of what the angels say, and how they never scold or criticize. They can't. Angels know only words of love, forgiveness, joy, and praise of God (Himself eternal, immutable, limitless). And just as they are able to express only feelings of love, so they are also attracted by love. In fact, they adore being adored! Try an experiment. Ask for something simple, and when you get it, give thanks and think, *It can't get any better than this!* and I swear the Universe will turn itself inside out—turn somersaults—to bring you something more!)

Here are other things that attract: innocence, wonder, purity of intent, praise, trust, delight. And prayer.

Do you want to know more about your angel?

Then ask.

It's as simple as that. Ask for what you want, no matter how small and inconsequential it may be—a lost glove or necklace. Ask to see an angel. And if you ask for something complex, then ask also to understand the answer when it comes.

What attracts them? Love, trust, faith, delight, and praise.

What pushes them away? Anger, violence, rage, revenge, and all the dark emotions of self-righteous hatred that we hold. I think they are like seagulls that are swept away by storm winds, and the rage of humankind can repel them just at the time when we most need their help. An angel can change all the physical laws of the universe, but it cannot interfere with our free will.

One last story. I've told this in another book but it bears repeating. One day I was talking with my angels, and I asked a particular question. The answer came back, "Pray."

I thought about that for a moment. "Why should I pray?" I then asked. "You already know what I want. What's the point of praying?"

The answer was seen all at once the way one views a painting, and then it divided into three separate parts.

The first was: "So that we will know what you want, in order that we may bring you what you need."

The second was: "Because when you pray—and you may be on your knees for fifteen minutes, but for only fifteen seconds of that time will you actually give in, surrender—for that instant you create a window through which we can fly to bring you the desire of your heart."

The third reason I could never have made up in my wildest imaginings: "Because your prayers give us the energy to do our work [of serving you]."

Until then, I had not realized that we are in a relationship with angels, with the spiritual dimension. We need them to help us with our work, but they need the energy of our thoughts, intentions, and prayers in order to bring us aid.

Therefore we are called to pray with all our hearts and minds and souls and strength, and to look upon all things as coming from God. We are called upon to love ourselves so as to open to the love of angels; and to love one another as we love ourselves, to open our hearts to love and accept that the Universe is on our side.

This brings us to the final question. Over and over we hear the angel story followed by the recipient's humble, questioning: *Why me?* Well, *Why not you?* Angels come to everyone; we all have guardian spirits protecting us—even the pathological killer on death row does. Why *not* you? Eventually, another question lifts its taunting head: *So what?* Or, *Now what?*

What does it mean that an angel came? What am I to do with that information? How do I respond? What now? In a way we're asking, *What's the meaning of life?* Possibly in the end all our questions are reduced to a single one: What happens to us after we die? Do we live on—or, more to the point—do *I? The whole, real me? With all my personality?*

I know people who don't believe in God for one simple reason. "How could God," they ask, "allow such horrors on this earth? *Ergo,*" they logically conclude, "there is no God." To them I say the same thing I say to those who do believe: good. Then go out now and act as God, the loving One. Repair the injustice. Love one another. Heal the sick and feed the poor.

And to those of us who have seen angels and commune with them, the same conclusion applies. What are we called to do, but be like angels on this earth? To comfort the grieving, laugh with the joyful, alleviate suffering, act like God. Oddly enough it means to love even the irritating neighbor, even the person who looks or dresses differently or comes from a different country or speaks a different language or who holds a different political opinion or worships (God help us) a different God in weird, wild ways and offensive practices. That's it. To treasure this little earth that is so loved by the angels. To act as if we care. For we are loved and adored and we are called to act ourselves as angels unawares.

Sophy Burnham

A Book of
Angels

PART I

Angels & Ghosts
I Have Known

· · · ·

CHAPTER 1

Angels & Ghosts I Have Known

· 1 ·

Once my mother saw an angel. She was five years old at the time, just a little girl in her nightie, getting ready for bed, when she looked up and saw an angel standing in the bedroom door.

"Auntie!" She pointed at the figure. "Look!" But her beloved auntie could not see.

"Go to sleep, child," she said. "There's nothing there."

I don't know what her angel looked like. When I asked her, my mother's face took on a dreamy and exalted look, simultaneously nostalgic and alight. She used words like *brilliance* or *radiance,* and I have the impression of many colors. But I have no idea what she saw.

The angel vanished. The grown-ups—her mother and father and aunts—explained that she was overtired and excited, that the vision was a figment of her imagination, and as the years passed, she doubted if she had really seen it. Hallucination or reality, though, she did not forget it.

My father, on the other hand, saw nothing, and it was in his intellectual spirit that we grew up. A lawyer, brilliant, warm, witty, intellectual, he loved to argue and debate. He liked to laugh and match his mind against others—and win!—in legal contests, chess, cocktail-party conversation. If he couldn't stand up in court (Supreme Court being his favorite), he'd exercise his skills on his family, us—his children. At dinner he would throw out a point of discussion like a bone on the table, then watch us leap like dogs to worry it, snarling and snapping joyfully. He'd make us defend our views against his assaults, and when he had us cornered, he'd say, "Switch sides." At which we raced to defend the very point we had shot down before. He was teaching us to think.

But he had no truck with the mysterious.

Once I asked my father if he believed in God. He put down his papers, removed his glasses, uncrossed his legs, and considered his answer:

"I have no reason to believe in God," he said. "I have never seen anything to convince me there is a God. *On the other hand,*" he continued, voice lifting in his legal lilt, "I've noticed throughout my life that all of the most brilliant minds of every generation believe in God—Tolstoy, Einstein, Marcus Aurelius—and who am I to say there's not? So I tend to go along with Pascal that if there's a God, I'm better off paying my dues, and if there isn't one, I haven't lost anything. You should hedge your bets."

I tell this to show that my environment did not encourage psychic experiences or the weird meanderings of a mind deranged. We were pragmatic.

Of course, if the conversation at the dining room table suddenly came to a halt for ten or twenty seconds, my mother or an aunt might say, "There's an angel passing through the room." For an instant we children would consider what an angel might look like and why we would all grow still at its approach. "There's an angel passing through the room," a grown-up would say; the silence would fracture like glass into laughter and the conversations pick up again, bright and sharp as wind.

So that was our childhood—my sister, brother, and myself romping with our dogs and clambering on the chicken-house roof when our mother wouldn't see, or jumping off the garage rafters; we climbed trees and swung green as apples in our Eden. We rode to school in a car pool, sat dully in overheated classes, stupefied by the hissing radiators and bored by the monotony of the teacher's voice. We learned the proper rules. We fought with friends, made up, sulked or laughed in perfectly normal, thoughtless, childhood life. The only thing that made us different perhaps was the isolation of living in the country during World War II. We listened to the radio, talked to one another, read.

We read constantly. We read the classics and were ridiculed

—Our doubts are traitors,
and make us lose the good we oft
might win,
by fearing to attempt.
*—*W ILLIAM S HAKESPEARE
Measure for Measure, I. iv

• • • •

for not having finished all of Shakespeare before the age of twelve, as our Aunt Kate had, or for not having opened Herodotus. I went away to boarding school, continued on to college, graduated, and got a job as a typist (which is what a woman did in those days when she graduated with honors from a major college). I married. I had children. I worked.

Then, when I was thirty, I saw a ghost.

—Who knows but life be that which men call death, And death what men call life?
—EURIPEDES
Phrixus, 830

• • • •

We had just moved to New York City. David, my husband, had taken a job with *The New York Times.* We rented a beautiful duplex apartment in Brooklyn, just across the river from Manhattan. It had high ceilings, an eat-in kitchen with a window overlooking a grassy garden. Upstairs, in a walnut-paneled bedroom, a bay window gave onto the Statue of Liberty. It was lovely! In addition to the master bedroom, we had a second bedroom, almost as large, for the two little girls, then aged three and about eight months. Anyone who knows the cramped boxes of most New York City apartments will appreciate our luck.

A week after moving there, David had to go out of town on assignment. He was gone for several days. One night I was in the little dressing room just off our bedroom, which I had taken over for my own, fitted out with my books and desk. I sat at the sewing machine that night, working on a dress for my three-year-old (the softest cocoa color, with a square neck and ribbon bindings—adorable). It was about ten o'clock at night. I was content and unafraid, concentrating entirely on this Lilliputian dress, when suddenly I had that shadowed sense one gets—there's someone in the room with me!

I looked up and saw in the doorway a man. I use the word *saw.* But I didn't see him the way I see with my eyes the usual material world; rather, I saw him with some inner knowledge, for he was there and also not there. I knew three things about him: that he was an older man, that he was troubled or concerned, and that he was "good." He would not hurt me. As those thoughts came, I turned back to the machine. I put my face in my hands, I remember, my elbows resting on the sewing machine. "Now I've gone bananas," I thought. "I'm flipping out. I've been alone too much." My eyes filled with tears (which is my physical response to any emotional strain). All the time I knew he was standing at the door and then that he was moving into the room. I was shaking with fear. I went so hot, my forehead broke out in beads of sweat.

He came right up behind me. I didn't look around. I could feel him there. I hated it.

Then he put one hand on my shoulder. I knew he meant to comfort me, but all I felt were the four fingers of his right hand on the front of my shoulder and his thumb at the back. His hand was freezing cold. It stung my skin like dry ice. I was burning hot except where his cold hand touched. Horrible. Then he left the room, walking like a normal man.

Flooded with relief, I sat shaking at the sewing machine— until suddenly it occurred to me that he had gone to see the children! I leaped out after him, through the bedroom and out into the hall. There I stopped. I couldn't go another step.

—There are four corners on my bed,
There are four angels at my head,
Matthew, Mark, Luke, and John,
Bless the bed I sleep on.

        —A CHILD'S PRAYER

• • • •

I danced from foot to foot. He was in their bedroom, and I knew it, but I could not go in. Why not? I turned back to my own bedroom. I was wringing my hands and pacing the floor. I didn't know what to do.

I have a blank in my memory at this point. I don't know how long he remained with them. Minutes? Seconds? Suddenly he materialized on the window seat of this beautiful bedroom. I say *materialized* as if I spoke about ghosts all the time. One moment he was in the babies' room and the next I was aware of him sitting on the window seat, watching me, still troubled. I could feel his questioning.

At this point I decided to take control. I spoke to him out loud.

"Now, listen. I don't know who you are," I said, "but we have just moved to this apartment, and I want you to know that it is mine. I love it. I intend to stay here for a long time. And you are welcome to live here with us, but if you do, I expect you to do no damage either to it or to us. This is a beautiful place. I will not tolerate its being hurt. Moreover if you decide to stay here with us, then you are to help me with the children. You are to guard and protect them and see no harm comes to them. And if you do this, you are welcome to stay."

He did not speak.

When I finished, he stood up, moved past me across the bedroom, out the door into the little upstairs hall. He went down the stairs, floating, myself following, through the kitchen, and out the closed back door.

I was shaken.

Why had he not simply vanished? Why had he walked down the stairs and out the closed, locked door?

And then, who was he? And what did this visit mean? As fascinating as the apparition, however, was the fact that as soon as he disappeared so did my anxiety. I returned to my sewing, calm and quite myself, my concentration back to normal. I think this upset me as much as anything. Here I was, running seams on my little girl's dress to the comfortable purring of the machine. As if I hadn't just seen a ghost.

And what did it mean that he'd left? Apparently he had been satisfied with my dictum. Or else decided living with me would be too much work.

The telephone rang. It was my landlady, Mrs. Rosenthal, an elderly woman, the former Mrs. Glass. I answered with surprise, because it was now after ten-thirty at night, much too late to call; and she was of the generation that knew these niceties.

"I'm sorry to telephone so late," she began. "I couldn't stop thinking about you in the apartment, and about my first husband . . ." Then she told me about her husband, Dr. Glass, who had kept his offices on the street level of the brownstone and built the two apartments above. He had adored this house. The man who paneled the Yale Club had put in the magnificent paneling in the bedroom. Dr. Glass had died in that bedroom. But his favorite little room, she said, was the tiny dressing room off the main bedroom—the one that I had taken over. It was his personal dressing room and study. She went on and on, apologizing, not knowing why she wanted me to know all this.

Annunciation (detail).
Leonardo da Vinci.
15th century.

I didn't tell her that I had just met her husband, but I had no doubt that Dr. Glass, having come to the house to meet us, had made her call to tell me who he was.

The next day David returned home. I told him what had happened. He is the most sensible of men. He said, "If anyone else had told me that, I wouldn't believe them, but if you say you saw a ghost, you did." This, though he believed in no ghosts or preternatural phenomena, spirits, or other dimensions beyond. It was part of what I loved him for—his trust.

We never saw the ghost again, but it pleased me to think he was there, protecting the children. I wondered what had happened to the other tenants, the ones before us. I knew that three or four families had moved in and just as quickly out. None had stayed longer than eight months. Had he removed them? Found them jobs in other states? Or broken their marriages to make them move away? However, he was good to us, for we stayed seven happy years in that apartment, and it was one of my private jokes with myself that he might have had a hand in that. After all, we'd never lived so long before in just one place. I liked it.

Was I mad? Actually the thought never crossed my mind. The man had appeared to me as plain as the palm of my hand. The fact that he had come and gone away, so that his presence could not be proved, was of no more significance than the fact that a sunset on a particular evening appears in brilliant reds while on another it's obscured by clouds.

—Millions of spiritual creatures walk the earth unseen, both when we wake and when we sleep.
—JOHN MILTON
Paradise Lost, IV

• • • •

I had seen a spirit. The fact interested me, but I was busy raising my children and working, and I didn't have time or maybe interest to give much thought to the implications—the fact of death and the metamorphosis of matter. After all, I had managed successfully to deny the angel a year or two before; how much easier the ghost of a stranger in the house?

• 2 •

*T*here's a problem in telling this story. Do I tell it as it happened, or disguise it so that it appears to unfold in a dramatic line, as if moving toward some final, dazzling revelation? Real life is messier than fiction, and things don't fall consecutively into place. Instead we live surrounded by all things. Like fish in water, we swim through the material and immaterial worlds, matter and thought; sometimes we perceive one movement, sometimes another, and sometimes it is only much later, after having passed through further currents and after having new experiences wash across our gills, that we can go back in memory to understand the meaning of an earlier moment. The only time sense we have, our chronology, lies in our ability to receive, and that is partly a matter of our openness. Which is to say, our trust.

Strange things have happened to me. But events did not flow toward a single momentous revelation, one blooming pyrotechnic end—Enlightenment!—with chrysanthemum fireworks bursting in the night. No, it was a great jumble of facts, instead, with ghosts on top of angels, and dreams and serendipitous coincidences, intertwining with the normal everyday. So covert was it all, indeed, that you'd think the other world was playing hide-and-seek, throwing up screens lest it be seen. Even the firework revelations were followed by the weary, dirty crowd straggling toward home, by worn-out parents dragging along their two-year-olds, picking up diapers and bickering about who left the thermos at the picnic site. There's always something more to attract our attention. That's how generous life is.

—It is said, and it is true, that just before we are born a cavern angel puts his finger to our lips and says, "Hush, don't tell what you know." This is why we are born with a cleft on our upper lips and remembering nothing of where we came from.
—RODERICK MACLEISH
Prince Ombra

• • • •

*T*hree times after she died, my mother came back. She was trying to tell me what it was like after death: We'd made a pact that she would try.

I want to talk of angels, but let me tell this quickly, because it applies. Her last visit was the most dramatic. I was lying in the pretty little canopy bed in "my" room, my childhood room, the room—the very bed—she had died in. It was ten or eleven at night. I was reading. The light was on. Outside the window (and in the country the night is very black) I could hear the ceaseless wind-washed murmuring of the trees.

Suddenly my mother was standing in the doorway. I looked up, saw her, and—

I burst into tears.

How can I live without my mother? I thought.

It was not her presence in the doorway that upset me, or that she had come to fulfill her pledge and tell me about The Other Side. It was that she stood there smiling at me with such unbearable love. She stood there, a phantom, without any of the barriers that had always separated us: barriers of culture and of our different memories, barriers of anger and judgmentalness or any of the petty hurts that we had inflicted on one another. This was the pure essence of my mother, distilled, and looking at me with such love I thought my heart would break.

How can I live without my mother? I thought. She took a step backward in concern: she hadn't meant to hurt me. In that moment I understood we are given physical bodies for a purpose, and we live in them like lobsters in the sea, struggling all our lives to reach outside our shells, to touch something else even for some fraction of a second and transcend our isolation. Making love, at the height of the act, will sometimes achieve this, and certain moments listening to music, and sometimes we can get outside ourselves when lost in artistic work or gazing at a mountain landscape or standing mesmerized by a waterfall. But for most of our lives we are straining to leap across our shells, and we cannot. On this material plane, I suddenly understood, we are not *supposed* to meet so totally: we are not strong enough to take such undiluted love.

Concerned, apologetic, she faded away. I have not seen her since—*not* in her own form—though now, years later, I think it would be fun to try. This time maybe I'd remember to ask about death and life. But I believe that possibly we are not supposed to know that either. We are put here with blinkers on our eyes, to play a game of blindman's bluff with God for reasons we do not understand, and I suppose it would ruin the game if we cheated and knew the reward.

We'd never be afraid.

We'd know there's always more.

We'd want to sling ourselves into the sea of love
    that's God,
        that we glimpse on the Other Side.

And this may also be why angel visits are so rare.

*A*t some point the matter of ghosts becomes incidental. The presence is either known or not known, and once known what does it prove except that life continues after death? Which is something that each of us must determine for ourself. To be told there's an afterlife gives no comfort to the person who does not believe, though religions have preached the fact for millennia. But once experienced, the question is not *whether* the spirit lives on, but in what form and why, and what it means in relation to God.

Or even, what is God?

Is there God? And if so, what is God doing there, the Atman, the Source, the Universal Force? What the hell's God doing, and what is our place in the scheme?

The question can be asked in a thousand other ways: Who am I? And why is there suffering and pain? If God is just and loving, then how come there's evil in the world? Am I (by chance) worshipping a capricious deity? Or worse, a figment of my own imagination—which is to say, no deity at all?

—Keep watch, dear Lord, with those who work, or watch, or weep this night, and give your angels charge over those who sleep. Tend the sick, Lord Christ; give rest to the weary, bless the dying, soothe the suffering, pity the afflicted, shield the joyous and all for your love's sake.

—The Book of
Common Prayer

• • • •

—*Thirty percent of the Americans who do not believe in afterlife say they have been in contact with the dead.*

—*American Health Magazine*
January/February 1987

• • • •

I go on at length about ghosts, because ghosts and angels are confused. The question we're asking is whether angels are really the spirits of the dead come back. It has taken me years to come to terms merely with the idea of their reality—there's something there!—much less be able to answer such questions. But let's dispose of it up front.

Ghosts are the spirits of the dead, but angels are messengers of the divine. Like angels, ghosts can come as a thought, nudging our minds, or as a *sense* of their presence, or perhaps as disembodied voices or balls of light, and sometimes invisibly as pranks. But when they materialize, they always take their own form. And this is different, as you'll see, from angels.

It is true that sometimes ghosts bring messages of love, and sometimes leave their loved ones with a patina of calm. But a ghost is not an angel. Ghosts are attached by their longing and troubled memories to this physical plane; or else they are lost shadows, unable to reach the other side. Ghosts are found in every culture, and all people agree on how they look. You can see through them, or else they appear as a milky, misty substance with rippling edges. They have no feet. Since they retain their own personalities, they are as dear or as wicked as they were in life. Some disturb because they are themselves disturbed or troubled. They come in on the channels of mediums, or they stand behind chairs in ancient houses, or they drift weeping and disconsolate through rooms, drawing plangent music in their wake. Or they play jokes, as if to show us dull, blind humans that they still exist. Some forces are truly evil, bordering on the demonic; they can possess you. They do great wrongs. But usually ghosts or spirits are our loved ones returning in concern or to tell us everything's all right.

When a spirit enters a room, you feel a chill, as if a door's been left ajar, and when it touches you or when its body passes through you, you feel an arctic cold. All these signs mark the characteristics of a ghost.

But angels are different, and no one who has seen an angel ever mistakes it for a ghost. Angels are remarkable for their warmth and light, and all who see them speak in awe of their iridescent and refulgent light, of brilliant colors, or else of the unbearable whiteness of their being. You are flooded with laughter, happiness.

And angels come to work, although I have three stories of angels who were seen simply standing around, chatting to one another quietly. Angels give aid, or bring messages of hope, but what they do *not* do is wander, earthbound, like the lonely spirits who are dead. Angels leave you with a calm serenity, and the people to whom they have come know, even when they could not see the figure itself, that they've been brushed by wings of silence, as Milton called them, invisible veiled wings.

George Washington is said to have seen an angel at Valley Forge. Johnny Cash was twice visited by an angel, once when he was twelve and again as a grown man, each time to warn him of a coming death. And I have the story of a college professor who saw and heard a group of female angels, and another story of six Russian cosmonauts—atheists, after all, in their communist state—who twice sighted a band of angels up in space with wings as big as jumbo jets!

I read it in the papers. The story comes, we are told, in a secret report smuggled out of Russia by a defecting scientist in early 1985. Who knows if it's true?

It was the 155th day aboard the orbiting Soyuz 7 space station; and we can imagine the weightless isolation of that party—day after day—enough to make anyone hallucinate. Three cosmonauts, Vladimir Solevev, Oleg Atkov, and Leonid Kizim, were performing medical experiments when suddenly they were blinded by a brilliant orange glow. Once their eyes adjusted to the light, they saw "seven giant figures in the form of humans, but with wings and mistlike halos as in the classic depiction of angels. They appeared to be hundreds of feet tall with a wingspan as great as a jetliner." Their faces were round, with cherubic smiles, and they were all identical. The band of angels followed the space capsule for about ten minutes and then vanished. But twelve days later all seven angels returned, and this time three more scientists saw them as well.

"We were truly overwhelmed," said Svetlana Savistskaya, the woman in the group. "There was a great orange light and through it we could see the figures of seven angels. They were smiling as though they shared a glorious secret."

—May I burst into jubilant praise to assenting angels.
—RAINER MARIA RILKE
Duino Elegies, 10

• • • •

• 3 •

Angels carry messages. The very word in Greek αγγελος means "messenger," and the Oxford Universal Dictionary gives this straight-faced definition of an angel: "A ministering spirit or divine messenger; one of an order of spiritual beings superior to man in power and intelligence, who are the attendants and messengers of the Deity."

Winged spirits—angels—are part of the mystery of every culture. I have a carving of a Balinese angel, looking like a winged mermaid. The Vikings called them *valkyries.* The Greeks called them *horae.* In Persia they were *fereshta,* and sometimes they were confused with *peri* or *horis,* which are sexless (yes) female celestial beings who give sensual delight to the inhabitants of Paradise; or with the Hindu *apsaras,* the beautiful fairies of heaven who dispense sensual and erotic bliss to the gods, though later (especially Christian) teachings insist that angels are without carnal lust, as some people think humans should be too. Still, in those early Indo-European myths, angels could have children, which sprouted like cabbages on their laps, already five years old at birth.

There are angels in Zoroastrianism, in Buddhism, in Taoism. There were angels in ancient Assyrian and Mesopotamian thought, and the belief in angels carried down through Manichaean, Judaic, Christian, and Islamic lore, all seeding one another's faiths. Shamanistic practices have their own intercourse with winged beings, though often they come in the form of eagles or ravens or spirits that we don't associate with angels.

It was Dionysius the Pseudo-Aeropagite who, writing in the sixth century about angels, influenced all later Catholic thought. He named the nine orders of angels, and though others tried as well, his remained the predominant hierarchy right into the eighteenth century—after which angelology fell out of favor, overtaken by the Age of Reason, or Enlightenment as it was called, a word claimed also by those on the spiritual path. But Dante, Milton, and Goethe each had their visions, as did Emanuel Swedenborg, the great eighteenth-century chemist and mystic, and the German philosophic genius, Rudolf Steiner, if you want to come right up to the twentieth century.

At the throne of God, the angels have no form at all, but come as pure, raw energy, great sweeping balls of fire, like supernovas, circling, whirling, wheeling in black space. They are called Wheels or Thrones and they cannot even be depicted except symbolically, although mystics who have seen and

Wheels or Thrones.

heard their stupendous silence know what they have seen and are humbled by that power.

Look: we know nothing about angels. We do not know what angels are or whether they stand in hierarchies in the skies. Nor whether they are assigned their duties according to seniority. We know nothing of this other realm, except that we are given brief, fleeting glimpses in our hearts. We hear its singing in lost memories. We see it at the edge of our eye, but so ephemerally that when we turn to face it, it's already gone. We feel it in our loneliness, the hollow hole at the heart that we try to fill with physical pleasures or danger or drugs or alcohol or war or work or love or friends or sex. It is the existential longing for surcease that makes us believe that something other must exist; for if we remembered nothing, if we had no sense of having once been filled, would we now recognize our present emptiness?

*S*ome angels have names, such as Michael or Gabriel. We know this only by the reports of those who saw them, or of various saints and mystics and prophets, people like the prophet Muhammad, to whom the angel Gabriel came, or more recently like Padre Pio, the stigmata-marked monk who died in southern Italy in 1968 and who, in the course of his contemplative life, battled devils and was washed by angels in his cell. He was recently named a saint.

But most angels come anonymously, as happened to

—Who if I cried out, would hear me among the angels' hierarchies? and even if one of them pressed me suddenly against his heart: I would be consumed in that overwhelming existence.

—RAINER MARIA RILKE
Duino Elegies, 1

• • • •

S. Ralph Harlow and his wife one day in Massachusetts. He taught at Smith College in Northampton from 1923 to 1953, and his story has been reprinted in several little magazines, including *Guideposts* and *Spiritual Frontiers Fellowship*. His story is unusual in that *two* people witnessed the angels when they came.

THE DAY WE SAW THE ANGELS

It was not Christmas, it was not even wintertime, when the event occurred that for me threw sudden new light on the ancient angel tale. It was a glorious spring morning and we were walking, my wife and I, through the newly budded birches and maples near Ballardvale, Massachusetts.

Now I realize that this, like any account of personal experience, is only as valid as the good sense and honesty of the person relating it. What can I say about myself? That I am a scholar who shuns guesswork and admires scientific investigation? That I have a B.A. from Harvard, an M.A. from Columbia, a Ph.D. from Hartford Theological Seminary? That I have never been subject to hallucinations? That attorneys have solicited my testimony, and I have testified in the courts, regarded by judge and jury as a faithful, reliable witness? All this is true and yet I doubt that any amount of such credentials can influence the belief or disbelief of another.

In the long run, each of us must sift what comes to us from others through his own life experience, his view of the universe, his understanding. And so I will simply tell my story.

The little path on which Marion and I walked that morning was spongy to our steps and we held hands with the sheer delight of life as we strolled near a lovely brook. It was May, and because it was the examination reading period for students at Smith College where I was a professor, we were able to get away for a few days to visit Marion's parents.

We frequently took walks in the country, and we especially loved the spring after a hard New England winter, for it is then that the fields and the woods are radiant and calm yet show new life bursting from the earth. This day we were especially happy and peaceful; we chatted sporadically, with great gaps of satisfying silence between our sentences.

Then from behind us we heard the murmur of muted voices in the distance, and I said to Marion, "We have company in the woods this morning."

Marion nodded and turned to look. We saw nothing, but the voices were coming nearer—at a faster pace than we were walking—and then we knew that the strangers would soon overtake us. Then we perceived that the sounds were not only behind us but above us, and we looked up.

How can I describe what we felt? Is it possible to tell of the surge of exaltation that ran through us? Is it possible to record this phenomenon in objective accuracy and yet be credible?

For about ten feet above us, and slightly to our left, was a floating group of glorious, beautiful creatures that glowed with spiritual beauty. We stopped and stared as they passed above us.

There were six of them, young beautiful women dressed in flowing white garments and engaged in earnest conversation. If they were aware of our existence they gave no indication of it. Their faces were perfectly clear to us, and one woman, slightly older than the rest, was especially beautiful. Her dark hair was pulled back in what today we would call a ponytail, and, although I cannot say it was bound at the back of her head, it appeared to be. She was talking intently to a younger spirit whose back was toward us and who looked up into the face of the woman who was talking.

Neither Marion nor I could understand their words, although their voices were clearly heard. The sound was somewhat like hearing but being unable to understand a group of people talking outside a house with all the windows and doors shut.

They seemed to float past us, and their graceful motion seemed natural—as gentle and peaceful as the morning itself. As they passed, their conversation grew fainter and fainter until it faded out entirely, and we stood transfixed on the spot, still holding hands and still with the vision before our eyes.

It would be an understatement to say that we were astounded. Then we looked at each other, each wondering if the other also had seen.

There was a fallen birch tree just there beside the path. We sat down on it and I said, "Marion, what did you see?

—Praise ye him, all his angels; praise ye him, all his hosts.

—Ps. 148:2

• • • •

Tell me exactly, in precise detail. And tell me what you heard."

She knew my intent—to test my own eyes and ears to see if I had been the victim of hallucination or imagination. And her reply was identical in every respect to what my own senses had reported to me.

I have related this story with the same faithfulness and respect for truth and accuracy as I would tell it on the witness stand. But even as I record it I know how incredible it sounds.

Perhaps I can claim no more for it than that it has had a deep effect on our own lives. For this experience of almost thirty years ago greatly altered our thinking.

—Our birth is but a sleep and a
forgetting:
The Soul that rises with us, our life's
Star,
Hath had elsewhere its setting,
And cometh from afar;
Not in entire forgetfulness,
And not in utter nakedness,
But trailing clouds of glory do we
come . . .
   —WILLIAM WORDSWORTH
      "Ode: Intimations
        of Immortality"

• • • •

*A*ngels are seen by children usually, those "still trailing clouds of glory," as Wordsworth wrote. Is that because later we aren't allowed to see? Or is our dullness of vision a sign of loss of innocence? This is the story of Hope MacDonald, who wrote a small treatise on angels for a Christian press.

Her sister, Marilyn, was eight at the time and Hope herself was four when her parents drove Marilyn as usual to school one day. An hour later Hope watched as they carried her big sister covered with bruises and blood back into the house. They put her on the sofa until the doctor arrived. It seems that in crossing the street to school, Marilyn had darted in front of a car and been hit and tossed high in the air. Her parents watched helplessly as she hit the pavement and rolled over and over toward a large, uncovered, open sewer. But instead of falling in, as expected, she suddenly stopped, right at the lip of the sewer.

The parents told this story to the doctor, and they all shook their heads in amazement. How could the child have stopped so suddenly, at the very edge of the sewer, when she had been rolling so fast?

In a voice filled with surprise, Marilyn spoke up from the sofa and said, "But didn't you see that huge, beautiful angel standing in the sewer, holding up her hands to keep me from rolling in?"

CHAPTER 2

Angels Unawares

In the beginning the immortals
who have their homes on Olympos
created the golden generation of mortal people
These lived in Kronos' time when he
was the king in heaven.
They lived as if they were gods,
their hearts free from all sorrow,
by themselves, and without hard work or pain;
no miserable
old age came their way; their hands, their feet
did not alter.
They took their pleasure in festivals,
and lived without troubles.
When they died, it was as if they fell asleep.
All goods were theirs. . . .
    Now that the earth has gathered over this generation,
these are called pure and blessed spirits;
they live upon earth,

and are good; they watch over mortal men
and defend them from evil;
they keep watch over lawsuits and hard dealings;
they mantle themselves in dark mist
and wander all over the country;
they bestow wealth; for this right
as of kings was given them. . . .

—HESIOD
Works and Days

• 1 •

*I*t is said that angels come as thoughts, as visions, as dreams, as animals, as the light on the water or in clouds and rainbows, and as people too. Are they walking on this earth as people in disguise? Or do they appear for that one moment and vanish into ether again? Or is it really us, mere humans, who for a moment are picked up by the hand of God and made to speak unwittingly the words another needs to hear, or to hold out a lifeline to another soul?

Once a man on the highway saw me pull over in my faltering car and stopped to help. This was on the New England Thruway, on my way from New York to Cape Cod. It was eight o'clock on a Saturday night in a slashing rain. My car kept stalling out at 60 miles an hour, which was the safe high speed. The motor would die and I would watch in terror as my pace sank to 25 miles per hour, while I stabbed on my warning blinkers, wondering if I'd be slammed from behind.

A man stopped his pickup, seeing me helpless at the side of the road, and accompanied my failing car in his truck for miles and miles out of his way, his flashers protecting me. That wonderful man spent six hours trailing me (imagine!), six hours of his time to ensure that I limped safely to my destination. I tried to find him later in New London, to thank him, but either I had misunderstood the address or he had left. There was no such man at that address.

For each moment of horror in the world we find these acts of goodness, by the hands of angels. Here is how another helped my reconciliation with my mother when she lay dying. My Jamaican angel, a charlady, come to give me back my life.

My mother was a great lady, small and muscular, endlessly active. She would haul the Gravely tractor around the lawn, then slap together a salami and tomato and lettuce and cheese sandwich on Wonder bread with imitation mayonnaise. She would eat two of these for lunch, standing at the kitchen counter, drinking several cups of coffee, as if sitting were a waste of time. Then off again to play a round of golf or rake up leaves or meet a friend in town or run to market or the bank. She was always moving, yet her favorite words to me were, "Relax! You're so jittery. Just sit down. You don't have anything to do here now but sit."

Which would set my teeth on edge, because the babies (her grandchildren) needed feeding or changing or something to divert them, and she was always picking, pecking at my skin.

And at her own. All her life she suffered from eczema. She was in constant pain and never talked about it.

Dream of the Magi. Gislebertus.
Capital from the church of
St. Lazare, Autun, France.
12th century.

There came a time when David and I moved from New York back to D.C., and I began an effort to mend my relationship with my mother. It took several years. She had had one bout with breast cancer and half her side had been lopped away. An Amazon removing her breast in order to draw her archer's bow would not have shown more disdain for her body than my mother did. After breast cancer she got lung cancer and had a piece of lung removed. That made her stop smoking, though she continued to sit in the study with my father, who lit one cigarette after another in the stuffy room, while the fire belched out clouds of smoke (the chimney held swallow nests which my mother decided would be too expensive to remove). At the end of her life my mother was so unhappy, stricken with grief by my father's stroke and her incapacity to help, embittered at the cruel trick fate had played, that her pain and anger often came tearing out at me, barbed and cutting.

"Oh, *journalists,*" she snorted. Both David and I were encompassed in that term. "*New York!* You're all so provincial."

Sometimes she would turn on my writing. One book in particular she loathed. She never explained its offense, but for several years she could hardly look at me without recalling it: "What an *awful* book." She said it again and again. "I was just ashamed reading that. Ashamed. I don't know how you can hold up your head in public, knowing you've written that."

"Well, what exactly didn't you like?"

"The whole thing. You can only hope it doesn't sell."

It would be a lie to say it didn't hurt. Once I fled the house before her assaults. But I also wanted a reconciliation.

One day she telephoned to say that she felt a little under the weather and had gone to bed. The doctor diagnosed it as walking pneumonia. Also she had slipped in the bathtub and hit her ribs, so she had a terrible pain in her side. My brother and his wife and David and I talked in whispers in the kitchen, as if she could overhear from upstairs. The sight of our mother lying down was still new to us. In forty years we'd hardly ever seen her sick, and then suddenly she'd had the two battles with cancer. We worried the pneumonia might be serious.

A month later she was in the hospital. I moved to Baltimore to be nearby. Every day I drove to see her in the hospital, and every day she bickered and quarreled with me. Reporters at the *The New York Times* had gone on strike: my husband was

—"Angel of God, my guardian dear,
to whom God's love commits me here,
Ever this day be at my side
to light and guard, to rule and guide. Amen."

out of work, our financial situation precarious. I had taken a job as a consultant to a federal agency and was keeping my sanity and reducing my grief with bouts of intense hard work.

My mother picked and picked at me. Why didn't I relax? Just sit in the garden? Take it easy and do nothing for a while? Did I *always* have to work? What was wrong with me? Intermittently she would worry about our finances: Were we all right? Could David find another job? But usually her attention focused on the fact that mine was divided. Looking back I see the quarrels were partly my fault. I didn't comprehend her fear. Why didn't I tell her I was scared for her—and for myself?

One day in the hospital she lit into me again. Peck-peck. Nothing I could do was right. I sank deeper in my chair, desolate: what was I doing there, when all she did was tongue-lash me? At this moment a broad-faced, black woman came in to mop the floors of this cramped hospital room, hardly big enough to fit a bed, a chair, a chest of drawers. My mother was sitting straight up against her pillows. She wore a nightgown with a little bedjacket over it. Her hair, freed from its customary bun, lay thin and loose on the pillow. Beside the bed stood an enormous oxygen tank with a plastic tube running to her nose, and this she had removed and waved in one hand like a pasha with his hookah as she shot off her charges at me, complaining about the way I dressed and my pathetic efforts to write, scorning my present assignments on urban affairs as trivial and pointless. Not even the entry of the hospital attendant quieted my mother's tirade.

I hunched in my chair, hurt and angry, wondering if I should simply get up and leave. Here was my mother, dying. There were things we should be saying to each other, not nagging, picking at me so.

"I grudge you the mother-talk." The Jamaican charwoman stopped her mopping. My mother and I both looked up startled. Neither of us had understood her lilting Island accent. But a thrill of recognition ran through me.

"What?" I sat up straight.

"I grudge you the mother-talk," she repeated, looking from one to the other of us, smiling with a broad, gold smile. "My own mother died when I was twelve," she sang, "and I've had no one in all these years to give me mother-talk. It is so nice to hear."

My mother looked embarrassed. I sat up even straighter, hit by joy. *Of course!* She was cuffing the cub, was all. I had not understood. It took only a few moments for that beautiful, dark-skinned woman to finish with the floor—three swishes of her mop and she had done. She left, but she left us in a different state.

I did not consider her an angel at the time, but marveled at the synchronicity of the encounter, this woman walking in to explain my mother's behavior and walking out again. From that moment our relationship took a turn.

We began to talk on another level. We could approach the topic of death, say how much we cared for each other.

A week later she was dead.

—Coincidence is God's way of performing a miracle anonymously.
—ANONYMOUS

• • • •

. . .

*I*s there anyone alive who has not had a similar experience, with strangers coming mysteriously to their aid?

I have a friend, Jack Moorman, an investment banker. He is by nature cheerful and optimistic and he has always expected everything to come out his way. When he was eight years old, he was alone in the house one day, woodworking with his new set of ultra-sharp cutting tools, when the knife slipped. It cut his finger to the bone. Pain! A flash of exposed white bone. Blood everywhere.

At that moment the doorbell rang. Wrapping his hand in a towel, he opened the door. It was a nurse in a white uniform asking for his parents. He says now, years later, that he never thought it was strange to see a nurse at the door for no reason. She came inside, cleaned his wound, bandaged his hand, and left. She never returned. He never thought anything of it—or bothered to tell his parents she had come.

It is only now, decades later, that he recognizes how strange was the encounter. Was she an angel come to minister to him, being all alone?

• CHARLIE AND THE TIRE •

*C*harlie is a young man still, with a fine blond mustache and a handsome wife. At the time of this story he was living in Takoma Park, a suburb of Washington, D.C.

"It was 1971," Charlie told me, "and back in those days we

were making like $37.50 a week, and we wanted to go to
Massachusetts to see my wife's mother, but we had a bald tire
on front, and in those days you couldn't go out and just buy a
tire, so it didn't look like we were going to make a trip. We
were canning food. This friend and myself were going to pick
pears, and I was telling him the story of how we wanted to go
to Massachusetts but the tire was bald and we didn't have the
money to buy a new one, so it didn't look like we were going
to go. So we were picking the pears, and then we came on
back home. We were living on this street that had a down-
sloping dead end into Sligo Creek, and when we pulled up
and were parking the car, there was a lady standing at the top
of the street rolling a tire and a wheel down the hill, and we
watched her let it go, and it rolled on down the hill and into
Sligo Creek. Not a great deal of a creek. I said, 'Well, I ought
to give that tire a chance,' so I got the tire and wheel and it fit
the car and we went to Massachusetts. I don't even remember
what the woman looked like; she was just a woman rolling a
tire and a wheel down the hill. At the time I didn't think much
of it, we just went to get the tire out of the creek. In those days
things like that happened a lot, but now they happen but you
don't notice them as much. Well, now I expect things like that
to happen, but in those days I didn't expect it. The perspec-
tive: 'When you need something, something makes it appear.'
But at that time I didn't know that yet.

"It just happens, and it's not as big a deal as it used to be.
I've had it happen so many times, that what you want you get.
I don't know how much intention has to do with it."

—The angels keep their ancient
*   places—*
Turn but a stone and start a wing!
'Tis ye, 'tis ye, your estranged
*   faces*
That miss the many-splendoured
*   thing.*
        —FRANCIS THOMPSON
        The Kingdom of God

• • • •

Oh, it isn't at all intention. Assistance can come even when you least expect it or don't believe you'd get it anyway. Harry Aylesworth was president of a financial consulting service in Clearwater, Florida, when he told me this story. At this time he was under great stress. He was driving late one night in Florida when his car broke down on an isolated road. He looked forward to a fifty-mile hike in the dark, and he was suddenly furious. He didn't believe in God or angels or any spiritual power, but the words burst out: "All right, I've had enough. I need help and I need it NOW!"

At that moment he saw headlights coming toward him. The car stopped. In it were two men—angels, he says now. They were driving to Boca Raton and didn't mind taking him down the road to a tow truck. Another queer thing: they were very quiet, very spiritual, and they let him talk, drawing him out about how his ex-wife's former husband's ex-wife was threatening to murder him—"family problems." When he left their car, he felt a new calm and peace.

"That was the beginning of my spiritual quest. I don't know if they materialized to give me a ride and dematerialized or whether they were people who were given the task of helping me, such as angels." Who could know?

This is one mark of an angel. It brings a calm and peaceful serenity that descends sweetly over you, and this is true even when the angel is not seen. Was that the sweetness that my aunts referred to when they would pause in the angel-silence? "There's an angel passing through the room."

It is remarkable how many people have had experiences,

been brushed by, the divine. Harry's pretty wife, Deborah (businesswoman; her own pilot license), listened quietly as he told his story, then told her own. She told it as everyone does who has had an encounter with other worlds—softly, with a little smile of remembrance at her lips. A little poignantly, as if regretful it had passed.

Her story, too, took place some years ago when she was opening the business with Harry and likewise under terrific stress. Her anxiety was so great that she lay down on her bed one afternoon. It was an uncharacteristic surrender for her. She was lying on her right side, she said, her arm forward, when suddenly she felt a hand on her left shoulder. It was warm. A comforting touch.

She knew it was something supernatural.

She couldn't say it was an angel.

But from its touch she felt a wave of inexpressible sweetness, the sense that everything would be all right.

After that she got up, knowing things were okay. And they were.

This is the second mark of an angel. Their message is always: "Fear not!" Don't worry, they say. "Things are working out perfectly. You're going to like this. Wait." Never once do you hear of an angel trumpeting bad news, and when we think about dying, well, that's what we want to hear from the Angel of Death: peace and joy and light.

Having said that, I should add that I know of two occasions when angels have inspired fear, but these are reserved for later in this book.

—"Fear not: for, behold, I bring you good tidings of great joy."
—LUKE 2:10

• • • •

. . .

*A*ngels come in all sizes and shapes and colors, visible and invisible to the physical eye. But always you are changed from having seen one.

And this is the third mark of an angel. You remember; you are never quite the same again.

Sometimes angels come in the shape of friends, but we recognize them best, it seems, when they come as strangers, shifting into our lives for a moment only, and dancing out again, sometimes without even leaving a name to know them by. I know a woman who should by all rights be dead. Her illnesses and her survival of repeated surgery have been a marvel to the doctors who have treated her.

Once she took a bus from New Jersey into New York to meet her husband and some friends for dinner. She had bought a one-way ticket to the New York Port Authority, and, since her husband was meeting her at the terminal, she had no money with her. For that matter, she didn't even know the *name* of the couple at whose house they were dining.

Unfortunately, because of major renovations to the building, the bus didn't arrive at the usual gate. She couldn't find her husband. All around lounged drunks and derelicts. No one knew anything. She walked for two hours, she says, moving up and down between floors and finally, of course, she began to pray.

Then a "cute little fat man" came by. He had a "sweet face."

OPPOSITE: The Angel Appearing to the Shepherds. Rembrandt. Engraving, 17th century.

• • • •

"Do you know where the departure gates to New Jersey are?" she asked in despair, thinking that if she found the departure gate, she could find the arrival gate.

"Yes," he answered. "I'll take you there." And he led her straight to her husband.

"We were so happy to see each other, we started to cry. Then I turned around to introduce this man, and he was gone."

• 2 •

*I*f angels come as people, or as invisible hands, they come also as presences. Sir Ernest Shackleton, the South Pole explorer who accompanied Robert F. Scott on one of his ventures, reported that during his return from the South Pole, he and his companions were accompanied by "one more," who traveled with them. And Francis Sydney Smythe, in his account of a 1933 ascent of Mount Everest, spoke of the friendly presence that climbed by his side.

"In its company I could not feel lonely, neither could I come to any harm. It was always there to sustain me on my solitary climb up the snow-covered slabs. Now, as I halted and extracted some mint cake from my pocket, it was so near and so strong that instinctively I divided the mint into two halves and turned around with one-half in my hand to offer it to my 'companion.' " Smythe attributed the presence to a hallucination.

But sometimes the presence can play an active role.

. . .

A friend, Gerry-Kay Talton—an acquaintance really, for I have not seen her in some years—told me her story. A follower of the Virgin Mary, she was praying, deeply depressed one day, when she heard a voice, the inner voice of Mary, kindly telling her to remember how many times she had been carried out of the way of harm. Later that afternoon she was crossing the street with a girlfriend when suddenly a car, backing up very fast, came straight at them. Her friend was already on the curb, but Gerry-Kay, paralyzed with surprise, stood, mouth open, watching the car barrelling toward her. Then to her surprise she felt two hands pick her up at the waist from behind. At which she came to her senses and jumped! The car missed her by a foot.

Her friend saw the whole thing. She said it was the queerest sight: Gerry-Kay standing rigid in the street as the car headed right for her, and then suddenly rising straight up into the air about three inches, hanging, momentarily suspended, and then leaping for the curb as if her feet had purchase on the ground.

Neither saw an angel, but Gerry-Kay could not forget the feeling of a pair of hands lifting her up. Or the sense of happiness that swept over her: giggles! She was reduced to laughter, and a feeling that everything was just fine! Perhaps she would have been less inclined to think the event had actually happened were it not for her friend's description, verifying what she'd felt.

—Angels can fly because they take themselves lightly.
—SCOTTISH SAYING

• • • •

But whose guardian was it—Gerry-Kay's, or that of the driver of the car?

Angels come most commonly, I think, to children, saints, and primitive people, to the innocents, who perhaps can perceive more clearly than we.

Bridget Maher, then eight years old, and living in Washington, D.C., told me she had an angel that accompanied her everywhere. She had pink wings, said Bridget, a yellow gown, and wings for feet. She had been with Bridget since about the age of three; and when Bridget went to sleep at night, the angel enveloped her body in a spiraling rainbow to protect her when she slept. I asked the little girl if the angel was always with her, even when she was in company or went to school, and she paused thoughtfully to answer: "No, unless I get a paper cut at school, and then she heals it." How? "With her magic wing."

This is not unusual. My niece Tory has a similar angel, who takes care of her, and any number of children I know talk quite openly about theirs.

This is Karen Hill's story:

"When my daughter was five years old and my son was seven, we were picnicking in the Colorado mountains.

"They were playing by a small stream when we heard our son scream: we turned to see our daughter being sucked into a nearby culvert. She had fallen on her head into the water. She was facedown holding on to the sides when my husband grabbed her out.

"On the way home I was holding her and telling her how

proud I was that she held on and how strong she was. Then I gave her a small lecture on danger—to never give up, and so on.

"She looked at me and said, 'But Mommy, there were three tiny angels helping me; they told me to hold on, and I felt so strong.' "

But adults have seen angels too. Some people describe them as radiating brilliant and luminous colors, and others describe them as dressed in shining white. It is baffling that even when they appear in their own celestial form, as *angels* (instead of invisible hands or balls of whirling energy or humans or dreams or visions or thoughts), still, no one quite agrees on how they look. Do the descriptions differ according to the perceptions of the person, or according to the angel which was seen?

Saint Francisca, a fourteenth-century French saint, had a guardian angel who never left her and who sometimes permitted her to see his incredible beauty. He had long, curly blond hair and wore a floor-length robe that was sometimes white and sometimes blue and sometimes red. His face was "whiter than snow, redder than the blush rose," and his radiance so luminous she could read matins at midnight in his light. His eyes were always lifted to heaven. She took him by the hand to introduce him to her confessor and spiritual advisor, who, oddly enough, could see the angel too. He said it had the proportions of a child of five or six.

One healer I know once saw an angel at the feet of the woman she was laying hands on. This was unusual, she said,

—Though they are so great, so glorious, so pure, so wonderful, that the very sight of them (if we were allowed to see them) would strike us to the earth, as it did the prophet Daniel, holy and righteous as he was, yet they are our fellow-servants and our fellow-workers, and they carefully watch over and defend even the humblest of us.

—CARDINAL NEWMAN

• • • •

because although she always prays, invoking Christ and the angels of healing for her work, and though she often senses them, she does not always *see* their forms. This time her eyes were closed. She opened them and saw the being faintly but with her inner eye. It was dressed in red and had the long, brown, mottled pinions of a hawk. She herself had entered the altered state of healing prayer. She acknowledged its beautiful presence, closed her eyes, and returned into her trance.

But the woman she was working with said, "There's an angel at my feet."

"What does it look like?" asked the healer.

"It's dippy," laughed the woman. And described a charming, cavalier young man with white wings and an unceremonious, rather scatological air. They saw, in other words, quite different angels thus at work.

What do angels do? They rescue, give aid, anoint us with calm and serenity. They deliver messages of warning or of hope. They guide us, teach us, answer our prayers, lead us to death. But always they are at the service of God, and not themselves.

A New York taxi driver told me that when he was a little child in Greece, of about three years old, he saw a flock of baby angels playing up and down a staircase! It was the outer stairway to the house of a saintly old woman who had just died; and indeed he and his mother were walking toward the house to her funeral, when he saw the baby angels, the *putti*—which we call cherubs in English and which are not to be confused with the magnificent cherubim of Scripture.

The baby angels are said to accompany the Virgin Mary, who is herself queen of the angels, seated at the throne of God. In all the visitations of the Virgin, angels abound. In 1858 the Virgin appeared to little fourteen-year-old Bernadette Soubirous at Lourdes and told her to dig the spring that ever since has poured forth holy water. Only three years later, in 1861, the first investigative commission pronounced fifteen of 100 cures at the spring "miraculous." By 1959, fifty-eight of 5,000 reported healings at Lourdes were declared to be miracles, including inexplicable recoveries from cancer, tuberculosis, and blindness.

In 1917 the Virgin appeared to three shepherd children in Fatima, Portugal, which has now become another site of pilgrimage, and there are rumors that she has popped up recently in Maryland, Georgia, Pennsylvania, and Texas. But one site is more famous than any others. Today in Medjugorje, in Bosnia-Herzegovina—part of the former Yugoslavia—she has been seen ever since 1981, when she made her first appearance to six twelve-year-old children: four girls and two boys. The children were chosen to receive the visions, says the Virgin, "because they were ordinary."

When the Virgin appears, the visionaries go into a trance state: they do not react to light, sound, or touch. Their eyes do not blink. "We see the Virgin as we see other people," said one of the visionaries. "We pray, speak, and touch her."

She is a beautiful woman with black curly hair, blue eyes, a crown of stars, and shining visage. She wears a gray gown or coat. She floats on a gray cloud, not touching the ground. She is surrounded by angels. The visionaries feel they are outside

—It is not because angels are holier than men or devils that makes them angels, but because they do not expect holiness from one another, but from God alone.

—WILLIAM BLAKE

• • • •

Two Angels.
Baptism of Christ (detail).
Verrocchio. 15th century.

of time and space when she appears, and those who are nearby, although they cannot see the Virgin Mary, are touched by . . . something.

An estimated 20 million pilgrims have traveled to Medjugorje since 1981. Dr. Susan Trout, Ph.D., of the Washington, D.C., Institute for the Advancement of Science, who visited in 1988, saw *putti* in the clouds there. Child-angels. But others have seen grown angels, and still others the Madonna, and some people report seeing into other realities—energies and swirls of color.

In Medjugorje, says Susan, you can look at the sun without hurting your eyes, because as you look, a disk—a round gray lozenge—moves in front of the sun to filter its rays and prevent any damage to your eyes.

The Madonna gives messages to the visionaries, and the messages are those of angels: Don't be afraid. Don't be anxious or worried; God will show you the way. . . . Give everything you do and all that you own to God, so that He can take control of your life, as the King of all you possess. . . . Rejoice in the Creator, who has created you so wonderfully, and give thanks unceasingly, so that blessings shall continue to flow down always from God upon your life.

For years the Madonna warned of the need for constant prayer, because something terrible was about to happen in Yugoslavia. But then it did, with the bloody massacres by the Croatians of Orthodox Serbs and Bosnian Muslims. Today her messages are often placid invitations to pray that Jesus "be born in all hearts."

*—Angels are not etherealized
human beings, evolving animal
qualities in their wings; but they are
celestial visitants, flying on spiritual,
not material, pinions. Angels are
pure thoughts from God, winged
with Truth and Love, no matter
what their individualism may be.
Human conjecture confers upon
angels its own forms of thought,
marked with superstitious outlines,
making them creatures with
suggestive feathers; but this is only
fancy. It has behind it no more reality
than has the sculptor's thought when
he carves his "Statue of Liberty,"
which embodies his conception of an
unseen quality or condition . . .*

*Angels are God's representatives.
These upward-soaring beings never
lead towards self, sin, or materiality,
but guide to the divine principle of
all good, whither every real
individuality, image or likeness of
God, gathers. By giving earnest
heed to these spiritual guides they
tarry with us, and we entertain
"angels unawares."*

—MARY BAKER EDDY
Science and Health

• • • •

Are the visitations true? The Vatican has taken no position on whether the visions are real, and there is at least one scandal associated with one Alabama organization called Caritas, which is charged with using the visionaries and the visions as a means of money laundering and defrauding pilgrims of millions of dollars. Other disturbing tales involve the sale of Nazi swastikas in tourist stalls, of rampant religious fanaticism and intolerance.

There are only three ways to know whether the visitations are true, say Catholic priests of the region. First is whether the visions lie within the traditions of established religion, and second is whether the contents of the visions are in accordance with the Gospels. The third is by the exaltation and ecstasy of the visionaries themselves. One has married and has three children, another became a nun. These young men and women are, says Susan Trout, "exquisite." They embody the peaceful, loving state; they radiate serenity, as one would expect from those who every day see angels and the face of God.

"I have not talked to a single person who was not changed by the experience of visiting Medjugorje," says Susan. "You find an inner connection, a deep *knowing*. Your worries are dissipated. A peace comes over your heart, and if you get that, no one can take it away again."

THE ANGELS OF MONS

I have heard that during World War II, some people claimed the Allied victory was due to angels fighting on their side.

But the most dramatic of the war stories, a *Song of Roland* of this age, concerns the angels at Mons in Belgium. The visitation occurred between the twenty-sixth and the twenty-eighth of August, 1914, during the first engagements of World War I. The French and British were retreating toward Paris, overpowered by the German guns. This was nothing like the slaughter that took place later in this war, when the average life expectancy of a British officer at the front was said to be twenty minutes, but it was nonetheless a sad and bloody retreat.

Then the stories began to dribble in—that the men had seen angels on the field. Nothing was clear about the tales.

The French had seen the archangel Michael, or else Saint Michael (or was it Saint Joan?) bareheaded, clad in golden armor and seated on a white horse, brandishing a sword. To the British it was Saint George, springing out of a yellow mist, "a tall man with yellow hair in golden armor, on a white horse, holding his sword up, and his mouth open, crying *Victory!*" And it was not just one or two men who saw this. The nurse in one hospital reported that she and her fellow nurses heard the tale again and again from the wounded, with men from both nationalities asking repeatedly for medals or pictures of either Saint Michael or Saint George. What the nurses found most curious was the air of exaltation or serene joy that accompanied these dying men.

One patient said that at a critical period in the retreat from Mons he saw "an angel with outstretched wings, like a luminous cloud," between the advancing Germans and

*—For He will command His angels
  concerning you*
*to guard you in all your ways; they
  will lift*
*you up in their hands, so that you
  will not strike*
your foot against a stone.
                    —Ps. 91:11,12

• • • •

themselves, and at that moment the onslaught of the Germans slackened.

Another reported "a strange light, which seemed to be quite distinctly outlined and was not a reflection of the moon. . . . The light became brighter and I could see quite distinctly three shapes, one in the centre having what looked like outspread wings, the other two were not so large, but were quite plainly distinct from the centre one. They appeared to have a long, loose-hanging garment of a golden tint, and they were above the German line facing us."

A year later rumors appeared from the German side: that at a certain moment the men were "absolutely powerless to proceed . . . and their horses turned sharply round and fled . . . and nothing could stop them." Back in Germany a severe reprimand was allegedly given to this regiment. But the German soldiers claimed they saw that the Allied lines were held by thousands of troops—"thousands," although in reality it was a thin line of two regiments, with men stationed fifteen yards apart or straggling down the roads in disorderly retreat.

Had the soldiers seen something? Who can tell? The stories cannot be confirmed. In some cases it was a single angel, in others several, hovering over the battlefield, in others a ghostly troop of cavalry riding guard for the retreating men.

Meanwhile back in England, a journalist, Arthur Machen, had been so moved when he heard on the radio the news of the retreat from Mons that he had written a short story. Entitled "The Bowmen," it appeared in the

London Evening News September 14, 1914, three weeks after the event, and it recounted how the retreating men had seen an apparition of "shining" medieval soldiers, phantom bowmen from the fifteenth-century battle of Agincourt, located right near Mons.

When the stories of angels began to sift back home, Machen thought the rumors came from his story. He spent considerable time trying to persuade people he had made it up—Untrue! he cried. No apparitions had appeared!

Yet the stories persisted. He never succeeded in quashing the tales.

One man suggested that the apparitions were the souls of the just-dead, still hovering near their comrades. Others said the tales were all untrue, the product of fever and fatigue in a war where the nurses in one field hospital were working forty-five hours without sleep; and, as the horse-drawn carts of the wounded rolled in, they pulled the living out from under corpses already cold. Some people said that the stories of angels resulted from the mass hysteria besetting an army of a hundred thousand that had set out only days before expecting instant victory and instead saw fifteen thousand men lost in the first engagement; and Machen, of course, egoistically took credit for the tales derived from his story of fifteenth-century longbowmen who covered the army's retreat.

But some people believe that angels were at Mons.

—For nothing worthy proving can be proven
Nor yet disproven: wherefore thou be wise,
Cleave ever to the sunnier side of Doubt.
—ALFRED, LORD TENNYSON
The Ancient Sage, 1:66

• • • •

CHAPTER 3

Turn a Stone/ Start a Wing

Eyes look but cannot see it
Ears listen but cannot hear it
Hands grasp but cannot touch it
Beyond the senses lies the great unity—
	invisible, inaudible, intangible
		—LAO-TZU
		Tao Te Ching, 14

· 1 ·

I suppose you cannot meet an apparition without having other psychic experiences: telepathy, clairvoyance, ESP. I'd had my share by the time I saw the Brooklyn ghost, but never thought much of them. For one thing, they arrived in so slight a form as to appear inconsequential. Easily ignored. Remember that I was the descendant of the Enlightenment, scornful of those who believed in séances and mediums, palmistry or charismatic preachers, all of which we lumped together with witches' covens and medieval alchemy.

Yet how to explain these flashes of the inexplicable? The telephone rings and you know who it is before you pick it up. Or your hand reaches out before the instrument rings, knowing that he or she is about to call. I have an Irish friend whose mother was a kind of seer. They lived in a house without a phone. "Go to market for me, Bill," she would say to her son; "we're going to have visitors this afternoon." How did she know?

For myself I noticed I had only to think of a friend, wonder how to reach that person, and he or she would run into me on the street. Or write. Or phone. It was creepy. Especially since the ability has increased with age. Another thing began to happen—or perhaps it had always been going on but I was too dull to notice and trust it: I would have a problem to resolve and find myself helpless to find a solution, when the answer would be given me. Someone would telephone. A book would drop off a table opening to a page with just the information required. It was as if I sent out a mental SOS and something answered it. The question is: Do we think of someone *because* they're going to call, *because* we are about to meet? In other words, are we dipping into future time? Or does the silent wish, our thought, pull that person to us? Are we physically manifesting our inner lives? Is the solution responding to the need?

Telepathy, I called it, and nodded as if something was explained by that word. ESP. If we can accept radio, that mysterious box that picks up silent sounds—or TV with its images—and transmits them at the switch of a dial into my room, then telepathy seems hardly mysterious. But how do we account for the fact that apparently certain messages do not require a *sender* in order to be received?

One day, when my babies were very small, I was working at my typewriter (no computer yet). We were living in Washington, D.C., at the time, not yet having moved to the Brooklyn apartment. One daughter was two and the other, Molly, was only a few weeks old. I was working on the third floor of our little house in a little attic room. Down the corridor Molly lay asleep on a bed. Though she was still too young to turn over (indeed had never tried to roll, though she practiced lifting her head), nevertheless I had caged her between three pillows, just in case. She slept like a stone, flat-out, as only dogs and babies can. In the other room I worked on an article, tap-tapping at my typewriter, totally absorbed and concentrating on the work when—

Molly's falling off the bed, I thought, and in a flash was pounding down the hall to her room . . . where I caught her in midair.

Now, this is disturbing. Even if we accept thought transference or telepathy, how do we account for the fact that the baby could not possibly have known she was about to fall,

—Good thoughts will produce good actions and bad thoughts will produce bad actions. Hatred does not cease by hatred at any time; hatred ceases by love.

—BUDDHA

. . . .

much less transferred the thought to me? After all, she'd never rolled over before, never fallen, didn't know she was on a bed three feet above a floor.

Moreover, I knew she was falling *before* the actual event. I had received information of a future act. Precognition, it is called.

Around 1250, the medieval philosopher Saint Thomas Aquinas wrote an entire treatise on angels. It was his contention that angels are pure thoughts, which assume corporeal bodies at will—quick as thought—but their bodies are also formed of thought. Pure intellect.

If that is so, then angels come as imaginings, as intuition, insights, the sudden bolts from the blue that give artists their visions and scientists the solution to their calculations. Einstein attributed his theory of relativity to intuition, and Nobel laureate Emil Fischer his discoveries in chemistry to a nagging intuition that "something was wrong."

We know nothing about intuition. We know it runs in families. We know it can be strengthened by experience and it can also be lost or forgotten from disuse. It is marked by *sudden* knowledge, *sudden* insight, a connection made instantly and unexpectedly, but usually only after days or weeks of fruitless work. Is that work a form of prayer?

Intuition has been explained from every point of view—historical, sociological, psychological. The Asians believe it is part of the Akashic records, a river of knowledge that encircles the earth and that certain favored people may dip into at times. The philosopher Spinoza saw it as union with God.

—That's all an angel is, an idea of God.

—MEISTER ECKHART

• • • •

—My brother used to ask the birds to forgive him; that sounds senseless but it is right; for all is like the ocean, all things flow and touch each other; a disturbance in one place is felt at the other end of the world. It may be folly to beg forgiveness of the birds, but the birds would be happier at your side—a little happier anyway— and children and all animals, if yourself were nobler than you are now. It's all like an ocean, I tell you. Then you would pray to the birds, too, consumed by an all-embracing love in a sort of transport and pray that they will forgive you your sin. Prize this ecstasy, however senseless it may seem to men.

—FYODOR DOSTOYEVSKY
The Brothers Karamazov

• • • •

It cannot be willed into being. It rides on desire, but it comes when you so forget your vanity, fears, and prejudices that you lose yourself in the idea or person or event—and at that moment, in a flash of understanding, comes the angel of insight.

We are told that prayer brings angels down. But if prayer is thought concentrated and distilled, the clear, pure yearning of the heart, is prayer itself also the manifestation of the divine? The desire itself being granted as a gift of God, in order that its satisfaction may be given us by God?

I was talking about this with my dear friend Jane Vonnegut. "Do you think there's a difference between prayer and angels attending?" The unifying part of me would answer no. It's all the same and single thing. One ocean, one dream, "in which all things flow and touch each other. A disturbance in one place is felt at the other end of the world," wrote Dostoyevsky. So a thought in the Atlantic creates turbulence in the Indian Ocean, and angels surely carry their messages in dreams and prayer, and by such invisible coincidences that we do not even notice the miraculous responses to our needs.

We are told that prayer brings angels down. Other people say it's grace that summons the angels. I read in the paper a year or so ago about a man who fell off a sailboat at night in the Pacific Ocean; or else his yacht sank, I forget, but he found himself swimming miles and miles from any land, climbing the rollers and swimming down the swells. He headed for Hawaii in the direction from which he had come, and which he knew was many miles away. Was it twenty miles or more? He swam all night. He must have been in strong condition, though he was said to be only a businessman on vacation. At one point, swimming, he knew he could not make it. There was no way he would have the strength to swim to land. Then he prayed, he said, with all his heart and soul—and felt a stream of power enter him. It buoyed him up. It gave him the strength to swim hour after hour more and to land on a beach alive.

I read about it in the papers. On the other hand, angels come without our prayers as well, so who knows why angels come? Or worse—why they so often don't?

Ed Shiver was fifty-three and a speechwriter for private industry when he told me this story. When he was a child of seven or eight, he had a series of dreams about angels. It was a stressful time. His parents were arguing. Like many children, Ed took the blame upon himself. But the visions did not clear up his guilt. Indeed they created more anxiety. Until he told his story to me, he said, "I've never told them to another living soul."

"I dreamed one night—and it is marked by extraordinary clarity even now—I dreamed I got out of bed one night and opened the bedroom door, and suddenly I was outside in the night. There was a quarter moon, and Christ was sitting in the crescent of the moon. I looked up, astonished. He looked down and waved to me and smiled. He was swinging in the crook of the moon. On his left was an angel holding a large

Angel Putting on Lipstick.
Edith Vonnegut. Painting, 2006.

book: *The Lamb's Book of Life.* And he looked at that and looked at me and smiled as if my name were in that.

"I've never told *anyone* about that. They'd think, 'The kid is a fanatic or sick, psychotic.' "

A week later he had the first dream of angels.

He dreamed that he walked up to a mirror that was in his living room. He could see himself in the mirror, and on either side of him stood two angels. They were grown-up. They were smiling. They had wings. They were brilliant and very white. The dream was in black and white.

"A few nights later I had the same dream over again. The thing that was so different—the dream was so . . . *crisp* and . . . *vivid.* It still remains that way. The other thing is, it scared me to death. It was taking me into something I didn't understand. I didn't want to be pious or special or set apart.

"Then it happened a third time, and I was terrified. I prayed that it would go away, and after that it didn't come back.

"Now I am divided about it. Logic offers the psychological roots of the dream, influenced by early religious training and coupled with stress . . . but another part of me—because the dreams are so vivid—thinks . . . something else.

"I can't see the angels now, but I like to think they're there. 'Would you guys please give me a hand?' I say. And suddenly a warmth comes over me."

Did it change his life? Was he different afterward?

"No, it didn't change my life. Or perhaps it did." Who knows?

• 2 •

By the time I had seen an angel and a ghost or two, I could no longer disbelieve. How could I? It would be like telling a man he's not burning his hand on the hot stove he's leaning on. Still, it seems perfectly correct to disbelieve in a Higher Power until you've got some proof. To believe in God or in a guiding force because someone tells you to is the height of stupidity. We are given senses to receive our information with. We are given experiences of our own. With our own eyes we see, and with our skin we feel. With our intelligence it is intended that we understand. But each person must puzzle it out for himself or herself.

And that seems to be what the joke of living is about.

Susan Lehman is a former actress and theater director. As a young woman, she was working as a singer in Saint Thomas in the Caribbean, living on the producer's ship while working on a show. There she got to know Howard and his two sons, Brian and Michael, who lived nearby on the yacht *Hypatia.* Howard had taken an early retirement from his job with BOAC, bought the *Hypatia,* a forty-foot trimaran, and sailed it with Brian from England to the Caribbean. There he put out his boat for charter. Michael had come to join him, and soon Susan came aboard and worked as crew on a ten-day cruise. They had such a marvelous time that she decided to continue to Miami with them on the first leg of their return to Canada.

Two occurrences upset their plans, and only later, looking

back, did Susan realize how small they were and what major consequences they were to have. The first seemed big, yet paled by comparison: Howard had a heart attack. The three young folk—Brian, Michael, and Susan—together with Susan's Scottie dog, Bonnie, would sail to Miami without him. The second event seemed minor, yet resulted in the shipwreck later on: the loss of a wrench.

While on that earlier ten-day cruise the two outboard motors had given them trouble, so when they returned to Saint Thomas, they replaced both outboards with two inboard motors. They lashed the two faulty motors inside the port pontoon, which served on the trimaran as storage space. Then they set sail for Miami, heading first for Puerto Rico, then to the island of Great Inagua, in the Bahamas, where they rested after the three-day passage. There the next of the troubles hit. The starter button on the new inboard motors wouldn't work right.

They were trying to fix the starter, when they accidentally kicked a five-eighths-inch spanner overboard. Oops. Susan remembers watching the small tool drop into the sea. There was not another spanner to be had on the island. That meant they had only sails to move them to the next Bahamian landing, Long Island, where they hoped to find another wrench.

Partway to Long Island they lay becalmed. They rocked on a quiet sea. Waiting. Had they had the spanner, they could have fixed the starter, turned on the motor, and continued under power. Instead they waited. Later that afternoon the wind picked up. It came with such force that it tore them up

—It is very important to pray for others, because when you pray for someone, an angel goes and sits on the shoulder of that person.

—THE VIRGIN MARY
to the children at Medjugorje

• • • •

the northeast coast of Long Island, past the entry into the harbor.

They were right on the ocean, with nothing to stop the hard east wind and unable to tack against it. Night fell. There was no rain on this bright, moonlit night, but the waves were so high and the wind so strong that inside the port pontoon the two outboards broke loose from their lashings and punctured the fiberglass. The boat foundered. It lurched so suddenly to port that Susan, in the back cabin, was thrown to the floor. She thought, "It won't sink, but it could tip over."

Brian, the more experienced sailor, threw out an anchor to hold the yacht into the wind. With each huge wave the boat was carried west, toward the island. But the main cabin was filling with water, and all the lifesaving equipment was in the torn pontoon.

Brian decided to abandon ship. The island was not far off. They could reach it in the life raft. He went on deck to inflate the raft. This was a twenty-person BOAC raft, complete with supplies, food, water. Insistently catastrophe hit again. Just as Brian pulled the cord to inflate the raft, a wave swept him overboard. He had no safety harness on, but the cord to the life raft was wrapped around his hand. In the darkness Susan and Michael strained to see him as the waves crashed against the foundering *Hypatia.* After a time they saw a light waved back and forth and knew that Brian had reached the shore. He was signaling them with a flashlight.

Michael and Susan, two inexperienced sailors, were alone on the sinking boat, with no way off.

Now the moon was setting. Michael said he was going to cut the anchor rope, that without the anchor the crippled boat would be washed to the island faster. Susan was no sailor, but she was gripped by certainty.

"If you do that," she said, "we'll go broadside to the waves and tip."

"That's possible," answered Michael stubbornly. "But I'm responsible. You can either jump or stay with the boat."

What was curious was her cold and certain knowledge. She knew what she must do. The wind howled. The twenty-foot waves combed in against the boat.

"I have to jump," she said. Susan had a cork life ring that Brian had given her. She drew the life ring under her arms, picked up Bonnie, her Scottie dog, and balanced the dog's hind paws on the ring, with its forepaws leaning on her right shoulder. She wound her fingers into the dog's harness. Once in the water, she knew—again with utter certainty—that she was being guided. The waves came at eight- or ten-second intervals and crashed over her head. But each time, she rose to the surface and gulped air, confident that everything would be all right. She told jokes to Bonnie.

Finally she felt seaweed underfoot, and then she started to scream for Brian's attention. He called back to her, came, and picked her up. She couldn't walk.

The dog promptly ran to a rock and peed.

They huddled in the life raft, trying to get out of the wind. Susan was chilled, in shock. The night was clear and starry, and she lay there thinking about Michael, certain that he was dead.

The next day they found the boat. A cobweb of ropes wound everywhere—Michael's elaborate, futile attempt to tie down the belongings. Michael had cut the anchor line. Did the boat tip? It was unclear. Did he fall overboard into thirty-five feet of water? No one knew.

It was the dog that found Michael's body. She was suddenly running down the beach, barking. Brian chased after her. He pulled his brother to the beach and covered him. Then the two survivors set off for help. They were on an uninhabited part of the island. Susan was barefoot in jeans with a bikini top and a windbreaker with a hood. They walked through thorns, and still Susan found herself in that tranced state in which she felt guided, led. She knew things she had no right to know. They had set off, for example, in one direction, when she stopped. "No," she said, "we're going the wrong way." She made them walk the other way.

Eventually they reached a house, a town, a constable, and told their story. Brian and the constable returned to the beach. They brought back Michael's body.

This was a British island. In the case of a drowning there had to be an inquest. Susan and Brian were ushered for interrogation into an inner office. Devoid of decoration, it contained a table, two chairs, and nothing else—not even a picture on the bare white walls. But on the table lay a five-eighths-inch wrench, the precise tool they had needed to fix the starter button! Had they had the spanner, they would have turned on the motor when becalmed and not been caught by the storm. Had they had the spanner, the outboards would not have broken through the pontoon fiberglass and sunk the boat. Susan stared at the tool, appalled.

Was everything ordained?

Michael was buried on Nassau.

A newspaper ran the story, dated April 15. "One person drowned and two were saved when the forty-foot yacht *Hypatia* struck a reef two miles offshore from O'Neill's near Simms Long Island at 1:30 A.M." The story does not conform to Susan's, but then she did not tell hers out loud.

She held hers to her heart. First that conviction that she must jump. Then the sense of being guided, a sense of having been in the water before, "as if I'd been a sailor in another life, and of knowing *precisely* what to do." Yet she had no previous experience with the ocean, beyond some gentle snorkeling.

In the water on that moonlit, windy night, she says she could *see* herself swimming. She knew she had something else to do with her life. Even as the waves crashed over her, she knew that she'd be safe. And this, more than anything, was the drama for her.

Later, at the interrogation, when she entered that empty room—a table, two chairs—and saw the spanner, she took it as confirmation, a sign that everything was as it was supposed to be. "You are where you need to be right now." That was the way she put it. As if what happened had been prearranged.

Sea stories bring up others.

This one was told me by a friend about another friend of

—I believe we are free, within limits, and yet there is an unseen hand, a guiding angel, that somehow, like a submerged propeller, drives us on.

—RABINDRANATH TAGORE

• • • •

• • • •

hers—a man who one day walked far out onto a jetty. He was deeply depressed. Contemplating suicide. Around him high waves lashed the jetty in tumultuous white froth and heavy green water. He stood on the pier, lost in despair, and thought how all he had to do was take one step. One step forward and his troubles would be over.

At that moment another wave curled in, enormous. It plucked him off his feet and swallowed him. It sucked him out to sea. He was held down, drowning under tons of water.

The next moment he felt the weight recede, then something solid under him—the jetty. The wave had brought him back. He lay on his stomach clutching the wet rocks and crawled weakly back along the jetty to safe land.

He took it as a sign. Some other dimension swinging down to ask if he really wanted suicide. He took it as a second chance at life.

Are we all given second chances? I have written in another book about a friend whom I called Anne, who is convinced she met with angels once. Dark angels. She is a poet and one of the luminous beings on this earth, the ones that make you proud of being human. For years, however, she was married to a man of old family, and they lived a rigid, formal style of life. She and her husband went every summer to the family's private island off the coast of Maine. One night, their son, Augustus, was flying from the Cape to join them, and Anne and her husband left the island in the Boston whaler to pick him up on the mainland. All day it had stormed; several times the plane had been delayed.

It was 9:00 P.M. and still stormy. The seas—building— would not have disturbed Anne's husband, but the increasing rain and lightning made him grab a couple of lifejackets off their lobster boat and throw them in the motorboat.

They set out. The waves were so steep the motor sometimes came out of the water entirely. Halfway to the mainland the whaler was filling with water. Rain poured from the sky. But it was the lightning hitting the water all around them that was frightening. It hit continually, in several places at once, light- ing the entire heavens and eerily guiding them past lobster pots and channel markers.

Anne was terrified. In atavistic fear that her husband would be hit by lightning, and feeling that if possible one of them should be saved for the children's sake, she huddled in the bow of the boat, as far from her husband as she could get. The waves poured over the bow, soaking through her oilskins.

She prayed, "Dear God, I don't know if you intend for me to die tonight, and if you do, that's all right. If you really do in- tend that. But if you're just enjoying a great storm and haven't noticed us out here, I want to remind you that we are here. And I don't want to die. Not yet. I have so many things I want to do. I haven't begun to live my life. But if you know that too, and if you've noticed that we are here, then it's all right with me, if you want us dead. But if I'm spared, dear Lord, I promise to change. I have so much work to do."

When the storm subsided, they were headed out to sea.

After turning back toward the village lights, they arrived, tied up, telephoned the airport, and were told that once again the plane was delayed.

Maine fishing villages can be tiny hamlets. They have white clapboard houses and decaying town halls and libraries. The churches are decorated with fine steeples and stained glass windows, and the houses have handsome wooden cornices, rectilinear and plain against an azure sky. Even in August some of them can be empty, especially at night. The couple had two hours to wait, and, as they were soaked through, Anne's husband went to see if he could rent a motel room.

Anne climbed up the steps of the Knights of Columbus building in the center of town and sat shivering under the street's only light. It was nearly midnight; the storm had cleared; the moon was scudding behind windblown clouds. She sat under the streetlight, an agamic figure in a yellow slicker, suit and boots. With the oilskin collar latched at her throat and the oilskin hat shading her face, only her nose was visible.

The street was dark. There were no signs of life. Then, from her left, appeared an enormous, black limousine. It slowed as it cruised past her, and she could see the man in the backseat lean forward to speak to the two men in front. There was no light on in the car, but she could see that all three wore dark suits. As the car glided by, all three looked at her on the steps. The car proceeded with brooding dignity and disappeared around the corner.

Unbidden, the thought came to her, "The car will turn around and come back." Being rational, she argued with herself. But she could not shake either the conviction or her fear.

In a moment the limousine returned—this time from the right. Still cruising noiselessly, it slowed almost to a halt as it passed. From the car, all three men stared at her, the yellow-slickered figure on the steps.

She was scared. "They're going to come for me," she thought, and as soon as the car had disappeared, she leaped to her feet. At the end of the street, she saw her husband. She ran toward him, shouting, "Hurry! Hurry! We haven't a minute!" Such was the intensity of her fear that, without a word, he responded. Together they raced to the motel room he had found, entered and locked it, and, gasping in urgency, pushed the heavy chest of drawers against the door. Even as she gave way to her fear, Anne knew it was irrational, that no three-men-in-a-car were coming for her.

But their barricade was not a moment too soon. Quietly the big car turned and stopped right outside their door. Except for the throbbing of its motor, there was absolute silence. No doors slammed, no footsteps, no crashing against the walls. No lights. But for a full forty minutes the long, black car throbbed there, menacing. Finally it pulled away.

Anne felt tears starting in her eyes. She had no doubts this episode had come in response to her prayer in the whaler.

"If you really meant what you said in the boat," warned these beings, "about wanting to change your life, then go ahead. But if you were not serious, if you intend to continue living as you are, then know what waits for you. And be afraid."

Anne began a long and intense examination of her views and values. She did change her life. She did accept the challenges and responsibility. She never deserted or neglected her children, but her marriage eventually came to an end.

This is the only story I know in which the celestial beings brought warning and fear and not the spillway of grace. Yet Anne felt nothing of the demonic in them: She came to believe they were merely Watchers, holding up a warning hand.

We hear of miracles a lot. We read about them, too, and I won't say that most of us, but many people, scoff and grimace with contempt or shrug off the impossible, as if each mystery occurred in our imaginations only: a fantasy. Skeptics believe that. They say we're subject to a microsecond's déjà vu, perhaps, as the brain's electrical impulses cross wires and thereby create for us the confusing impression that we've participated in a mystery. I remember once asking an editor at *The New York Times Magazine* if I could do an article on spiritual healing, examining whether it was true or a hoax. He stared into his vodka martini as if it were a crystal ball and allowed as how he thought the idea interesting—certainly there were plenty of things out there we didn't understand, he said; but he couldn't imagine suggesting it in an editorial meeting. The very idea embarrassed him.

Yet the same paper in early 1983 reported the statement of

—Angels and ministers of grace defend us.

—WILLIAM SHAKESPEARE
Hamlet, I.iv

• • • •

Jacob wrestling the Angel.
Marc Chagall. 20th century.

*—Why, who makes much of a
miracle?
As to me I know of nothing else but
miracles,
Whether I walk the streets of
Manhattan,
Or dart my sight over the roofs of
houses toward the sky,
Or wade with naked feet along the
beach just in the edge of the
water,
Or stand under trees in the
woods. . . .
Or watch honey-bees busy around
the hive of a summer forenoon,
Or animals feeding in the fields,
Or birds, or the wonderfulness of
insects in the air,
Or the wonderfulness of the
sundown, or of the stars shining
so quiet and bright,
Or the exquisite delicate thin curve
of the new moon in spring;*

a Connecticut woman who was in a car accident. She was knocked unconscious and could not move. She heard a voice:

"Get out," it said. She felt invisible hands pulling her from the car. Once free, she crawled away. The car exploded.

A shiver runs down your spine when you realize it is not our imagination. Something is watching us out there.

*N*ita Colgate told me of a New York psychiatrist whose husband is also a psychiatrist. Both strict constructionists. One night she had a dream that her husband's car had stopped at the side of a highway at sunset. She saw it clearly: the highway with its traffic, the car, her husband sitting in the car, the Howard Johnson's up the hill, and then the truck bearing down on him, the crash. She woke.

She didn't tell him about the dream.

The following Monday she got a phone call from her husband. His car had given out on the Connecticut Thruway, and he would be late getting home. He had walked up to a phone booth to make the call, he said, and since he had already called a tow truck, he was going to go back and sit in the car to wait. It wouldn't be long, he said. She grew agitated. She didn't want to tell him about her dream, but she was horrified at the idea of his returning to the car.

"Why don't you go up to the Howard Johnson's," she said calmly, "and get a cup of coffee. Don't wait in the car."

"How did you know there's a Howard Johnson's here?" he laughed. "Well, maybe."

"No, really," she said. "I mean it." But what information did she have to go on? A dream? She wasn't going to tell him that a truck might run him down. They hung up. Her husband returned to the car, got in, began to wait. And suddenly he felt a terrible urge to leave. Perhaps he would get coffee. He could see the orange roof of the HoJo's just over the rise. He got out of the car, walked off a few steps. And at that moment the truck came barreling down and smashed the car to bits.

*S*ara Michaels lives in Memphis. The story she told in her soft, southern accent, happened when she was twenty-two, and "it feels like yesterday."

She had dropped out of her senior year in college to travel with some friends, and with a pack on her back had gone first to Israel and then to Greece. They landed on a small island, Ios, and there they rented rooms in the house of "Mama" in a village on a hill. Their rooms had a terrace with a slate floor overlooking the harbor; the four friends spent their evenings on that terrace playing charades and drinking coffee.

"I have never been so happy either before or since. I was not in love with anyone but life. The month was May, the colors so striking and vivid, and everything was heightened, it seemed to me."

I asked if she was doing drugs, which brought a laugh: "Oh no. I was just happy. My drug of choice was caffeine."

These with the rest, one and all, are to me miracles,
The whole referring, yet each distinct and in its place.
To me every hour of the light and dark is a miracle,
Every cubic inch of space is a miracle,
Every square yard of the surface of the earth is spread with the same,
Every foot of the interior swarms with the same.

To me the sea is a continual miracle,
The fishes that swim—the rocks— the motion of the waves—the ships with men in them,
What stranger miracles are there?
　　　　　—WALT WHITMAN
　　　　　　"Miracles"

• • • •

One evening the sun was going down. They were watching a ship come in at the harbor and the people climb on donkeys to ride up the hill into the village. Sarah saw a man whom she'd known earlier in Oak Ridge, Tennessee. She recognized him by his hat and ran down the hill to welcome him. He was staying at the one hotel on the island, on the beach, which was a twenty- or thirty-minute walk from the village. She told him she knew a shortcut along a rocky cliff to the hotel and she took him there and had a cup of tea with him, and then it was time to go back home.

"By then it was pitch-black dark. He walked me partway back, and said, 'Aren't you afraid to walk alone?'

"I smiled. 'You don't know this island,' I said. But because it was so dark, I decided to take the road instead of the shortcut, which meant a half-hour walk. I don't know if the seed had been planted by his comment, but I began to feel afraid. I was talking to myself: 'Don't let these thoughts in; don't ruin a beautiful walk.' But the thoughts kept pushing at me, crazy thoughts: 'What if I step on a snake,' or 'What if I meet a mountain lion coming from the left and here's the ocean on my right.'

"So these scary thoughts were creeping in. I was singing to myself. Ten minutes from the village there was a rope footbridge over a canal, lit by a bare lightbulb, and on this side of it a cemetery. Near the bridge were these windmills. Mama had told me her husband was buried there.

" 'Okay, so it's a graveyard,' I said to myself. 'Don't get spooked,' I said, knowing I was spooking myself all this trip.

"Suddenly I heard a scream. I froze, it was so horrible. Have you ever heard two cats mating? Thinking about it afterward, I think the only sound it could have been was wildcats mating. It was eerie. It was pure evil. It scared me stiff. I was frozen to the road. I literally couldn't move.

" 'In the name of Christ, save me,' I began repeating like a mantra. 'In the name of Christ, save me. In the name of Christ, save me.' I have no concept of time. It could have been two minutes or five minutes or thirty that I stood there repeating those words out loud, over and over.

"I call it 'he,' but I never saw anything. I didn't see anybody. He came down from up above and lifted me under each arm. He lifted me off the ground about six inches and carried me to the bridge with the light bulb and carried me over the bridge.

"What was strange, it was so familiar. It was like the most normal, right occurrence, with nothing unusual about it, and a feeling of utter peace, as if—*of course!*—as if it happens every day. The minute he came, I said, 'Thank you.'

"It was as if your mother picked you up as a child. As soothing as that.

"Then he dropped me. On the other side of the bridge.

"I was barefoot in a short little skirt. I fell and skinned both knees. And then I got to my feet and ran like a jackrabbit, like a deer, into the village, stepping in donkey-doo, and up to our house and up to our room and onto the terrace, where my friends were.

"They looked at me. 'What in the world is the matter with you?' they said.

" 'Just fix me some coffee,' I said. 'I got spooked out there, but I'm all right now.'

"There was one girl, Rowena, from Israel. She pulled me aside. 'You've *got* to tell me what happened,' she said, and I wouldn't, and she kept insisting. 'You have to tell me. You saw God out there.'

"I just looked at her.

"She said, 'When you came in, the light about you was so bright we couldn't look at you.' "

I asked Sara if she had ever seen her guardian angel since.

"No." When she got home she had told a minister at her church. His response was, "Don't tell people. It needs to be private."

But she told her family. The story made an impression especially on her mother, who never doubted it for a minute. Sara shared the story with others. "I'd tell some people and some I wouldn't. I told a bricklayer in a restaurant where I was waitressing. A total stranger. But then other people, close friends, I wouldn't tell."

It's been important to Sara to tell her story, and to tell people also that since then terrible things have happened to her, and she has not been protected or felt directed or guided in any way.

Years later, she was raped. Tied, bound, a knife at her throat, she kept waiting for her angel to appear—"Now my guardian angel will come . . . now my angel will save me"—

and he didn't. We talked about it, she and I. She thought that maybe she needed the experience in order to grow, to learn more compassion—perhaps forgiveness, even for her rapist.

"And I survived. I didn't die. Or perhaps we go through horrible events for reasons we don't know. We can't expect that every time we prick our finger we'll be saved."

Or perhaps she was saved at the cemetery from something worse than rape.

*O*r perhaps it has something to do with our free will. Angels can change all the physical laws but they cannot prevent the murderer from plunging in his knife. They can, however, deflect the blow, call for the doctor, bring the ambulance quickly, guide the surgeon's hand, warm, comfort, heal.

Since writing Sarah's story all those years ago, many people have offered me their own, and I've thought a lot about the questions raised. I was giving a talk once in a Washington suburb, when a young woman rose to tell her tale. I will call her Laura. She said that as a teenager walking down the road one evening, she was kidnapped by three soldiers, and I won't even tell you what country this happened in, because soldiers in every country can be drunk, violent, brutalized by blood and war. This story can happen anywhere.

She was hauled into a car, driven to a deserted woodland, and there the three soldiers spent the next several hours beating her up and doing unspeakable sexual acts. They raped her again and again. They penetrated her with a stick—the tale is

—Are they not all ministering spirits, sent forth to minister for them who shall be heirs of Salvation?
—HEB. 1:14

• • • •

horrific—and finally as the night wore on they agreed to kill her with a tire iron in the trunk of the car. At this point, she struggled, and bit her next assailant in a sensitive spot. They flung her to the ground, and ran over her with the car back and forth, to kill her.

No angels came. But now come the coincidences. First, it had rained the day before, and the ground was soaked. When the car ran over her, she sank into the mud. She was left for dead, covered with mud and leaves.

She came to and saw through the slit of a closed eye the full moon, and when she saw the moon she knew she was still alive and was so full of joy to be alive that she began to cry: "Alive!" With one collapsed lung, a broken arm and leg, a crushed pelvis and internal bleeding, she dragged herself almost three hundred yards down the dirt road toward a tarmac one, thinking that if traffic came by, somebody would see her.

At the same time, an old man who lived a few miles away decided uncharacteristically to go fishing. It was late at night with a large and floating moon. He'd never gone night fishing in his life at that particular spot on the river. He didn't usually tramp through the woods at night. He collected his gear and set off. Walking to the water, he heard the girl's moans and found her, dying.

He didn't know what to do. She was in shock. If he left her, she might die; if he didn't go for help she surely would. He held her gently in his arms and whispered that he had to go for help, that he'd be back, then he covered her with his coat.

—Nothing in this world is single;
All things by a law divine in each
other's being mingle.
—PERCY BYSSHE SHELLEY
"Love's Philosophy"

• • • •

But what help could possibly come at 1:00 in the morning and miles from any town?

Just then they heard a motorcycle, and a moment later a rider came around the bend. The old man waved his arms, flagged him to stop, told about the girl and her need for help. The cyclist roared off, to call the hospital from a pay phone some distance away. It would take hours for an ambulance to arrive. The man returned to the girl, barely alive, who in his absence had sunk dying into a tunnel of light, where beings of light surrounded her and telepathically gave her a choice: die then or later. She chose later.

Then came even stranger happenings, for soon after the old man returned they heard the wail of a siren, and then the ambulance itself appeared. But how could the ambulance have come so fast? The hospital was miles away—in fact, so distant that the hospital dispatcher who talked to the motorcyclist started to order a medivac helicopter to that remote site.

It seems that earlier someone had made a prank call, asking for an ambulance at an abandoned barracks in that general area, and when the ambulance arrived and found no accident, the angry driver had called back to the hospital to report a nasty joke, at which the dispatcher directed him to the nearby girl.

The motorcyclist was never seen again. Who was he, driving in the night?

The ambulance took her to the military hospital on the base. The girl suffered multiple fractures and interior damage.

It required many surgeries and months to recover. The soldiers were found, tried, sentenced, sent to prison. She thanked the fisherman, but afterward she would not speak of her ordeal. She didn't want to be marked. Now here she was, fifteen years later, a beautiful young woman, engaged to be married and standing in a suburban living room, telling for the first time in her life of the horrors she had suffered and how she was saved. She had never told the story before. Tears poured down her face.

PART II

Angelology, or the Knowledge of Angels

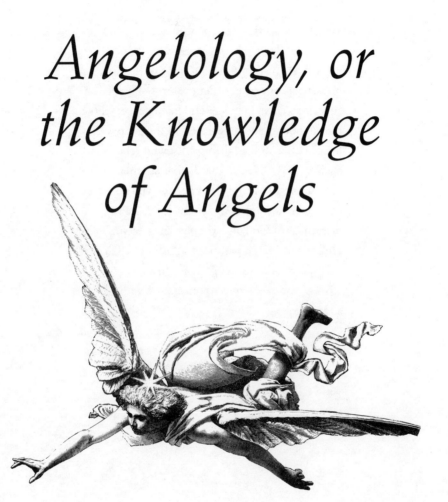

. . . .

ANGEL: [ME., a OF. -ele, repl. OE. engel:— * angil—, Com. Teut. loan, a L. angelus, Gr. αγγελος messenger.] 1. A ministering spirit or divine messenger; one of an order of spiritual beings superior to man in power and intelligence, who are the attendants and messengers of the Deity OE.; hence b. one of the fallen spirits, who rebelled against God OE.; c. a guardian or attendant spirit (*lit.* and *rhet.*) ME.; d. *fig.* a person who resembles an angel in attributes or actions 1592. 2. Any messenger of God, as a prophet or preacher (a Hellenism) ME.; a pastor or minister of a Church ME.; *poet.* a messenger ME.; *fig.* in *angel of death* 1574. 3. *transf.* A conventional figure with wings 1536.

—*The Shorter Oxford English Dictionary*
on Historical Principles

• • • •

CHAPTER 4

The Sons of God

So many wings come here
dipping honey
and speak here
in your home Oh
God.

—AZTEC POEM

· 1 ·

Were there angels among the cavemen? Neanderthal and Cro-Magnon angels? Angels of Australopithecus? More visible perhaps in those days, when people lived closer to nature and their intuition? By the time we come to recorded history, the traces are visible in art and pictographs. The city of Ur in the Euphrates Valley, about 140 miles from Babylon, was settled around 4000 B.C., flourished around 2500 B.C., and continued for another fifteen hundred years or more. There, archeologists have found a stele that depicts a winged figure descending from one of the seven heavens of Sumerian belief to pour the water of life from an overflowing jar into the cup of the king. Some scholars say it is the earliest known representation of an angel, but we find other precursors in the giant winged griffins of Mesopotamia, or in one Egyptian tomb painting that shows a winged Isis (is she the angel of death?) enfolding her devotees in the sleep of her wings. In Greece, both Iris, the rainbow of Zeus, and Hermes, the divine herald, who wore wings on his cap and feet, served angelic functions, carrying messages and giving humans aid. Indeed the idea of angels appears all over Asia Minor, our ancient civilized world, and extends westward into Italy, where centuries later the winged Greek Nike of Victory would be transformed into the Renaissance angels we think of when we think of angels today.

In our Judeo-Christian culture the word *angel* signifies their work as *messenger,* but other words for angels signify their *essence.* They are called gods, the sons of god, ministers, servants, watchers, the holy ones. They constitute a court of heaven. They are called spirits, the heavenly army, hosts, cherubim, seraphim, living creatures. In the Book of Job they are called "morning stars" and in Psalms "the chariots of God."

—The chariots of God are twenty thousand, even thousands of angels: the Lord is among them, as in Sinai, in the holy place.

—PS. 68:17

Angels have existed from the beginning of time. They were there before Adam and Eve walked out spellbound to explore their Garden, "in the first, spinning place, onto the fields of praise"; and after the first humans were driven from Eden for having eaten of the Knowledge of right and wrong, the cherubims (the *s* constituting a double plural), which are one of the three orders of angels closest to God, stood guard at the east gate. Their fiery swords turned every which way to keep us—Adam and Eve—from returning to eat also from the tree of Immortal Life.

Cherubim (a plural noun) means "fullness of God's knowledge." The concept is Assyrian in origin, where *karibu* means "one who prays" or "one who communicates." In Islam they are *el-karrubiyan,* those "brought near" to Allah. They praise God night and day unceasingly.

In Assyrian art, cherubim are depicted as winged creatures with either human or lion faces and the bodies of eagles or of bulls or sphinxes. At first they were conceived of as palace guardians rather than angels.

In the Middle Ages, cherubim were often described as blue or wearing blue, as befits the possessors and bestowers of wisdom: They pour forth wisdom in floods. We speak of them more fully later on.

As time went on, cherubim changed into babies, or *putti,* an idea taken over from Roman lore. In English they are "cherubs," childlike in form and appearance and usually hovering, cupidlike, around a lovely woman. They are vastly different from the awesome beings of Ezekiel's vision or of those cherubim who guard the east gate to Eden.

Who knows if the image of angels arose in different cultures independently? Or which idea was seeding whose, for wise men and merchants and scoundrels and mercenaries and gypsies and the refugees of famine or war were wandering restlessly for thousands of years across all of Asia from Byzantium to Cathay. We forget how rootless ideas are. So we find this concept of angels in Aryan, Mithraic, Manichaean, and Zoroastrian myth, and it runs on down the centuries of time, through Persian thought to Judaic to Christian to Islamic.

In the Bible the first angels were men. They came, like the guides or "familiars" of the American Indians, to walk a few miles beside a hungering human or to help a man or woman at a task. Three came to Abraham, we are told in Genesis, when Abraham had his tent by the oaks of Mambre. What did they look like? They had no wings, no shining garments, no halos around their heads. They were three ordinary-looking men, sitting under the oaks, while their host washed their feet with water and served them veal and bread and cheese. Moreover, unlike later angels, "they did eat." It turned out one was Yahweh Himself, with two angel attendants, and when the meal was over, God disclosed that Abraham's aged wife would bear a son whose descendants would forge a great nation.

And that's all. This visitation is similar to those the Greek gods made to favored mortals, though in this case without the

—So great is the power of angels in the spiritual world that, if I should make known all that I have witnessed in regard to it, it would exceed belief. Any obstruction there that ought to be removed because it is contrary to Divine order the angels cast down or overthrow merely by an effort of the will and a look.

*—*EMANUEL SWEDENBORG
Heaven and Its Wonders and Hell, s.229

• • • •

Abraham Entertaining the
Three Angels. Rembrandt.
Engraving, 17th century.

personal impregnation that Zeus was so fond of undertaking.
It resembles the appearances that come, right up to this very
day, in the devotion of Hindus—not a visit from angels bearing messages from a distant deity but from the god or goddess

—And the angel of the Lord called unto him out of heaven, and said, Abraham, Abraham: and he said, Here am I.

　　　　　　—GEN. 22:11

• • • •

itself, taking on a form and appearing lovingly to the devotee. One-on-one. A personal encounter with God.

During that same visit Abraham bargained unsuccessfully to save Sodom and Gomorrah, and the two cities were destroyed a little later by two more ferocious angels; and a few years later still a gentler, kinder angel kept Abraham from slitting the throat of his new son, which ended that particular practice of human sacrifice, but also goes to show how far a religious zealot will go when he thinks he's heard the voice of God. It's dangerous, this concourse with God.

Abraham's wife Sarah, old and barren, finally had the son announced by the Lord himself under the oaks of Mambre. He was named Isaac. One day Abraham heard the voice of God telling him to sacrifice his boy—to take him to a remote mountain and slit his throat and offer the boy to God as demonstration of Abraham's devotion and total surrender: to give up what was most valuable to him. And he did it. Abraham walked off with his child and one servant, without telling his wife, of course, indeed telling no one what he was going to do. After a while he left his servant and went ahead with the boy, ostensibly to sacrifice a lamb. They had wood for the fire and a knife, and Isaac trustingly speaks out, curious: "Father?"

Abraham answers, "Here I am, my son."

"We have the fire and wood," says Isaac, "but no lamb."

"God will provide," says Abraham, thinking that his own son was to be the lamb. Did his heart twist in his breast? Or was he happy in his driven, rigid surrender to God? They went on a little farther and built the altar and lit the fire, and

Abraham suddenly grabbed his own boy and bound his hands and feet and laid him on the altar, the knife at his throat—when the voice of the Angel stopped him.

"Lay not thy hand upon the lad." At which moment Abraham saw a ram caught in the bushes by its horns, and he took the ram and killed it thankfully and offered that to God instead of his own son.

Angel Preventing Abraham from Sacrificing Isaac on the Rock Moriah. Woodcut, 15th century.

*T*he earliest angels had no wings, not even the Judaic ones. So Jacob, the son of Isaac, saw in a dream-vision a ladder of angels, and some of the angels were climbing and some descending as they hurried about their work between the realms of man and God: they did not fly.

In those days angels acted more as the kind of interior guides that people work with today in their dream journals rather than as external beings. They could be counted on to appear when you called on them, and if Jacob wrestled all night with an angel who would not reveal its name, what do we learn from this strange tale except that even in that nomadic time men (and women, too, I hope) wrestled with their guilty inner selves?

As a young man, Jacob had cheated his brother, Esau, out of his inheritance and run away and later married two wives and sired twelve sons and I don't know how many daughters, including the illegitimate children out of various maids. Then he'd decided to go home. He was scared. He camped a half day's distance from his brother's place and sent presents to

Esau: whole herds of goats and sheep, and thirty milk camels with their foals and ten bulls and twenty jenny-asses and ten foals and forty cows. Still, he couldn't sleep, not knowing if he'd be killed the next day; he deserved it. And that night the angel came and he wrestled with it all night long.

If we take that angel literally, we imagine that in those days angels had real bodies, which grunted and groaned and were thrown to the ground and broke out in glistening sweat as the silent combat continued all throughout that desperate night. And when it was over and Jacob found himself still alive, he demanded a blessing of the being, which was given, though he never learned the angel's name. And then he took his wives and cattle and sheep and servants and many riches down into the valley and across the plains to meet his brother, Esau, who had come out to meet him with 450 armed men; to his relief Jacob discovered that his brother had forgiven him and was glad to see him after all.

The angel never appeared again to Jacob, and I, for one, don't believe it was a true manifestation, having myself wrestled many times with my inner angels as well as the inner spirits or daemons that are confused with them. Sometimes I, too, have found it hard to put a name to what was troubling me and thereby rid myself of it. For when I can name my anguish (guilt! anger! fear!), it loses power over me. In truth, it has never occurred to me to ask my fear or shame or envy or loneliness or anger to bless me when it comes rushing in to grip me by the throat. . . . Will it go away if I ask a blessing of my fear?

In almost all later encounters (and everyone agrees on this) the angel of God comes clothed in radiance and light, and all you want to do in the face of that divinity is to fall down in reverence and joy.

The Sadducees thought angels did not exist except as human fancies. The Pharisees believed in angels.

We have come a long way from the dignified messenger-men of Abraham's time to the sentimental and often cloying imagery of the nineteenth and twentieth centuries—vapid fairies flickering through the air. We have moved in just a few thousand years from the Voice of an Angel telling the runaway maid, Hagar, not to be stupid, but to get out of the wilderness and go back home, to the ox-faced creatures of Ezekiel's vision, to Dante's transcendent beings of light and song, which swing in endless, sparkling circles of praise to God, to Milton's amplified angels, humans incorporeal, cavaliers speeding posthaste at the bidding of God. In modern times they might have ridden on motorcycles, so human seem the eating, drinking angels of Milton. Indeed the archangel Raphael blushes describing angelic sexual intercourse in Milton's poem. Jump a few more centuries and you find modern mystics giving no descriptions, really, except of beauty, and making no attempt to translate into our impoverished human language of nouns and facts the qualities of the spiritual creatures that they saw and heard: angels who advised them, stayed with them, loved and cared for them on a daily basis.

—Their garments are white, but with an unearthly whiteness. I cannot describe it, because it cannot be compared to earthly whiteness; it is much softer to the eye. These bright Angels are enveloped in a light so different from ours that by comparison everything else seems dark. When you see a band of fifty, you are lost in amazement. They seem clothed with golden plates, constantly moving, like so many suns.

—PÈRE LAMY

• • • •

A Seraph, *"Siencie Plenitudo,"* One
Rank of the Choirs of the Angels.
From the cupola of the baptistery.
Mosaic, 14th century.

In the history books of the Old Testament, almost the only
angel mentioned is the Angel of Death. It destroyed 90,000
people at the time of David and on another night slaughtered
185,000 in the camp of the Assyrians, that army being ranged
against the Jews. This was such an extraordinary event that it
is mentioned in no fewer than three different chronicles, with
a wondrous use of pronouns.

Sennacherib, king of Assyria, was invading Judah. His
armies camped outside Jerusalem.

And it came to pass that night, that the angel of the Lord
went out, and smote in the camp of the Assyrians a hundred
fourscore and five thousand; and when they arose early in
the morning, behold, they were all dead corpses.

So Sennacherib went back to Nineveh, much to the relief of the Jews.

Another time an angel stopped the prophet Balaam and frightened his poor donkey with its drawn sword and made it shy and balk and run away. The prophet beat the poor creature mercilessly, not being able to see the angel himself (I've felt the same way with my pony as a child, and it never occurred to me either to blame it on an angel, donkeys and horses being balky beasts at times). And of course we have the visions of the two prophets Isaiah and Ezekiel, on which we base much of how the seraphim, another of the exalted hosts of heaven, appear.

Isaiah lived sometime between the eighth and seventh centuries B.C. In his vision the seraphim had six wings, each pair with a function of its own:

> In the year that King Uzziah died, I saw also the Lord sitting upon a throne, high and lifted up, and his train filled the temple. Above it stood the seraphims; each one had six wings; with two he covered his face and with two he covered his feet, and with two he did fly. And one cried unto another, and said, Holy, holy, holy is the Lord of hosts: the whole earth is full of his glory.

Then Isaiah was struck with his own uncleanness in contrast to the glory and purity of God, but one of the seraphim flew to him carrying a live coal in his hand (though he had taken the coal off the altar with a pair of tongs), and he touched the lips of the holy prophet with this coal, saying, "Your sin is purged."

The angel Raphael is said to be a seraph, and in Milton's *Paradise Lost* he is described:

> . . . six wings he wore, to shade
> His lineaments Divine; the pair that clad
> Each shoulder broad, came mantling o'er his brest
> With regal Ornament; the middle pair
> Girt like a Starrie Zone his waste, and round
> Skirted his loines and thighes with downie Gold
> And colors dipt in Hev'n; the third his feet
> Shaddowd from either heele with featherd maile
> Skie-tincturd grain.

According to medieval symbols, seraphim are red, with three pairs of wings and swords of fire. Their business is to inflame humans to divine love. Dante says seraphim are related to the presence of "gladness of God."

Two hundred years after Isaiah, the prophet Ezekiel saw not seraphim but the very chariots or Wheels of God. It is from his vision that the medieval scholars derived the class of angels known as wheels or thrones, the highest of the high.

His vision took place very precisely on the fifth day of the fourth month of the thirtieth year of the Captivity of the Jews in Babylon, about 560 B.C. It was by the River Che'-bar that the heavens opened:

—The highest ranks [cherubim, seraphim, thrones] do not join in our struggle against our vices, but dwell with us only when, above all conflict, we are with God in peace, in contemplation, and in perennial love.
—JAN VAN RUYSBROECK
Seven Steps of the Ladder of Spiritual Love

• • • •

The Temptation of Christ.
Mosaic, 13th century,
San Marco, Venice.

And I looked, and behold, a whirlwind came out of the
north, a great cloud, and a fire infolding itself, and a brightness was about it, and out of the midst thereof as the colour
of amber, out of the midst of the fire.

Also out of the midst came the likeness of four living
creatures. And this was their appearance; they had the likeness of a man.

And every one had four faces, and every one had four
wings.

And their feet were straight feet; and the sole of their feet
was like the sole of a calf's foot: and they sparkled like the
colour of burnished brass.

And they had the hands of a man under their wings. . . .

Their wings were joined one to another; they turned not
when they went; they went every one straight forward.

Seraphim Standing on Winged and Fiery Wheels. Byzantine Mosaic, 13th century.

Each of the four had the face of a man as well as three other faces on their helmets—of a lion, an ox, and an eagle. They moved on wheels in the middle of wheels, blue-green in color, or aquamarine, and when the creatures lifted off the earth, the wheels lifted too. Above their heads was "the likeness of the firmament," which was the color of crystal, and under this were their wings, two on each side of their bodies. Ezekiel is helpless to describe the tremendous noise of their wings, "like the noise of great waters, as the voice of the Almighty, the voice of speech, as the noise of an host." A voice came from this "firmament" over their heads when they stood and let down their wings. Above the firmament was a throne blue as sapphire with what appeared to be a man in it surrounded by amber and fiery tones, and a brightness as sharp as a rainbow.

When Ezekiel saw all this, he fell on his face before the glory of the Lord.

This is a condensation of some of his incredible vision.

Thrones wheel around the High Fixed Point of God, inspiring confidence in the power of God. The Virgin Mary herself is poetically said to be a throne: "True throne of God, she exalts the throne of God." This, of course, is merely a manner of speech, since she is actually not considered an angel. In Catholic dogma she was a human being conceived without original sin (thus the immaculate conception) and also without personal sin, and therefore she is glorified and raised above all the angels in heaven. As the mother of God she is considered to be the queen of the angels.

I know one astrophysicist, Robert Jastrow, who teaches at

Dartmouth. He postulates that what Ezekiel saw was not an angel at all but a spaceship with people from outer space, who moved rigid as robots in their space suits, turning their whole bodies so their feet were always "straight." Jastrow, at least when I knew him, did not believe in God. But he did believe in the evolution of mankind climbing to ever higher orders of intelligence and that we are now moving to a new and exciting Intelligence, which will replace us, ultimately . . . the computer!

*I*n the earliest accounts of the Old Testament (Genesis 6), around 2000 B.C., angels stayed close to earth. Indeed, so close were they that the Sons of God had intercourse with the beautiful "daughters of men," producing thereby the race of Nephilim, "the famous men." It was common folklore. The Greeks and other peoples also held to the underground belief that angels and humans can consort together, have progeny. By the time of the Captivity of the Jews in Babylon, however, around 600 B.C., the angels and archangels had moved to higher spiritual spheres, though they could still appear as men sometimes, and in another six hundred years, by the time of Jesus, angels were clearly perceived as above sexual union with women, no matter how seductive the women may be.

*T*hree times following the conquest of the kingdom of Judah by King Nebuchadnezzar II, the factious, rebelling Jews were deported to Babylon: in 598 B.C., in 586 B.C. (when the Temple of Jerusalem was destroyed), and again in 582 B.C. after still another uprising. Troublesome people, the Jews. They were brought to Babylon, the capital city of their Persian conquerors, and there they began to fall under the spell of the luxurious ways of the wealthy, urbane Persians, even beginning to worship false gods.

This was not the first time the Jews had fallen away from their God. Some two hundred years earlier, when Ahab was king of Samaria, it was up to righteous prophets like Elijah to make them toe the mark—and a hard time he had of it, his outlaw life in constant danger. Jezebel killed 450 of his fellow priests. On one of his outcast wanderings in the wilderness, though, an angel itself came to feed him, under a broom tree, when the poor, discouraged prophet was ready to give up, burned out. "Eat," said the angel. "You'll need your strength." Or words to that effect. And then the holy man went another forty days, fasting and meditating in the desert, before walking down into Samaria and killing four hundred priests of Ba'al.

During the Captivity, Nebuchadnezzar, the king of Babylon (607–587 B.C.), undertook a vast building program, which included the hanging gardens and the great Temple of Marduk or Venus with its associated ziggurat, the tower of Etemenanki, known to us as the Tower of Babel; and it was for that he needed slaves. It rose in seven stages to three hundred feet—one of the wonders of the world. There were temples to Ishtar and Ninmalsh and Gula. According to the historian Herodotus, Babylon was the most splendid city in the world.

During the Captivity, Nebuchadnezzar, the king of Baby-

*—With silence only as their
benediction
God's angels come
Where, in the shadow of a great
affliction,
the soul sits dumb*
—JAMES GREENLEAF WHITTIER
writing to a friend on the death
of his sister

• • • •

lon, had an image of God built. It was all gold and sixty cubits high and six cubits wide. A cubit is the length of a man's forearm, roughly twenty inches long, so the image stood one hundred feet high and ten feet wide, and it was set up on the Plain of Dura, sparkling and flashing in the sun. Nebuchadnezzar told his princes, governors, captains, judges, treasurers, counselors, sheriffs, and all the rulers of the provinces to come to the dedication of the image and then at the sound of the music to fall down and worship it. For instruments he had cornets, flutes, harps, sackbuts, psalteries (a stringed instrument played by twanging), dulcimers, and "all kinds of musick." And when this cacophony began, everyone fell down on their faces as they were told, for fear of being burned alive in a fiery pit, which is what the alternative was.

All, that is, except three saintly men, Jews, and we even know their names: Shadrach, Meshach, and Abednego, for they were not only governors or satraps in the administration of Babylon but holy men, devoted to Yahweh, and they knew better than to worship graven images, when God is limitless, formless, and so magnificent that the concept cannot even be grasped by the limited human mind.

These three, together with Daniel, had been brought as children into the palace of the potentate, as was the custom in those days, to be reared for three years, eating the best meat and drinking good wine, to build their health and beauty and see if they found favor at the court; but the three youngsters and Daniel had begged the head eunuch to let them remain vegetarians, saying that neither their health nor their beauty

—Those who are in a state of innocence attribute nothing of good to themselves, but consider themselves receivers, and ascribe all things to the Lord; they wish to be led by Him, and not by themselves; they love everything that is good, and delight in everything that is true, because thus . . . is to love the Lord. . . .

—EMANUEL SWEDENBORG
Heaven and Hell, 278

• • • •

would suffer by the diet. They undertook a ten-day fast to prove their point, which so persuaded the head eunuch that, against the king's commands, he had permitted them to eat only pulse, or beans, instead; which is the diet of all true holy people throughout the world—all Indian gurus and sadhus, all hermits and monks and nuns and yogis, all who by prayer and contemplation seek to develop a conscious connection to God. At the end of the three years, Nebuchadnezzar had found these four young men full of wisdom and understanding, and with powers "ten times better than all the magicians and astrologers that were in his realm."

We don't know where Daniel was at the time, but these three others, standing before the golden image on the Plain of Dura, refused to prostrate themselves full-length. So they were bound hand and foot and the fires were stoked in the fiery furnace until it was seven times hotter than usual, and then they were thrown in—hats, coats, shoes, stockings, and all (says the writer, obviously relishing the detail). The fire was so hot that the soldiers who cast the three men into the flames caught fire themselves and burned to death. Imagine!

Then the king looked down into the fire pit and saw the three men and another as well, walking about in the flames. They walked right out. The princes, governors, captains, and the king's counselors all saw these men untouched by fire. "Nor was a hair of their head singed, neither were their coats changed, nor the smell of fire had passed on them." Nebuchadnezzar, having learned nothing about the love of God, or that there is One God Only, though called by many names, praised the God of these men and the angel who delivered them and immediately decreed that anyone saying a word against the God of these three holy Jews should be cut in pieces and their houses made into dunghills, because no other god could deliver the way this one could.

By the time this story is told, we are aware that the story-tellers are telling stories, and moreover they have a purpose: to show that angels reward those faithful to God. The earlier angels weren't concerned with rewards. They appeared with news of one sort or another, or they destroyed a city, or they cared for and watched over some man or woman (usually a man). But they weren't much up to rewarding people for adherence to the faith. Perhaps because such stories weren't needed until people got lax and memories began to fade under the influence of the luxuries of Babylon; or perhaps because these angelic duties were added with the passage of time.

The same impetus lies behind the story of Daniel and the lions—a gentler and more loving tale, because King Darius is a finer man than Nebuchadnezzar. The Book of Daniel is the only Old Testament book that mentions angels by name: Gabriel and Michael. They are "watchers," and they appear to Daniel in various visions, but the angel that "shut the lions' mouths" is still anonymous. (In the Apocryphal *Book of Tobit,* the angel named Raphael accompanies Tobias on his journey to find a wife and heal his father's blindness. But *Apocryphal* means "hidden writings, secret"; and this book is technically not part of either the Hebrew Bible or the Christian Old Testament.)

By then there'd been some power changes. Nebuchadnezzar had died, and his grandson, Belshazzar (who, remember, saw the handwriting on the wall and asked Daniel, this holy prophet, this seer, this man who walked hand-in-hand with God, to interpret it for him)—Belshazzar had lost his empire, conquered by Cyrus. *His* successor, Darius, was about sixty-two years old when he took office in 522 B.C.; and Daniel, having survived four Oriental potentates, was by now one of three great presidents, ruling immediately under Darius and governing 120 princes of the kingdom. Of the three presidents, Darius loved Daniel best, recognizing "an excellent spirit was in him."

So the other princes, governors, presidents, captains, and counselors tricked the king into signing an edict that for thirty days no one could petition any god or king except Darius himself; or else they'd be thrown to the lions, which was possible because in those days Oriental satraps kept zoos of wild and rare animals, much as present-day potentates collect rare art. Darius signed it in the rush of business without thinking that according to the inflexible law of the Medes and Persians he couldn't take it back: no decree signed by the king could be changed. (Thus my grandmother's old saying, "After all, it's not the law of the Medes and the Persians!")

When Daniel knew the edict was signed, he went home to his house, opened the windows onto the street, and prayed loudly three times a day on his knees, giving thanks to God, as he always did.

Daniel in the Lion's Den. Copyright © The British Library Board. From a commentary on the Book of Revelations by the Spanish Monk Beatus (d. 978).

Of course Daniel's enemies raced to Darius with the news that Daniel was petitioning someone other than the king and had to be thrown to the lions. Darius was horrified and angry with himself. He worked all day trying to figure out a way to save Daniel, only to find he couldn't undo the law. Sorrowfully, then, that night he ordered Daniel into the lions' den, telling him that he hoped Daniel's God would deliver him. Did he also direct his men to feed the lions extra helpings of their evening meat? Who knows? Darius himself spent that night in the palace fasting and praying, awake till dawn, when he rushed out to the lair to see if Daniel was still alive; and then he threw the advisors who had tricked him into the den with their wives and children (which was excessive perhaps, but they didn't have Welfare in those days, so perhaps it was a kindness), and the lions ate them all. Then the king directed everyone to worship the god of Daniel, who could perform such miracles. Daniel remained in prosperity throughout the reign of Darius and into that of his successor, too.

> My god has sent his angel and hath shut the lions' mouths, and they have not hurt me.
>
> —DAN. 6:22

• 2 •

*A*ngels are frequently mentioned in Judaic lore. These tales allude to four angels at the throne of God and name them:

Raphael

Gabriel | Throne | Michael

Uriel

Uriel brings the light of the Knowledge of God to men. He is interpreter of prophecies, the Angel of Retribution. His name means "Light of God," and in Milton's *Paradise Lost* he is called a regent of the sun.

Tobias and the Angel Raphael.
Fillippino Lippi. 15th century.

Gabriel is the chief ambassador to humanity. His name means "Hero of God." He is the Angel of Revelation. He is majestic, richly attired, and depicted in Christian iconography as kneeling before Mary, hands folded on his breast or carrying a scroll, scepter, or lily.

It is Gabriel who brings good news. It was Djibril, the Islamic name for Gabriel, "the Faithful Spirit," who brought a revelation to Muhammad in a clear Arabic tongue on the "Night of Power and Glory." Gabriel, the Judaic Angel of Judgment became under Christianity the Angel of Mercy. He is made of fire.

Michael is the prince of the heavenly hosts, despite the fact that archangels rank second-to-last in the celestial hierarchy. Michael is the commander-in-chief of the celestial army. His name means "Looks Like God" or "Who Is As God." He is strong and young and handsome, and in Renaissance paintings is depicted as wearing armor. He is the protector of the Roman Catholic Church, as well as the patron saint of the Hebrew nation. Though the Bible does not say so, folklore holds that it was Michael who liberated Peter from prison and led him past the guards. Michael appeared together with Gabriel to the prophet Muhammad. Just as great sadhus and holy men can bilocate and levitate, Michael can appear in three of the seven heavens simultaneously. (We know little about these divisions of heaven, which date back to the origins of Zoroastrianism, although we know that Saint Paul was carried to the third heaven and that to be in "seventh heaven" is the highest state.) Michael is made of snow.

— . . . The Night of Glory,
more opulent than a thousand
moons!
Then angels and revelations waft
down
by the grace of their Lord.
*—*KORAN, XCVII

• • • •

The Angel Israfil (angel of music). Islamic manuscript painting.

Raphael is a seraph and also the chief of guardian angels, the Angel of Providence who watches over all humanity. His name means "Divine Healer," or "God Heals." Often he is depicted with the young man, Tobias, and his dog, the travels of whom he accompanied as faithfully as the supernal helpmate of a fairy tale. He is especially concerned with pilgrims—meaning not only travelers but those on pilgrimages toward God. He walks, therefore, with staff and sandals, water gourd, and wallet held by a strap over his shoulder. He is a friendly being. Here is Milton's description of Raphael in *Paradise Lost*:

> Down thither prone in flight
> He speeds, and through the vast ethereal skie
> Sails between worlds and worlds, with steady wing
> Now on the polar winds, then with quick Fann
> Winnows the buxom Air; . . .

These are the first four, the archangels. In addition, legend and Jewish mystical tradition have hundreds of other angels, some with a hundred variants on their names, of which more will be said below.

Islam, too, knows many angels and by name. They guard heaven's gates from the "listening" of demons, djinns, and shaitans.

Israfil, "the burning one," is the Angel of the Day of Judgment. He glorifies Allah with many tongues in a thousand lan-

—Thrice he assayd [to speak] and thrice in spirit of scorn Tears such as Angels weep, burst forth.

—JOHN MILTON
Paradise Lost, I

• • • •

Angel with Trumpet.
Lucas Cambraso. Drawing,
16th century.

guages, and Allah creates from his breath a million more angels to glorify Himself. Israfil looks each day and night toward Hell and weeps with such grief that his tears "would
inundate the earth if Allah did not stop their flow." Israfil is

also the Angel of Music, and his trumpet or horn has the form of a beast's horn and contains dwellings like the honeycomb of bees, and in these cells repose the souls of the dead.

Mika'il (Michael) was created by Allah five thousand years after Israfil. He has saffron hair from his head to his feet and wings of green topaz. Each hair has a million faces, and in each face are a million eyes from which fall seventy thousand tears. These become the Kerubim, who lean down over the rain and the flowers and the trees and the fruit. Mika'il has a million tongues, each speaking a million languages. Mika'il does not laugh.

Djibril (Gabriel) was created five hundred years after Mika'il. He has 1600 wings and also saffron hair. The sun is between his eyes. Each day he enters the Ocean 360 times, and when he comes out, a million drops of water fall from each wing to become angels, who sing the praise of Allah. When he appeared to the Prophet on the Night of Power and Glory, to reveal the Koran, his wings stretched from the east to the west. His feet were yellow, his wings green, and around his neck was a necklace of rubies. His face was of a radiant brightness. Between his two eyes were written, THERE IS NO GOD BUT GOD, AND MUHAMMAD IS THE PROPHET OF GOD.

Azrael or Azaril is the Angel of Death. To the Muslims he is another form of Raphael. He is veiled with a million veils. He has four faces, one before him, one on his head; one behind him, and one beneath his feet. He has seventy four thousand wings and his body is covered with eyes. When one of these

—None sing so wildly well
As the angel Israfel.
And the giddy stars (so legends tell)
Ceasing their hymns, attend the spell
Of his voice, all mute.

—EDGAR ALLAN POE
Israfel

• • • •

eyes blinks, a creature dies. He is vaster than the heavens. Between his hands lies all the world, like a dish from which he can eat whatever he wishes; and thus the Angel of Death turns the world this way and that. He sits on a throne in the sixth heaven.

The Koran also mentions by name: Harut and Marut, who yielded to sexual temptation; and Malik, the angel in charge of hell. In addition, nineteen angels stand as guards of hell. They are called the "Violent-Thrusters" (*al-Zabaniya*), an otherwise unused word. They are called "rough" and "violent." The tortured in hell call to the keeper of hell, "O Malik!"

In the Koran, Isa or Jesus stands in the company of angels nearest Allah, and is himself of semi-angelic character.

The angels of Islam, *malaika,* meaning "messengers," are guardians over mankind, writing down what they do, although in one passage of the Koran the writing is done by Allah Himself. Tradition says they are formed of light, as Satan or Iblis and all the demons and djinns are created of fire. But there is no reference in the Koran to what angels are made of, and since fire and light as so closely allied, can change into one another, give each other off—light to fire, fire to light—we are left with the despairing knowledge that Allah alone knows the truth.

Like Christian angels, the Islamic ones are not described as either masculine or feminine, and if they have a particular gender (and some people think they do), they may not take advantage of it. In that respect, therefore, humans are said to have a higher potential for excellence even than the angels above us, for we must learn to curb our lust.

CHAPTER 5

A Thunder Like Drumming

· 1 ·

Why is it that angels like disguise? It seems they take whatever form the visited person is willing to accept; and sometimes no form at all—a dream, a thought, a surge of power, a sense of guidance. They don't seem far removed from natural events. This explains why angels are easily explained away, and why skeptics can pad down the corridors of their intellect, unhindered by the intrusion of the inexplicable: because (we observe) nothing whatsoever happens to such rationalists that cannot be naturally explained. And this is the most miraculous marvel of them all! It is not that skeptics do not experience the mysterious and divine, but rather that the mysteries are presented to them in such a flat and factual, everyday, reasonable way as not to disturb; for this is the rule: no one receives more information than he can bear. Therefore it seems that angels bring messages in the form—even in the dialect—that each recipient can hear.

Likewise the deeply religious or those spiritually inclined may or may not see visions, depending on their sect and perhaps on the openness of their hearts. But even in such circumstances we are struck by the extraordinary fact that these visitations and insights are usually in accord with the upbringing and conditioning of the recipient. A Hindu rarely sees a vision of Christ, and Protestants don't often dream of the Buddha, though odd to say it happens. I have a Jewish friend who, to her horror and confusion, kept witnessing Jesus Christ together with all the Christian symbolism whenever she smoked pot. Christ's face glimpsed through the darkness of a window, or a shining cross. It changed her life. I know another woman, raised an Episcopalian, who one day had so violent a vision she was termed insane. She was driving down the New Jersey Turnpike when her revelation came—Saul knocked off his horse and blinded on the road to Damascus. She was picked up by the police driving the wrong way down the road. She'd seen into other worlds, she said, and when she recovered from the resonances of her trance, she changed her dress, her diet, desires, prayers, and went to India and became a Hindu, um, priestess. She now maintains an ashram on the east coast. Her story is interesting because it is so rare. Angels and gods usually come in the cultural clothing of the people to whom they appear.

Two Spirits Coming for Black Elk. Native American painting, 20th century.

To some people they come as animals. Elijah was fed by ravens in the wilderness, the birds flying to him both morning and evening with sustenance from God. Were they angels?

Among the American Indians, great winged birds, Raven and Eagle, help little mankind, or play tricks, or heal or bring fire or carry messages from God; and "familiars," sometimes winged, sometimes not, walk in friendly fashion among humans, guarding them from harm and helping them with shamanistic practices.

Patti Lipman is a former anthropologist who studied the Northwest Coast Indians for the Smithsonian Institution. She always felt an affinity for crows. They can taunt you, tease you,

—I looked up at the clouds, and two men were coming there, head-first like arrows slanting down; and as they came, they sang a sacred song and the thunder was like drumming. I will sing it for you. The song and the drumming were like this:

"*Behold a sacred voice is calling you;*

All over the sky a sacred voice is calling."

—BLACK ELK SPEAKS

• • • •

she says. They chase away predators. They are smart and people can tame them. Crows are Patti's totem. Whenever times are bad, she looks for crows, and if she sees one, she knows everything is going to be okay. They are her angels.

One year at Vail she had a ski accident. She smashed into a tree, shattered her ribs, and occasioned nerve damage to the right elbow and hand. It was the kind of high-speed accident that is usually fatal, and every year three or four expert skiers die by slamming into trees.

After that, she was alone all day, recovering, and the pain, she says, was intolerable! She was sitting on the sofa in her condominium watching TV with a channel changer. She couldn't stand up. She was lamenting, "Why me! Why, God, did this happen to me?"

Then she saw two crows on a nearby roof. She was surprised, for you rarely see a crow in Vail, she says. They flew to the railing of her balcony, and then clear as day she heard a voice: "But, Patti, we let you live."

Later I'll tell you my own encounter with a swan, and Hope MacDonald, a writer, tells the story of a young girl, Laurie, who late one night found herself being followed home on the bus by a suspicious-looking man. She was terrified and began to pray. At her stop a great white dog stood at the curb, a Great Pyrenees, which put its head under her hand and paced beside her all the way to her house. The man took warning and drifted off. At her door the dog then disappeared.

To people who live close to the earth, spirits live everywhere—in rocks and stones and trees and rivers and animals and desert scrub. Divinity shines forth everywhere, so why shouldn't guardians walk beside us too? And why shouldn't simple nomads, innocent as children, trust their own senses?

People who live close to nature are bound to it, and this idea of the connectedness of things cannot be put aside. Nor can death, which surrounds you in the country; you can't stop seeing it: the death of ducks and pigs and snakes and fish and cats and fine horses and good hunting dogs, the death of babies, the death of family members. And in that silence that comes of living solitary as a hermit far from urban centers you come to see as a mystic sees, to hear with more acute ears, until you, too, are a part of the simple miracle of living and dying and growing and fading. It takes days and months and even years. Monks, hermits, shamans, all rishis and holy people, search out this solitude and time for prayer (unendurable labor) because it is the only gateway to the direct experience of God.

—The world is charged with the grandeur of God,
It will flame out like shining from shook foil.
—GERARD MANLEY HOPKINS
"God's Grandeur"

• • • •

Be still, and know that I am God.

But when it comes—we are transformed!
In a letter to President Franklin Pierce in 1853, Chief Seathl of the Suwamish tribe wrote,

The white man must treat the beasts of this land as his brothers. I am a savage and I do not understand any other way. I have seen a thousand rotting buffalos on the prairie, left by the white man who shot them from a passing train. I

—If we had a keen vision and feeling of all ordinary human life, it would be like hearing the grass grow and the squirrel's heart beat and we should die of that roar which lies on the other side of silence.

—GEORGE ELIOT
Middlemarch

• • • •

am a savage and I do not understand how the smoking iron horse can be more important than the buffalo that we kill only to stay alive.

What is man without beasts? If all the beasts were gone, men would die from great loneliness of spirit. For whatever happens to the beasts, soon happens to man. All things are connected. . . . Whatever befalls the earth befalls the sons of the earth.

• 2 •

*I*n ancient Babylon, the people worshipped a pantheon of deities: winged bull-men, a god named Nebo, another moon god and various *sukalli,* or angel messengers, who were sons of the deities. It was Zoroaster who introduced a monotheistic deity and transformed the old Babylonian and Assyrian gods into archangels, whence they crept irrevocably into Judaism and Christianity. By the time of the Babylonian Exile of the Jews, Zoroastrianism held sway. It was the official religion of King Darius, and much of our present Western lore on angels dates from this early influence.

Zoroaster, or Zarathustra (the name meaning "rich in camels"), lived sometime between 1000 and 600 B.C. He was born in Medea and was active in Bactria, a prophet who protested the religion which was probably close to the Hindu Vedas and which included fire worship, the sacrifice of cattle, and possibly the worship of the Goddess and of Ba'al or Ba'lim. Zoroaster sought to wean people toward an ethical or moral monotheism. As the Buddha would do half a millennium later, he emphasized good thoughts, good words, good deeds; he taught that the world is polarized in a perpetual battle between good and evil and that we are supposed to choose between them.

In Zoroastrianism the good is ruled by one Supreme God, Ahura Mazda, the "Wise Lord," the supreme Pure Light. Against him is ranked the evil spirit Angra Mainyu or Ahaitin (Satan), the spirit of darkness, surrounded by his demons or *daevas*. But Ahura Mazda is helped by seven *amesha spenta,* archangels or holy spirits, emanating from him and representing seven fundamental moral ideas. These seven angels have various names, but one grouping translates them as Good Knowledge (or Wisdom), Truth (or The Way), Piety, Salvation, Immortality (or Delight in Beauty), Obedience, and Deserved Good Luck, and each protects something: Wisdom is the protector of Earth; Truth the protector of Fire; Delight in Beauty the protector of Plants, and so on. *Ashi* the Good is the Angel of Blessings, she being the feminine form of *Asha,* who is Truth, Justice, Virtue, Holiness, Cosmic Law and Order. Ahura Mazda bestows His abundant blessing (Ashi) on those who follow Asha, His Truth, His Divine Law. Ashi is protected and mothered by *Armaiti,* the Angel of Devotion or Love of God in our hearts. Her three brothers and playmates are *Sraosha,* the Angel of Divine Intuition, *Rashnu,* the Angel of Justice, who weighs the good and evil deeds of the soul at death, and *Meher,* the Angel of Light and Mercy who sustains and comforts the soul during this terrible time.

A Winged Being Kneeling beside the Sacred Tree. From a wall panel at the palace of Ashur-nasir-apal II at Nimrud, 9th century B.C.

In addition there are other angels, or *yazatas,* including *Psychopomp,* the "Celestial Escort," Lord of the Material Plane; *Vata,* who rules the Air and Winds; *Mithra* of ten thousand eyes, who later became the Persian God of Light, a god in his own right. In Zoroastrianism, Mithra is the angelic mediator between heaven and earth, the judge and preserver of the world. He is represented on ancient monuments as a handsome youth plunging a dagger into the neck of bulls and he was worshiped in underground catacombs with a ceremony that involved baptism, the eating of consecrated bread and water, and anointing with honey.

It appears that until the time of Zoroaster, the Supreme Deity, by whatever name, contained within itself both good and evil, without the concept of right or wrong. God flung upon the earth events that were perceived and named by people as either good or evil but that are neither one or the other, or else that contain the seeds of both. With Zoroastrianism came the duality we're familiar with, with the good angels on one side and the bad demons on the other. They wage an uneven battle, since good is assured the ultimate victory.

In 330 B.C., Alexander the Great almost wiped out Zoroastrianism. The Muslim conquest of Asia Minor in the seventh century A.D. pretty much finished off what remained, and the majority of Zoroastrians migrated to India in the tenth century A.D., where they became known as the Parsees, still a small sect today, strictly intermarrying and therefore growing smaller all the time.

Today they have been assimilated into the Hindu milieu, dress, and customs. About 250,000 of them remain, mostly around Bombay.

Zoroaster wrote some 21 hymns to his angels. Here are two songs from the *Gathas* of Zarathustra:

—Where wast thou when I laid the foundations of the earth? . . . When the morning stars sang together, and all the sons of God shouted for joy?

—JOB 38:4,7

• • • •

When I held Thee in my very eyes, then I realized Thee in my mind, O Mazda, as the First and also the Last for all eternity, as the Father of Vohu Mana, the Good Mind, as the true Creator of Asha, the Divine Law, and as Lord over the actions of life.

—YASNA, 31.8

She (Armaiti, Angel of Devotion to God) indeed will give us good shelter. . . . she, the Beloved of Vohu Mana (the Good Mind). Hence for her did Mazda Ahura . . . make plants flourish in the birth of primeval life.

—YASNA, 48.6

Four or five thousand years ago (around 2500 B.C.) the Aryans, or Indo-Europeans, settled in Iran and India. Their supreme god was Dyeus (thence *Zeus, deus, deity,* and other words). Dyeus was the shining God of Sky, the giver of rain, the vanquisher of enemies with thunderbolts. His divine consort was Mother Earth, and around them revolved the other gods, the sun, moon, and dawn. These early peoples worshiped fire as well as a host of devas and nature deities. The word *deva* itself means "shining one," but such beings were not exactly considered angels then, as they are not considered angels in India today.

Are there Hindu angels? I cannot get a direct answer. For angels appear mostly in monotheistic religions, which need an intermediary between the human world and a far-removed and distant deity. In polytheistic religions the gods themselves appear. In India, people don't see angels; they see God, just as the greatest Christian mystics—Saint Teresa, Saint John of the Cross, or Julian of Norwich speak little of angels and much of Christ: because it was the Godhead that appeared to them and Whom they adored. The angels are ancillary.

I once asked a great Hindu teacher about whether angels appear in Hindu thought. He spoke instead of the Almighty God, the Creator, which is beyond our puny imaginations. God is absolute knowledge, absolute wisdom, absolute love. By one thousand names He is known, but is only One. In godness there is neither right nor wrong, but only pure being. Limitless, formless, boundless, shapeless, God nonetheless wants a relationship with humankind, and because God cannot be seen without a form, God in boundless compassion takes on a body to appear to the worshiping devotee. This realization of God, said this teacher, comes in the form of energies, or *shaktis*. Often the shakti appears as a goddess, a devi, such as Parvati. (A devi, by the way, is not to be confused with the masculine *deva*, which is a lowly nature spirit in India and which, under Zoroaster and later Persian folklore, was denounced as a *daeva, div, djinn*, or *demon*.) Durga is the greatest of shaktis, but there is also Kali, who appears naked as a black-faced hag, smeared with blood and with a protruding tongue. Not your usual angel. In her four hands Kali holds sword, shield, the head of a giant, and a strangling noose. She wears a necklace of skulls and dances in a wild God-ecstasy so

—God alone suffices.
—Saint Teresa of Avila

• • • •

abandoned and powerful that at one moment she crushes the head of her own husband underfoot and then in horror at her blind impetuousness revives him lovingly. She drinks the blood of demons. She is one of the many aspects of God.

There are other devis—Lakshmi, or abundance; and Surasuti, a white and peaceful shakti. Devis are always feminine, the manifestation of God in female form, and the yogi, the holy mystic, attains liberation and wisdom by *being made love to* physically and spiritually by this *shakti* or devi—by the goddess herself. I will come back to this sexual point about angels later, but we find the same language in Christianity, when the saint throws herself onto the arrows of God's love and calls Christ the Bridegroom, herself the Bride, to be enjoyed.

The devi don't appear to function as messengers, but Hindus also acknowledge the existence of winged beings, the *kinpuru'sh,* who hover worshipfully about the gods, and these may be angels of a kind. They live in the same place as the gods, but on another plane of consciousness, and I can't tell you either what this means or what they do. There are also the *apsaras,* the beautiful geishas who pleasure the gods with music and dance and adoration and sexual and erotic bliss. Apsaras were created for lovemaking. They are the perfect dispensers of amorous bliss, copulating endlessly with their beloved. Apsaras usually stay in heaven. Sometimes, however, they are sent by the gods to seduce and distract men who are disturbing the peace of the universe (and we can only wish

—In the Pilgrimage of the Spirit, it is the strong and steadfast aspiration to meet God face to face that is the pathfinder, first and last.
—DILIP KUMAR ROY
Pilgrim of the Stars

• • • •

that they'd be sent more frequently). Apsaras adore adoring, and adore having their adoration adored. They adore giving pleasure, which comes in all divine and loving forms and without troublesome bodily fluids or menstruation or pain or pregnancy, pain, birth, or nursing. But if they once were angels, apsaras no longer hold title to that state.

"Are there angels in ancient Hindu religious thought?" I persisted.

"Yes," the Master answered. But he could not come up with the name for them, though he mused on the Persian concept of *feresh'ta,* the winged spiritual counselors that praise and worship God both in story and in art. And yet angels abound in modern Hindu practice. Were they brought by Western merchants and Portuguese missionaries after the Renaissance?

As with Christian angels, modern Hindu angels are closer to God than to humans, but they honor human saints and prophets as well as God. In his beautiful book, *Autobiography of a Yogi,* Paramahansa Yogananda tells of visiting a holy woman in India in the 1920s. She was the wife and lifelong companion of the enlightened master Lahiri Mahasaya, and she described to Yogananda, then a young man, how one night she dreamed—and the dream was vividly clear—that there were angels in her room. She woke up only to discover the room radiating with a dazzling light and her husband levitating in his meditation in the center of the room. Off the floor! She was so astonished, she thought she was still dream-

—At the end of the 1890s the great Indian saint, Sri Ramakrishna, was asked:

"Do you believe in God, sir?"

"Yes," he replied.

"Can you prove it, sir?"

"Yes."

"How?"

"Because I see Him just as I see you here, only more intensely."

—PARAMAHANSA YOGANANDA
Autobiography of a Yogi

• • • •

Shiva and Parvati with angels.
Hindu wood carving from the
façade of a building in Nepal.

ing, because surrounding him were angels, palms folded, worshipping his worship.

Lahiri Mahasaya spoke to his wife, saying she was not
dreaming, and she fell to her knees in awe and fear, humbly
asking her husband's forgiveness for not having recognized
the saint he was. He asked her to do reverence then to the angels, too, who returned her greeting with all their celestial
voices sounding together; after which they disappeared. The
room returned to blackness.

She became her husband's disciple, and he never slept in
her bed again.

That's a hard resolution to the story. Sad by our way of

thinking—that the angels and her husband's great spiritual force should have separated them from conjugal love. It reinforces all the reasons we distrust the celestial world. Fear.

Fear of loss.

Fear of loss of something good.

Fear that it's not really on our side.

I tell the story, though, to show that apparently angels do appear in Hindu visions, and like the Christian angels they sing with their voices and also make obeisance—imagine!—to humans who surrender their lives to the Universal Force. Moreover, like Christian angels, they are never to be worshipped, nor mistaken for God, but nonetheless to be revered.

—The man form is higher than the angel form; of all forms it is the highest. Man is the highest being in creation, because he aspires to freedom.

—PARAMAHANSA YOGANANDA
Autobiography of a Yogi

• • • •

• 3 •

*I*n Malaysia freckles are called angel kisses. Taoists give no official place to angels as we know them, but if by angel is meant a ministering spirit, a spiritual being attendant upon and worshipping a supreme deity, then angels are a constant theme in Chinese and Japanese religions too. They are the Immortals, originally human beings who have attained such heights of spiritual clarity that they never die. They are classified as "gods" (in Chinese, *shen*), yet are subordinate to them, in close relationship to the human world. Like angels, they can fly, travel between worlds, perform miracles, heal, cast out demons, and teach. Like angels, they appear in human or animal form to aid and advise, and like angels they are them-

Altar Shrine with Maitreya and angels. Northern Wei Dynasty, 6th century.

selves the message. But all these things are done by saints as well. . . .

Indeed the farther we move East from Persia, the more unclear grow our notions of just what angels are. Under Buddhism, the bodhisattvas, the holy Buddhas-to-be, are also likened to angels, for they, too, like the Immortals, have chosen to come down to guide and lead us to Enlightenment. But in each of their bodies resides the energy of God, which is called a *dakini* or angel and which corresponds to the Hindu shakti. There is a slight difference between the bodhisattvas of Buddhism and the Taoist Immortals. Taoist immortality exists on a physical plane: the body does not die, and there is a whole catalog of names for these beings, that, mixed with local shamanistic and Buddhist traditions, creates a mishmash of legend and folklore.

The Buddhist bodhisattvas, on the other hand, are high beings, who, having achieved salvation (which means having been given the opportunity to get off the wheel of reincarnated lives), have elected, out of their great love and compassion, to return to earth to teach and guide us mortals.

Bodhisattvas make love to and enjoy the delights of the spiritual world; but they are also agents of the Divine. Not only do they do angelic things—bringing healing, guidance, rewards, and punishments to human beings—but they also guide the souls of the dying to their appropriate place at death. Still, they do not claim the physical immortality of Taoist Immortals, for when their time is up, they die, just as the Buddha died. They die a holy death, at an advanced age, peacefully, as they lived, undisturbed by violence and never (as in Christian history) martyred or suffering for their god. Sometimes their bodies do not rot.

Those who have seen a Living Buddha in China or Tibet describe the aura of peace and energy, the warmth and love they emanate. Some people see light flaring from their skin.

Do other angels attend the bodhisattvas? In one bronze at the Metropolitan Museum of Art a bodhisattva is shown surrounded by winged deities hovering in worship and joy. Both the Immortals and bodhisattvas can travel out of body, levitate, and bilocate, and live for weeks without food, as if they had no physical needs. Yet I must admit that this activity is undertaken by the holy men of every culture, by all of those who dedicate their wills and lives to the care of a loving God.

It is told of the Christian hermits of the fourth and fifth cen-

A Mahasiddha Enjoys the Delights of Spiritual Flight with His Dakini-angel. Tibetan tanka (detail).

turies A.D. how one day a magistrate came to Pelusia to tax the monks, as if they were a secular group. It caused consternation, there being some separation of church and state even then. The monks thought they should go see the emperor about it, but Abba Ammonathas, a holy one, told them to go to their cells and fast for two weeks, that he would deal with the matter with the grace of God. So they did. At the end of two weeks the brothers were dissatisfied. The old man had merely sat in his cell, doing nothing about the business. On the fifteenth day the monks assembled according to their agreement, and the old man gave them a letter bearing the emperor's seal. They were astonished.

"Where did you get this?" they asked.

"Believe me," said Abba Ammonathas, "I went that night to the emperor, who wrote this letter; then going to Alexandria, I had it countersigned by the magistrate. Then I returned to you."

—By miracles we don't mean contradictions to nature. We mean that left to her own resources, she could never produce them.

*—*C. S. Lewis
On Miracles

• • • •

• 4 •

*H*ow many times have I been asked if those we love become angels when they die? It is an old, old idea, for many cultures and many philosophers hold to this belief that human souls evolve into protecting angels, as angels themselves rise to higher and higher forms. Thus angels come as "manes," the souls of departed spirits, to help us on the way. I heard of one German woman who was in a terrible car accident ten days after her husband died. The car was crushed between a truck and a tree, yet she and her sister miraculously crawled out of the wreckage unharmed. She attributes her survival to the protection of her husband, only ten days dead, because she felt his presence so powerfully at the crash. It is old, this idea that our loved ones look after us, or enjoy our lives on earth, though the departed spirit is not always kindly:

The manes of my son shall smile this day,
While I in blood my vows of vengeance pay.
— JOHN DRYDEN

I know of no culture on earth that does not believe the soul lives after death. I suppose the idea is carried to the extreme in the ancestor worship of Confucianism. Here each spirit lives for ten generations, but the surviving descendants must keep it alive by honoring and remembering it. And this is no mean task, for in ten generations you have 1,024 ancestors to care for and make offerings to and burn incense to. Gradually, as it pales in memory, each spirit pales in form as well, until it simply disappears. But while healthy and "alive," this grand-parent-spirit concerns itself with its descendants. It is never depicted as having wings or coming from a higher deity. It is far closer, from what I can gather, to the "shades" of the ancient Greeks, who upon death had immortality only so long as their heroic deeds rang down the halls of Time in the songs of bards. Achilles, therefore, in the *Iliad* has life only so long as the memory of his deeds reaches to our hearts, and otherwise he is one of the unhappy shadows wandering gray Hades and thirsting for blood sacrifice.

Temple banner, Avalokitesvara. Chinese, Hien-lung period, 18th century.

Unlike the Chinese, the ancient Greeks could not call on the shade of Achilles or Agamemnon to help them in times of trouble. The lives of poor humanity came under the casual supervision, or even the intrusion at times, of a pantheon of gods, who sent them dreams or visions or came directly as Zeus or Apollo or Athena; while the spirits of the dead were simply dead.

Well into this century, I am told, the Copper Eskimos in the central Canadian arctic held that every child has its personal guardian spirit. The baby is called by the name of the person who died most recently, whose spirit is thought to have entered the infant's body at birth. If the spirit was the grandmother, the baby is addressed as Grandmother, if an uncle, then as Uncle, for the child is too young at first to have a personality of its own. Moreover the baby is treated with the respect accorded to the adult. It can do almost anything it wishes—play with a skinning knife, for example—and no one screams at it, because Grandmother or Uncle knows perfectly well how to use a knife. Around the age of six the child may be punished for the first time. By then it is believed to have acquired its own personhood and name.

This ancestor-spirit, however, does not represent the presence of a guardian angel as we think of it, for the spirit leaves as the child grows older.

The major Eskimo worship is of raven and crow, bear, whale, seal and the creation myths of gods appearing as nature spirits, fixing things up for little humankind, and fighting the demons or evil spirits that stalk the earth hunting for a person to possess.

—The question is this: Is man an ape or an angel? Now, I am on the side of the angels.

—BENJAMIN DISRAELI
in a speech on Charles Darwin's
Origin of Species

• • • •

CHAPTER 6

The Battle of Heaven & Princes of Hell

Let them praise the name of the Lord:
for he commanded, and they were created.
—Ps. 148:5

· 1 ·

*A*fter God created the angels, He created humans and told the angels to bow down to humankind, to revere and care for them. By some accounts, it was this that brought about the Battle of Heaven and the fall of Satan, who out of pride or jealousy refused the task. By other accounts the demonic was already alive and well long before Adam and Eve awoke.

St. Michael and the Battle
of Heaven. Albrecht Dürer.
Woodcut from the Apocalypse
series, 15th century.

The story is not told in the Old Testament. Those books make no mention of fallen angels or of battles in heaven, but the New Testament, including the Revelation of John, then living on the island of Patmos (12: 7–9), tells of the war in heaven in which Michael and his angel soldiers fought against the dragon, Satan, and his evil horde, and how the serpent, which deceives the whole world, was cast out into the earth, an army of angels raining from the skies.

Jesus mentions it, too, in the Book of Luke: "I saw Satan fall like lightning from heaven," he said.

Five hundred years later, it was transformed under Islam into a poignant love story. In the Persian account, God created the angels to praise and worship God. Then God made humans, man and woman, and told the angels to serve his newest creations. But Satan, or Iblis, loved God best of all the angels, and he refused to bow to humans, but only to the God who had created him.

God said, "Get out of my sight," and instantly the angel was cast into hell, for to be out of sight of one's Beloved—to be sent away—is hell. And how does he stand the pain of separation from the Beloved? By the memory of the echo of God's voice saying, "Go to hell."

Thus we are to understand that the Evil and Good Angels dwell near one another, and yet there is the greatest immense Distance between them. For the *Heaven is in Hell* and the *Hell is in Heaven,* and yet the one is not manifest to the other; and although the Devil should go many Millions of Miles,

*—And He created you, then fash-
ioned you, then told the Angels:
Fall ye prostrate before Adam!
And they fell prostrate, all save
Iblis, who was not of those who
make prostration.*

*He said: What hindered Thee
that thou did not fall prostrate
when I bid thee? (Iblis) said: I am
better than he. Thou createdst me
of fire, while him Thou didst create
of mud.*

*He said: Then go down hence!
It is not for Thee to show pride
here, so go forth! Lo! Thou art of
Those degraded.*

—KORAN, VII

• • • •

desiring to enter into Heaven, and to see it, yet he would be
still in Hell and not see it.

—JAKOB BÖHME
Mysterium Magnum

By the second century A.D. the Christian view prevailed
that every man and woman (and especially every child) had a
guardian angel at its side; and some people believed that we
each have one good angel and one bad one, balancing out our
deeds: a good angel on your right shoulder and a bad one on
your left, and you get to choose between the two at every moment of your life. However, the Catholic church has never of-
ficially declared how angels sinned to become demons; nor
defined as dogma that every man has a guardian angel, nor
even that angels are divided into orders.

• 2 •

I think that all religions have satanic or demonic figures, who
lie and cheat and twist the truth and tempt weak humankind
with vanity, fear, doubt, obsessive lust, and avarice. I cannot
speak with any authority, but three times now I have seen
cases of demonic possession or exorcism, and, arguing from
that limited base (and glad to know no more), I believe—I
have come to believe—in evil, not as the mere absence of God
but as a palpable force in its own right. It is accompanied by
certain signs. First, the people possessed know it: they know

Angels Bow Down to
Adam and Eve.
Islamic manuscript painting.

—Demons are animals with a rational mind, a passive and immortal soul.

—APULEIUS

• • • •

that "something is wrong," as if another force were gripping them; they're out of control; and something is living underneath their skin. Second, they hurt. Their anguish is intolerable, both physical pain and the terrible isolation they feel. Third, they are afraid, but with a fear beyond the normal anxiety that we all experience at times. These people live in the grip of the most ferocious fear—and sometimes anger—that I have ever seen. And so I think the devil himself must live, tortured by anger and fear. Finally, and most interesting, these people, all three whom I saw, were beautiful—were physically so attractive that I stood in admiration of their exquisite form, and in one case of a lustrous softness of the eyes . . . and yet they were not happy. Their souls cried out in rage and loneliness.

Blake thought the demonic was another aspect of God, which the enlightened soul recognizes in its archangelic, shining glory as another messenger of God.

I have no theories on the difference between possession and madness, and indeed even to contemplate the concept of evil, or the demonic, in our society is to be considered mad. I would say that drug addictions and the damage they inflict are demonic, and whether it's a reality or a metaphor I hardly care.

*J*ust when the angels were created was a matter of concern in the Middle Ages. No one could decide. Was it when God divided dark from light? Was it when He divided the oceans from the skies? Saint Epiphanius thought angels were created *after* heaven and earth, but Saint Augustine decided that it was simultaneous with the creation of heaven and earth.

> And God called the firmament Heaven. And the evening and the morning were the second day.
> And God said, Let the waters under the heaven be gathered together unto one place, and let the dry land appear; and it was so.
> And God called the dry land Earth; and the gathering together of the waters called he Seas: and God saw that it was good.
>
> —GEN. 1:8–10

So when did evil arise? And how? With God? From someplace else? And do demons get salvation too—do they get to enjoy the love of God?

In Hindu philosophy a demon does bad deeds because he doesn't know right from wrong. But in Christian dogma (the religion of the most Loving Lord), demons know right from wrong straight from the beginning—and always choose wrong.

> Fall'n Cherub to be weake is miserable
> Doing or Suffering: but of this be sure,
> To do ought good never will be our task,
> But ever to do ill our sole delight,
> As being the contrary to his high will
> Whom we resist.
>
> —JOHN MILTON, *Paradise Lost,* I

In the Bible, Satan as Adversary appears only under the influence of Zoroastrianism, after the Exile to Babylon. Before that he is still in the Court of Heaven, the servant of God. Indeed, in the *Book of Job,* Satan acts as the comrade of God, casting doubt and challenging God's judgment in order to prove the power and goodness of God. Only under the influence of Babylon, then, did Satan move to an opposing and almost as grand a power as God.

Origen, the compassionate Greek philosopher and church father, saw the demons as being on a wheel of evolution, climbing through numerous lifetimes away from the desolation of loneliness and up toward God. But others say that not even the angels can help the demons find God. Or release them from their awful pain. Still, I am a romantic. I comfort myself that in Islam the *shaitans* as a class are created for evil, but that one *shaitan,* a great-grandson of Iblis, appeared to Muhammad and was taught certain suras, or chapters, of the Koran, thus taking a first step toward happiness.

Islamic angels fell after the creation of humans, but the Judeo-Christian angels fell *before* God fashioned humankind. When exactly? "Before time," says Dante, in *The Divine Comedy,* written from 1300 to 1320, "before the heavens over which they rule," and the evil angels fell instantly—"before you could count to twenty"—cast out through Satan's pride. Milton, however, writing *Paradise Lost* another 350 years later and caught in the physically grounded Renaissance of human space and time, saw the Fall as occurring after a terrific three-day battle in heaven, and even then the rebellion was quashed

Expulsion from Paradise.
Albrecht Dürer. Woodcut,
16th century.

only because the Son of God Himself intervened (at His Father's command), grasping ten thousand Thunders. The rebellious angels, "all resistance lost, all courage; down their idle weapons drop'd;" and wished the very mountains would be thrown on them to shelter from His wrath. They plunged down the crystal walls of heaven,

> Hurld headlong flaming from th'Ethereal Skie
> With hideous ruine and combustion down
> To bottomless perdition

Satan took a third of the vast angelic host of heaven with him in this rebellion "numberless were those bad Angels seen"—a multitude—and they were the very highest of the high: "The great Seraphic Lords and Cherubim."

> Thrones and imperial Powers, off-spring of heav'n
> Ethereal Vertues; or these Titles now
> Must we renounce, and changing stile be call'd
> Princes of Hell?
> —JOHN MILTON, *Paradise Lost,* II

Satan lay nine days recovering from his fall before rallying himself to go stalk Adam and Eve, newly formed in Paradise. The poem is actually about *their* loss of Paradise.

Milton's Arch Fiend lies chained on a burning lake, and he is huge. When he moves, he cuts a tree taller than the mast of a ship for his staff. He pulls on swift wings to fly, and he has not yet lost, as a former seraph, all his original brightness and angelic glory. But later in the poem, when he straps on his bat wings and goes searching for Eden, the other angels recognize him by "his looks with passions foul obscur'd" when unexpectedly touched by the angelic spear of the angel Ithuriel, he turned in surprise, his face twisting into its natural state—hatred—and becomes "the Grieslie King."

A Dungeon horrible, on all sides round
As one great Furnace flam'd, yet from those flames
No light, but rather darkness visible
Serv'd only to discover sights of woe
Regions of Sorrow, doleful shades . . . with ever-burning
   Sulpher, unconsum'd.
          —JOHN MILTON, *Paradise Lost*

He lives in his palace Pandemonium, surrounded by chaos. Yet who can say where this place is? It comes and goes.

Lucifer, King of Hell. Gustave Doré. Engraving, 19th century.

The Fallen Angels, in Milton's poem, formed a multitude, one-third of the heavenly host, and came from all the angelic ranks: principalities, virtues, cherubim, seraphim, thrones. Only a few are named:

SATAN himself, the Foul Fiend

BEËLZEBUB—who is next in rank to Satan; In other contexts he is Lord of the Flies or Dung, holds dummar our idolator

MOLOCH, a horrid King besmeared with blood of human sacrifice

CHEMOSH, dread of Moab's sons, also called Peor

BAALIM, a male spirit

ASHTAROTH, a female spirit

ASTORETH of the crescent horns (known also as Astarte, Queen of Heaven)

AZAZEL, "a cherube tall"

MAMMON

THAMMUZ

DAGON

RIMMON

BELIAL, the most Lewd, who appears at first both graceful and humane and whose tongue drops Manna

The mind is its own place, and in it self
Can make a Heav'n of Hell, a Hell of Heav'n.
—JOHN MILTON, *Paradise Lost,* I

They lie in Hell together with the pagan gods Osiris, Iris, Orus, the Golden Calf, and the Greek gods.

Six others fought beside Satan, but are not listed as being in Hell. Were angels killed in that terrible clash? They are:

ADRAMELEC and ASMADAI—two Thrones
ARIEL
ARIOC
RAMIEL
NISROC, who was a Principality.

The Good angels who did not side with Satan are:
URIEL
GABRIEL
MICHAEL
RAPHAEL
UZZIEL
ITHURIEL
ZEPHON
ABDIEL (who at first was tempted and then refused to join Satan's horde).

Milton termed the archfiend Satan; Dante called him Lucifer or Dis, and placed him not in a fiery pit but frozen in a lake of ice, for ice is suitable to the cold, cold heart of one who cannot love. Again, Dante's Lucifer is gigantic, and as ugly as once he was beautiful. He has three faces on his head. The one in front is red, the other two adjoin this at the middle of each shoulder, one yellowish-white, one black.

> Under each there issued forth two mighty wings of size befitting such a bird: sea-sails I never saw so broad. No plumes had they; but were in form and texture like a bat's; and he was flapping them, so that three winds went forth from him.
>
> —DANTE, *Inferno, 34*

These bat-wing winds froze the lake in which Lucifer is trapped. With six eyes he weeps blood. In each mouth he champs a traitor . . . and one is Judas Iscariot.

In the *Divine Comedy,* Dante answered all the metaphysical questions that the medieval mind fretted over—about the creation of the world and how such pain could exist if God is good; about the beginning of angels, and why some fell, and what angels are made of and whether they think and reason logically or whether they are merely the dumb instruments of God—automatons, as it were, or wind-up toys, without free will to choose to love or not, as humankind can do.

Do angels think? Angels see all things at once, always, said Dante, and therefore don't need memory or logic or the faculties of reason.

And yet humans, who think and exercise free will, are especially loved by God. It is this that fueled Satan's wrath against

. . . the happy seat
Of som new Race call'd *Man,* about this time
To be created like to us, though less
In power and excellence, but favour'd more
Of him who rules above. . . .

—JOHN MILTON
Paradise Lost, I

*I*n the Jewish tradition, angels are masculine; in the Christian tradition they are androgynous. As the Middle Ages gave way to the physically oriented Renaissance, Christian angels took on an airy and more feminine appearance. In the seventeenth century, however, when people's attention was focused still further on earth (long after Dante's sparklers of circling light), Milton depicted a sensuality among angels that was thrown in his teeth, for his all-male angels eat and defecate and make love joyfully, although with an embodiment so much finer than ours that they can be seen only by clairvoyant eyes. So Raphael sat down with Adam and Eve, who were naked as the day is warm and innocent as babes, and ate heartily what was fed him.

Then he told the humans how angels have sex. For spirit, Milton wrote, can at will assume either sex, or both, so "uncompounded" is their pure essence. Moreover, "without love no happiness," Raphael explains, and love demands that it be shared. How they do it is by interpenetrating each other's bodies in an impulse of mutual desire, mixing like two wines.

Whatever pure thou in the body enjoy'st
[said Raphael] . . . we enjoy

In eminence, and obstacle find none
Of membrane, joynt, or limb, exclusive barrs:
Easier than Air with Air, if Spirits embrace,
Total they mix, Union of Pure with Pure
Desiring: nor restrain'd conveyance need
As Flesh to mix with Flesh, or Soul with Soul.

—JOHN MILTON
Paradise Lost, VIII

This is very different from the sexual acts of demons, which Milton also describes, for one of the masks of evil is the misuse of sex. Satan, while still a seraph at the throne of God (and before he took up arms against Him), had a splitting headache one day, from which erupted a beautiful woman angel. Satan fell on her (pure seraph though he was) and took her with mutual, grappling, loathsome lust. Her name was Sin, and from their incestuous coupling came Death. Sin (now changed from beauty to incredible hideousness) and her son, Death, guard the gate of Hell in Milton's poem. She stops Satan momentarily when he crawls up out of the pit to search for Adam and Eve.

In some early rabbinical writings, Satan was himself the Angel of Death, since death was considered an evil. But death and evil are no longer connected, the Angel of Death coming today as a holy herald at the bidding of God.

—There is but one freedom, to put oneself right with death. After that everything is possible. I cannot force you to believe in God. Believing in God amounts to coming to terms with death. When you have accepted death, the problem of God will be solved—and not the reverse.

—ALBERT CAMUS
Notebooks

• • • •

• 3 •

*D*emons are not to be confused with angels of death. What demons (real or metaphorical) do is lie and make us think no

The Dance of Albrion.
William Blake. Engraving,
18th century.

order exists in the universe beyond our pain and doubt. And if we believe it even for a fraction of a second, we are cast into hell in despair; we feel an emptiness so terrible we plunge into drugs or sex or murder or war or greed, anything to numb the pain. But ah, the bright wings of the Angel of Death; that's another matter.

Johnny Cash, the country singer, was twice visited by an angel announcing death. Once, when he was twelve, an angel, its magnificent aura filling the room, came to tell him that his older brother, Jack, was going to die; and again many years later it appeared with the same radiance to foretell the death of his best friend, Johnny Horton. The first angel, "I can only describe . . . as faceless and surrounded by a brilliant, glowing light. There were no wings or halo. It spoke softly, saying, 'Your brother Jack is going to die.' Then it disappeared." Both times he felt such a sweet rush of peace that he was prepared when the actual death occurred.

Beth Peacock lives in Washington, D.C. Her father once saw several angels of death.

It happened in July. Beth's grandmother had a ninety-first birthday, so Beth flew to Wilmington, North Carolina, to bring her grandmother up to the family in Virginia Beach to celebrate, since her grandmother's only child, Beth's mother, was dying. Of liver cancer. It was all so unexpected. Six months earlier, in January, Jessiebeth had gone into the hospital for a minor operation, only to discover a cancer of the colon that had already metastasized to her liver.

Beth's father met his daughter and mother-in-law at the airport, and as they were driving home he told them what had happened the night before. He told it as innocently and simply as he would mention farm prices or the stock market, common conversation for an astute, retired businessman.

"When I went to bed your mother was resting quietly. Suddenly I was startled awake. Jessiebeth wasn't in bed, and I had the most terrified feeling. I ran into the den. The room was full of angels.

"It seems like a dream, but it wasn't. Jessiebeth was leaving with them. I was frantic. I called her to come back. I begged them not to take her. Then they vanished.

"I went into the living room, hoping to find them. Nothing. I was devastated. I went back to the bedroom, and there I found your mother, asleep, as she had been earlier. I was so relieved."

"What did they look like?" asked Beth, curious.

"They were angels. With wings and robes. They didn't speak."

"How high were they?"

"Very high. Thirty to fifty feet. As if there were no ceiling."

That was in July. As the months passed, Beth became aware that, although her mother had accepted dying, she was staying alive "for our sakes." Except for brief business trips, Beth stayed in Virginia Beach. "It's a time I cherish."

Finally, four months after the vision, her mother passed away. "She chose not to die until we could accept it," Beth told me, then paused, reflecting.

"The last gift our parents give us," she said, "is their dying. They give us so much . . ."

—The eternal silence of these infinite spaces terrifies me.
—BLAISE PASCAL
Pensées, 206

• • • •

. . .

. . . .

Angels occupy my mind. They walk the corridors of my past, ageless shadow forms, appearing and dissolving, and who could ascertain which are real, when all are merely memories?

When I was living in New York, a woman pushed her little girl, aged five, in front of the F train at the West Fourth Street Station in New York. She wanted her daughter "to be with the angels." That was how much she loved her and how horrible she found her dirt-black, grimy days of sidewalks in New York. The garbage in the gutter contained more protein than she could afford in a day—rotting heads of lettuce and the shells of scooped-out grapefruits lying yellow by the curb. My hands in dishwater in the sink, I cannot turn my thoughts from her. I imagine how she dressed her little girl in her Sunday best. I visualize the white starched dress with a red waistband. Her hand-me-down shoes were only a little too big for her tiny feet, and she pranced beside her mother to the subway, tugging at her hand. "Where are we going, Ma?"

Through the pitted streets, then down the stairs into the pit of hell itself, with a stop at the gate to push into the slot the token that permits you to pass the River Styx. And down more stairs, for the platforms go deep underground at West Fourth Street, and your ears are filled with the roar of trains echoing in the chambers and with the scream of brakes and sometimes—it is unsteadying—with silence, in which you hear only the whispering of countless feet on the cement, scuttling toward entrances or down the platforms to a bench. No sound but this soft scratching of the feet of prisoners. It lasts for only seconds at a time . . . ten seconds . . . twelve, before the next train bursts through a tunnel, tearing at your eardrums and thundering against the bones of your chest.

"Where are we going, Ma?"

"Is this our train?"

Did she lean down and kiss her child good-bye? Did she reach out to hug her to herself one last time, her darling one, small enough to fit still into the crook of an arm that stretches like wings to brood her one last time. And did she wait for several trains before making her decision? Not this train, not yet. . . . She stands, her fingers nervously snapping in anxiety, and the pain in her breast increased by the thunder of the trains, the pain of loneliness and fear, the abuse of humankind against its own.

"Now look what you've done. You've got dirt on your face!" She spits on the hem of her own dress and scrubs the little girl's thin cheek, while the child squirms to get away.

"Stand still. You can't go like that. Let me get you clean."

And then another train is rushing in, right on top of the last. The platform shudders with its strength. She pulls her little girl toward the head of the platform, where the trains plunge full-speed out of the black tunnel of arched cement. There are two lights stabbing at the dark, two brilliant yellow lights coming right at them.

"Come on. Hurry up."

The child toddles after her, pulled by her mother's hand, and tries to catch up, this little one, tripping in her shoes too big. Then comes the swing from those strong grown-up arms,

A Father's Memoirs of His Child.
William Blake. Engraving,
18th century.

and the babe is thrust into the train, splat into the brilliant yellow eyes. She beats against the metal as a bird against a pane of glass. It's much too fast for the motorman to stop. He knows only that he felt a thud, like a hand on the flat of his chest, and the sidewise lurch of the train as one wheel lifts over an object—a stick perhaps. Already his brakes are on and screaming in the chambered vaults, together with the scream from the woman's throat.

Her act was seen.

Passersby caught at her.

The police came.

"I sent her to the angels," she said. "I wanted her to live among the angels, not down here."

They sent her for observation to Bellevue, the hospital for the insane.

THE DELICATE, PLUMMETING BODIES

A great cry went up from the stockyards and
slaughterhouses, and Death, tired of complaint
and constant abuse, withdrew to his underground garage.
He was still young and his work was a torment.
All over, their power cut, people stalled like streetcars.
Their gravity taken away, they began to float.
Without buoyancy, they began to sink. Each person
became a single darkened room. The small hand
pressed firmly against the small of their backs
was suddenly gone and people swirled to a halt
like petals fallen from a flower. Why hurry?
Why get out of bed? People got off subways,
on subways, off subways, all at the same stop.
Everywhere clocks languished in antique shops
as their hands composed themselves in sleep.
Without time and decay, people grew less beautiful.
They stopped eating and began to study their feet.
They stopped sleeping and spent weeks following stray dogs.
The first to react were remnants of the church.
They falsified miracles, displayed priests posing
as corpses until finally they sneezed or grew lonely.
Then governments called special elections to choose those
to join the ranks of the volunteer dead—unhappy people
forced to sit in straight chairs for weeks at a time.
Interest soon dwindled. Then the army seized power
and soldiers ran through the street dabbling the living
with red paint. You're dead, they said. Maybe

tomorrow, people answered, today we're just breathing;
look at the sky, look at the color of the grass.
For without Death each color had grown brighter.
At last a committee of businessmen met together,
because with Death gone money had no value.
They went to where Death was waiting in a white room,
and he sat on the floor and looked like a small boy
with pale blond hair and eyes the color of clear water.
In his lap was a red ball heavy with the absence of life.
The businessmen flattered him. We will make you king,
they said. I am king already, Death answered. We will
print your likeness on all the money of the world.
It is there already, Death answered. We adore you
and will not live without you, the businessmen said.
Death said, I will consider your offer.

How Death was restored to his people:

At first the smallest creatures began to die—
bacteria and certain insects. No one noticed. Then fish
began to float to the surface; lizards and tree toads
toppled from sun-warmed rocks. Still no one saw them.
Then birds began tumbling out of the air,
and as sunlight flickered on the blue feathers
of the jay, brown of the hawk, white of the dove,
then people lifted their heads and pointed to the sky
and from the thirsty streets cries of welcome rose up
like a net to catch the delicate and plummeting bodies.

—STEPHEN DOBYNS

• 4 •

Oh sovereign angel,
Wide winged stranger above a forgetful earth,
Care for me, care for me. Keep me unaware of danger
And not regretful
And not forgetful of my innocent birth.
—EDNA ST. VINCENT MILLAY

I don't believe in hell. I don't believe we are tortured for eternity in fire or locked for eternity in ice. We make our own hells here on earth, in our minds and in the prisons of our hearts, and it is to escape these hells and our howling demons that the angels come—to tell us we have freedom, that we are not *supposed* to live in terror and hate.

Some people discover this through a near-death experience, and Hugh Hildesby is one of these. Hugh is an Englishman, enormously tall with big, rangy movements and expressive hands. He is rector of the Church of Heavenly Rest at Fifth Avenue and Ninetieth Street in New York, and before that he was an auctioneer with the international auction house, Sotheby Parke-Bernet.

"But I didn't see an angel," he told me. "There may have been angels in attendance, but the spirit of God was so present that the angels were not in view. Still, I felt so strongly the force of spirits taking care of one, that it confirmed the angelic for me."

Raymond Moody wrote a whole book, *Life After Life,* collecting these extraordinary experiences, though what it means is unclear, for none of the subjects, after all, actually completed the job and died! They do tell us that there is no death and nothing to be afraid of when we're wrenched into another dimension. I don't know what happens, but I do know now that we live on, not merely as static electricity or sparks but with our very personalities too. Some people say we "go over" immediately and are met by friends and relations, and some say that it takes weeks or months, but everyone agrees life doesn't only end. Euripedes thought that we are dead when we are in this life on earth and born to life only once we do what's known as "die."

Dr. Hugh Hildesby's experience will illustrate. He lay on the operating table and shot out of his body. It was not frightening. "I was washed in light. I felt the absence of weight, and this pulsing, flowing light of incredible brilliance—gold and white, but with a white so pure and scintillating it was alive. It came in wave after wave over me.

"Around the light were 'angels,' but they were not angels as we conceive of them. They were spirits without form. I was aware of their company. They were people I knew who had died and whom I looked forward to meeting.

"The other thing was that I was laughing. The whole thing was humorous—all the people down there looking at my body. 'I'm not there,' I thought. 'Why are they concerned with that object?' I was struck by the humor of it. 'Thank goodness I don't have to take all that stuff with me.'

—This is what you are to hold fast to yourself—the sympathy and companionship of the unseen worlds. No doubt it is best for us now that they should be unseen. It cultivates in us that higher perception that we call 'faith.' But who can say that time will not come when, even to those who live here upon earth, the unseen worlds shall no longer be unseen?

—PHILLIPS BROOKS

• • • •

"I felt very strong. It was wonderful. I was held in the arms of God. I was absolutely, completely taken care of, in a way that we can't be in this life. There was no anxiety. I was totally protected, and the angels are part of that, a community formed together by this perfect love, and you then recognize," he continued, "that you are one of the angels. You have found your identity."

· CHAPTER 7 ·

The Angelic Doctors

*I*n the New Testament we find no Angels of Vengeance or Death, and angels perform no heroic deeds, nor blast cities with fire, nor kill Assyrians or Egyptian children, nor give kings leprosy. Instead they seem simply to appear at moments of high glory. It is true that angels comforted Christ in the desert when he was worn out after the temptations by Satan, but the New Testament doesn't record angels taking any real action until after the death of Christ. Then one (the *Gospel of John* mentions two angels) is described as sitting lonesome inside Christ's tomb, on the right. It has no wings. It looks like a man. It has "a countenance like lightning" and garments "white as snow." It is the women who see it. Mary Magdalene and Mary, mother of

James, and a woman named Joanna have gone up to the tomb and, to their wonder, find Christ's body is gone, and this angel telling them that Jesus has risen from the dead. They run breathlessly to the men, who hurry up to the tomb and find it empty, including of angels. Each of the Gospel writers tells the story a little bit differently, but that's the gist of it.

In the Acts of the Apostles, an angel (Michael) springs Peter from prison, appearing suddenly in his cell, breaking his chains and leading him, to Peter's amazement, out past all the sleeping guards, and no one there to stop them. And another angel is seen by the centurian Cornelius, "a man in bright apparel," telling him to send for Peter.

They are still male, these angels, the wingless patriarchs who supplanted the supple goddess forms that had ruled in early times. Not for another millennium will we see angels depicted again as feminine, or even mildly sexed.

Around A.D. 300 we find an angel painted in the catacombs of Rome, and more images appear under the rule of Constantine the Great (306–337). Constantine was the emperor of Byzantium, who after a vision of a Cross in the sky converted to Christianity, and with him a lot of people who understood which side their bread was buttered on. (It was Helen, his devout mother, though, who brought back as souvenirs from her pilgrimage to the Holy Land not only splinters of the True Cross but the very manger in which the baby Jesus was born!) Under the rule of Constantine we find carved angels on the sarcophagus of a child. They are wholly Greek in tradition, taken from the flying Nike.

—Every visible thing in this world is put in the charge of an angel.
ST. AUGUSTINE
Eight Questions

• • • •

Meanwhile the Church was growing by leaps and bounds. With each martyr killed in the circuses by lions or sadists, more people flocked to join the despised sect. By the end of the fourth century, angels were being painted with wings, halos, and the nimbus of light with which we think of them today.

By the fourth century A.D., theological arguments were breaking out. At the first Ecumenical Council at Nicaea in 325, the doctrine of "coinherence" was formulated, sharply dividing body and soul. The corporal, physical, material world was denied value. The truly Christian life was elevated to the spiritual plane, and it was the duty of humans to aspire to heaven, not to the earthly kingdom of God. Oh, but there was no holding to our delight in the physical, the pleasure we share in this pretty world.

> Praise this world to the angel . . .
> show him
> something simple which, formed over generations,
> lives as our own, near our hand and within our gaze.
> Tell him of Things. . . .
> —RAINER MARIA RILKE, *Duino Elegies*, 9

It was hard for the Church, coming to terms with angels. The impulse of angel-interest surged up from the peasants, out of folk roots, sometimes seeming to overwhelm the adoration of Christ. Of course a hierarchy had to be established, with the Son of God at the top, and it was done early on by

Saint Paul, with his usual zealous righteousness. He attacked "the worship of angels which some enter into blindly, puffed up by their mere human minds." The First Council of Nicaea in 325 declared belief in angels part of the dogma of the Church, which must have loosed a renewal of angel worship, because less than twenty years later, in 343, another Council claimed it was idolatry. Finally in 787, the Seventh Ecumenical Synod established a *limited* dogma of the archangels, together with their names and their special duties, and this took firm root in the Eastern church, though distrust still flared up in the West.

By the High Middle Ages, angels were considered to govern the four elements of earth, air, water, and fire. They moved the stars, tended plants, and graced the procreation of all living creatures, including the births of humankind. Each day of the week had a protecting angel, each season, each astrological sign, each hour of the day or night, in fact everything you ever thought of or did or wrote or watched was governed by an angel of its own.

The idea still persists. I have a friend in New Mexico whose garden is astonishingly beautiful. Asked how she can grow such flowers and giant vegetables at that high altitude, she describes how she talks to the devas and angels of the earth, asking the spiritual protectors of each plant what to do. She follows their directions precisely. Is this much different from the concepts of the High Middle Ages, whereby each plant or planet was governed by an angel?

As the Catholic church grew, an entire angelology devel-

THE COMPASS POINTS
Michael rules EAST
Raphael rules WEST
Gabriel rules NORTH
Uriel rules SOUTH

oped. It was fashionable throughout the Middle Ages, when questions about angels were hotly debated and our relationship to angels was of powerful importance, too. We ridicule these early thinkers now—grown men fighting over what the angels were made of and how many could stand on the head of a pin (actually that image was never discussed), declaring each other heretics and arguing passionately for their ideas about angels, which, after all, can hardly be said to be provable material, so that a little tolerance and nonattachment might have been more appropriate. But it was a scientific question to them, as important as the laws of chemistry or gravity to us: they wanted to know their relationship to nature. Can two things occupy the same space simultaneously? What about incorporeal ones?

In the thirteenth century the two rival schools were represented by the Scottish theologian John Duns Scotus and the Italian scholastic philosopher, St. Thomas Aquinas—himself known as the Angelic Doctor, not only for his goodness and brilliance but for his discourses on angels.

The question was: what are angels made of? Scotus thought they were composed of "spiritual matter," vaporous as that might be; they were incorporeal and immaterial but dense and material in comparison to God. Earlier, around 500 A.D., St. Fulgentius, the North African bishop, had suggested that good angels had bodies of fire and evil angels bodies of air, which is similar to but unlike the later Islamic tradition that angels are made of light, while demons or djinns are of fire!

Then in 1259 Aquinas gave a series of lectures on angels at

—Out of that stream there issued living sparks, which settled on the flowers on all sides, like rubies set in gold; and then, as if intoxicated with the odors, they again played into the amazing flood; as one spark sank, another spark emerged.

—DANTE
Paradiso, XXX

• • • •

ANGEL	MONTH GOVERNED	ASTROLOGICAL SIGN GOVERNED
Gabriel	January	Aquarius
Barchiel	February	Pisces
Machidiel	March	Aries
Asmodel	April	Taurus
Ambriel	May	Gemini
Muriel	June	Cancer
Verchiel	July	Leo
Hamaliel	August	Virgo
Uriel	September	Libra
Barbiel	October	Scorpio
Adnachiel	November	Sagittarius
Hanael	December	Capricorn

ANGEL	CELESTIAL BODY GOVERNED	DAY OF WEEK GOVERNED	TREE	DUTY
Raphael	Sun	Sunday	Broom Tree	to warm or scorch
Gabriel	Moon	Monday	Willow	to foster or blight
Sammael	Mars	Tuesday	Kermes Oak	to strengthen or weaken
Michael	Mercury	Wednesday	Almond Tree	to make wise or foolish
Zidkiel (Aniel)	Venus	Thursday	Terebinth Tree	to make fruitful or barren
Hanael (Kafziel)	Saturn	Friday	Quince Tree	to grant or withhold heart's desire
Kepharel (Zadkiel)	Jupiter	Saturday	Pomegranate Tree	to make whole or accursed

Boy Angel. Italian wood sculpture,
18th century.

the University of Paris. In those days, when most people could not read, *thinking,* the use of the mind, was itself a game, a spectator sport, and great teachers such as Peter Abelard or Thomas Aquinas attracted tremendous crowds who came to hear them discourse upon a subject with arguments and counterarguments that involved long quotations from memory of the classics or Scripture and the complex use of logic and reasoning. People poured in like spectators at a football game or kibitzers at a chess tournament, for the sheer admiration of style and clarity of thought. Such talks might even take several days. Thus, Thomas held fifteen discourses on angels over a period of a week, setting out everything known or asked about them and answering the audience's questions. His lectures were written down as he spoke them and formed the foundation of our knowledge about angels for the next eight hundred years.

Angels are "all intellect," said Aquinas, who was himself one of the greatest intellects ever to have walked this earth; thus leaving us wondering if our perceptions of angels are simply reflections of our own strengths and desires.

Pure intellect, he said, without matter. On the other hand, he also believed that angels were animals without bodies (as demons are), but that they could assume bodies at will, and even eat, as is known by the fact that they ate with Abraham under the oak trees of Mambre. (All Thomist arguments are drawn from logic and readings from Scripture, not from personal experience, while the mystics who entertain angels don't seem as interested in these ancillary questions as in the messages the angels bring, in that brush with divinity that leaves only endless, overwhelming, and consuming love.)

There was another question: Are angels eternal? Are they born, like stars, and do they die as stars are now known to die, blow up or fade coldly out? Many of the church fathers discussed this problem. (The answer, *yes,* was given by the Vatican Council in 1870.) And the other questions that each raises: If they are born and die, do they also evolve, grow into different stages of angels? If they are intellect, do they think and have they the capacity of logic, reason, which brings us to Free Will? It's an important point. Can angels *choose* God? Can they *choose* evil as a path? Can they continuously "fall"?

The Greek theologian, Origen (185?–254), believed that angels, like humans, not only are born and die, but also are subject to the laws of karma and evolution over repeated lifetimes, that they not only evolve to higher and higher states, but that they can fall once they've chosen God. But St. Thomas Aquinas, one thousand years later, believed that angels, despite being pure intellect, do not reason. They are given one brief exercise of free will at the moment they come into existence, although their perfection gives them the instantaneous life-choice for God. And this was the accepted concept at that time:

> These beings, since they first were gladdened by the face of God . . . have never turned their vision from that face, so that their sight is never intercepted by a new object, and they have no need to recollect an interrupted concept.
>
> —DANTE, *Paradiso*

—I throw my selfe down in my Chamber, and I call in and invite God and his Angels thither, and when they are there, I neglect God and his Angels, for the noise of a file, for the rattling of a Coach, for the whining of a doore.

—JOHN DONNE

• • • •

Unlike Aquinas, Scotus held that angels think and reason and that they form one species with thousands of individual personalities within that group: like people. Aquinas removed them to a higher sphere. They do not belong to a species as humans or dogs do, he said, but each one is a distinct substance in itself, a kind of species in itself.

I don't know what he thought about whether angels die.

But I'm interested in another question: Where do guardian angels go when they're not around? And is the guardian always the same angel? And does one angel have responsibility for one person or does it take care of many—in which case is it simply busy when it fails to ward off harm? At another level: Does your angel call in reinforcements, when needed, from the general pool, the hosts who have been simply hanging around? Because I have the idea that an angel may be able to multiply itself like smashed mercury—scattering into a hundred thousand aspects of its very self, each a living hologram, or like a mirror, which shatters into pieces that each reflect as if it were the whole.

So Elisha opened the eyes of his servant to see an army of fiery chariots drawn by horses of fire—angels ranked against the Assyrian enemy. And another time the Syrian army—which had lain a single, long siege against Samarica that was so severe that it had driven inflation inside the city to incredible levels and reduced the inhabitants to cannibalism—the Syrians suddenly fled, leaving tents and gold and silver and horses and wagons and weapons and flour and food and clothing: everything abandoned in the frenzy of their depar-

—Every angel is terrifying.
—RAINER MARIA RILKE
Duino Elegies, 2
• • • •

ture. They had heard the noise of an angelic army thundering down on them. So who were these angels coming down in crowds? There are no answers to these questions. You hardly ever hear them asked!

Since Aquinas, the formal study of angels has shifted from the scholastics to its own sort of theology. Treatments of angels are usually found now in insipid tracts, which are simpering and dogmatic simultaneously. They lay out information which was questioned and debated a thousand years ago, as if it has been proven, as if we actually know; so that the subject of angels has been removed to another plane—faith. You're supposed to take it all on faith.

*T*he numbers of angels are uncountable. They are spoken of as armies. Legions. Hosts. Their numbers range from a small 100,000 to the 49 million of the Jewish Kabbalah. According to one count, there are 496,000 angels ranked in seven divisions. Matthew's Scriptures note that Christ could ask his Father for more than twelve legions of angels—a legion ranging from 3,000 to 6,000 men, including cavalry—while Daniel in one vision saw that "thousands of thousands ministered to him and ten thousand times a hundred thousand stood before him." Saint Augustine thought angels "breed like flies."

No wonder they were divided into a heirarchy as strict as that of feudal lords. The only trouble was that there was more than one idea of how the hierarchy worked, so that the ranking of angels was itself disputed until Saint Thomas presented

Angels at the Battle of Ascalon (detail). Gustave Doré. Engraving, 19th century.

his discourses and, seventy years later, around 1320, the Florentine politician and poet Dante Alighieri published *The Divine Comedy* with its definitive ranking of all creatures bad and good. These two texts established the hierarchy of angels once and for all. Both men followed the order proposed around 500 A.D. by Dionysius the Pseudo-Areopagite.

(Keep in mind, however, that three hundred years after these two medieval giants, in 1664, the English poet John Milton ignored the tradition entirely in his *Paradise Lost*. There Satan's army came originally from the highest orders of angels, and Raphael, a high-born seraph, delivers messages like a common courier.)

Dionysius the Pseudo-Areopagite was a Syrian. He wrote four obtuse books of mysticism, full of literary artifice, one being *De Hierarchia Celesti,* about the nature and properties of angels. In this he pretended to be Dionysius the Areopagite, the first-century Greek who was converted by Saint Paul at Athens (Acts 17:34). Later he was thought to be the first bishop of Athens, and later still he was identified with Saint Denis of France, until around 1450 it was discovered he was a fraud. To avoid confusion, therefore, he's called the Pseudo-Areopagite, or the Pseudo-Dionysius for short. Nonetheless, his influence in the Middle Ages was enormous, and the best-known hierarchy of angels is his.

According to the Pseudo-Dionysius, the three highest angels are the Old Testament seraphim, cherubim, and thrones. The next two triads come from the various lists that Paul poetically tossed off in the first century to the new Christian disciples when he was touring the Mediterranean basin, building a young Church; and like any writer who finds a good line, he repeated it in different letters to the Ephesians, the Romans, and the little church at Colossos.

> For by [God] were all things created that are in heaven, and that are in earth, visible and invisible, whether they be thrones or dominions, or principalities, or powers: all things were created by him, and for him.   —COL. 1:16

Far above all principality, and power, and might, and dominion, and every name that is named, not only in this world, but also in that which is to come . . . [is God].
—EPH. 1:21

I'm no biblical scholar, but I'm not sure that Paul was necessarily talking about *angels* when he wrote those lines.

"Who shall separate us from the love of Christ?" he wrote to the Roman church:

Shall tribulation, or distress, or persecution, or famine, or nakedness, or peril, or sword? . . . Nay, in all these things we are more than conquerors through him that loved us. For I am persuaded that neither death, nor life, nor angels, nor principalities, nor powers, nor things present, nor things to come; Nor height, nor depth, nor any other creature, shall be able to separate us from the love of God.
—ROM. 8:35; 37–39

Now, why would angels want to separate us from God? And why would the church fathers assume that principalities, powers, and mights, were angels instead of just good strong words, like height, depth, famine, peril, Roman soldiers, and future time?

At any rate, and Pseudo-Dionysius arranged the angels into three groupings, using Paul's list, and everyone else took them up:

1. Seraphim, cherubim, and thrones
2. Dominions, virtues, and powers
3. Principalities, archangels, and angels (lowest)

Some people substituted *mights* for *virtues,* and Pope Gregory the Great, who lived in the sixth century, reversed the order of principalities and virtues—and was sharply taken to task for it by Dante, too, in *The Divine Comedy,* when the poet makes him actually apologize to Dante in heaven and admit how wrong his order was!

Dionysius was not the only person to attempt a catalog of angels. Saint Ambrose, a fourth-century bishop of Milan, had proposed a different hierarchy: seraphim, cherubim, thrones, principalities, dominions, powers, virtues, archangels, and angels. In various Judaic works and apocryphal literature other orders popped up: four orders in something called the Sibylline Oracles, six in the "Shepherd of Hermes," seven in the work of Clement of Alexandria, seven in folk piety—all of which goes to show only that we know nothing whatsoever about angels and cannot hope to.

According to early medieval thought, dominions, virtues, and powers wear long albs, or gowns reaching to their feet, hitched with a golden belt and adorned with a green stole. They carry golden staffs in their right hands and the seal of God in their left.

The lowest group, principalities, archangels, and angels are dressed in a soldier's uniform, with golden girdles, hatchets,

Miracles happen when you don't plan in advance. If you dot all your i's and cross all your t's, then you will find no miracles.

—SUTISH KUMAR

• • • •

and javelins; later they were painted by medieval and Renaissance artists carrying lilies or floating streamers with their messages of hope or else simply with folded, praying hands.

By the fourth or fifth century a lot of angels had been named, and more kept cropping up all the time, both in Judaic and Christian lore until there were literally thousands. In the Roman Catholic tradition, the names (and indeed the numbers) of the archangels fluctuated a bit, wobbling between four and seven, until the church finally decided that only seven angels are known by name.

Yet, true to tradition, the names of the seven vary also, depending on which text you read; so that actually only the four archangels remain constant: Raphael, Michael, Gabriel, and Uriel. The others, leaking in from Judaic or folk thought, are: Simiel, Oriphiel, and Zachariel, sometimes called Chamuel, Jophiel, and Zadkiel, while the Council of 745 mentioned them (disapprovingly) as Uriel, Samiel, and Raguel. It was this council, the Ad Lateran Synod of 745, that condemned the practice of giving names to angels, for all agree that the proper worship of God is God, and to worship the angel is like concentrating on the finger pointing instead of on the Light at which it points. (My dog used to do this, looking with adoring puzzlement at my hand pointing to his dinner dish, and never making the connection that it was the food I was directing him to.)

This is still the position of the Church, and it shows how angels have moved during the centuries not only farther from man but farther from God as well—far from those early days

SERAPHIM, the highest order, the six-winged ones, surround the throne of God, singing ceaselessly, Holy, Holy, Holy. They are angels of love, light, and fire.

CHERUBIM are the guardians of the fixed stars, keepers of celestial records, bestowers of knowledge. In the Talmud cherubim are equated with the order of wheels, also called ophanim. Chief rulers are Ophaniel, Rikbiel, Zophiel, and, before his fall, Satan.

THRONES bring God's justice to us. They are sometimes called *wheels* and in the Jewish Kabbalah, CHARIOTS or the MERKABAH. The occult book, the *Zohar,* ranks wheels above seraphim, but other sources place them as cherubim, the whole thing being confused. The ruling prince is Oriphiel or Zabkiel or Zaphiel.

DOMINIONS or DOMINATIONS regulate angelic duties. Through them is manifested the Majesty of God. They hold an orb or sceptre as an emblem of authority, and, in Hebraic lore, the chief of this order is named Hashmal or Zadkiel.

VIRTUES work miracles on earth. They are bestowers of grace and valor.

POWERS stop the efforts of demons to overthrow the world, or else they preside over demons, or perhaps (according to St. Paul) they are themselves evil. Ertosi, Sammael, or Camael (depending on the source) is chief of the Powers.

PRINCIPALITIES are protectors of religion. Nisroc, in Milton, is "of principalities the prime," and others, according to various sources, are named Requel, Anael, and Cerviel.

ARCHANGELS and ANGELS are guardians of people and all physical things.

*—Angels are spirits, but it is not
because they are spirits that they
are angels. They become Angels
when they are sent. For the name
Angel refers to their office, not their
nature. You ask the name of this
nature, it is* spirit; *you ask its office, it is that of an Angel, which is
a messenger.*

—SAINT AUGUSTINE

• • • •

when an angel was considered the incarnation of God, the
physical manifestation of God's word. In the first century
after Christ, the Alexandrian Jewish philosopher Philo Ju-
daeus (20 B.C.–A.D. 50) wrote that God shows Himself to people as an angel—not that God changes, but that each soul
receives the impression of His presence in a different and angelic form, just as the formless, impersonal Hindu Brahma
takes on the form of a god to visit the devotee. Likewise, Saint
Augustine said that the word *angel* connotes God: "It is the
name of the indweller, not the temple."

I might add that many people today are just as interested in
naming their angels. "How do I learn the name of my angel?"
is a question often asked. I myself think it unnecessary to
know, especially because in my experience the angels don't
care. They don't claim separation from one another or from
God. But if an angel appears to you, and if you want a
name . . . just *ask!* The angel (so obliging are these beings)
will come up with a name. Then of course you'll have another
problem: whether to trust the message you received or laugh.

By the seventeenth century the role of angels in man's salvation was no longer of prime importance, the mediation having passed to Christ. The one thing left for angels is to move
us along by their will and intellect, directing our actions invisibly, and this, according to the Church, they do. Yet angels
kept cropping up visibly: they would not go away.

It's time for a story.

I was giving a talk recently in a Georgetown Presbyterian
church. One of the audience members told how, when he was

a young boy, he had been playing with his pals on his front lawn, while the neighbor's two-year-old played on the front porch. The baby stood up and tottered to the steps, wanting to play with the big boys, then stood there balancing, one foot out—about to tumble down the stairs. All the children saw him, and so did this boy's mother, who was babysitting. They saw the infant sway, stagger, start to fall down the steps—and then his T-shirt was pinched as if held by two fingers, pulled backward. The baby righted himself, and by then the mother had raced up the steps and caught him. But they had all seen that T-shirt pulled back by an invisible hand.

• THE KABBALAH •

*I*n the meantime the Jewish population in Europe lived side by side with Christians yet totally separate. I don't know what kind of mystical knowledge could have passed between these peoples, when the one loving group was exterminating the other like angels among the Assyrians or sending them out of their countries wholesale—the expulsion of Jews from Spain, from England; the isolated massacres in Germany and in France; the laws against Jews owning land; the pogroms in Eastern Europe, where they were slaughtered both individually and as whole townships. Merely maintaining their identity as a people, their language and culture, forced the medieval Jews into religious isolation. So it is possible that the teaching of the Kabbalah (also spelled *Kabala, Kabbala, Cabala,* or *Cabalah*) never touched the great medieval Christian masters.

On the other hand, at least in Spain, both Jewish and Muslim mysticism influenced Christian mystics before the year 1492, when Queen Isabella expelled some half a million Jews. During the preceding centuries, when Arabs ruled Spain, all three religions lived in harmony, and that period was one of high learning, culture, and tolerance. The grandfather of St. Teresa of Avila was Jewish, a *marrano* forced to convert for fear of the Inquisition. In that diaspora, in which the Jews were not allowed to take out of Spain any gold or silver from the sale of their cattle, vineyards, houses, furniture, or lands, the one thing they could take was learning.

The word *Kabbalah* derives from the Hebrew root *kbl,* meaning "to receive," and the term is used to designate mystical writings so secret (as all true mystical teachings are) that they are handed down only orally, from one master to the next. The Kabbalah is so sacred, so complex, so difficult to interpret, that no one should grieve at not being able to understand it. Indeed one book I read on the subject said that "in one city, only three persons can interpret it, and two are in one family."

The Kabbalah is centuries old. Flourishing in Palestine in the first century A.D., it evolved around the ecstatic contemplation of the divine throne of God or "chariot" seen by Ezekiel. But the major texts did not appear until the twelfth and thirteenth centuries, especially from Spain, where the *Zohar,* the "Book of Brightness," appeared.

There are various other books, beginning with the "Book of Creation," the *Sefer Yetzira,* written between the third and the

—And they that be wise shall shine as the brightness [Zohar] *of the firmament.*

—DAN. 12:3

• • • •

sixth centuries, and followed in the thirteenth century with the "Book of Splendor" and the "Book of the Image."

The Kabbalah is the guide on the path to God, taking you through a series of heavenly halls with angelic assistance. It is filled with long descriptions of how to make the safe journey up through a tree of angels. It requires secret passwords to overcome the demons on the way.

The tradition of the Throne Chariot of God, known also as the *Merkabah,* spawned other Kabbalistic traditions, with angels playing central roles. One twelfth-century German school taught a doctrine of four "worlds," each emanating from God, and also the recognition that God is so far beyond our comprehension that all attempts to understand that grandeur are futile. The four worlds are:

1. The physical or material world we live in
2. The place of ten hosts of angels, specified by name and presided over by the highest, Metatron, who himself has seventy-six names
3. A world of lights that stream from the highest world of God
4. The world where God is united to his feminine counterpart, or *Shekhinah,* a word that does not occur in the Bible but in mystical literature only and that means "shelter" or "dwelling."

In the Kabbalah, the angel Metatron is called the Angel of the Lord. He began his journey as Enoch (son of Adam and Eve's son Cain), a prophet in the Book of Genesis, who led such a holy life that God transported him physically to heaven, into the first rank of angels, and named him Metatron, which means "closest to the throne."

Enoch is written of in two other occult books of doubtful authenticity, each describing the secret pathway to God that was revealed to this holy patriarch. The first Book of Enoch is an Ethiopian translation of a Greek translation made in Palestine from the original Hebrew or Aramaic. It is a compilation of several works. The oldest portions were written shortly before the Maccabean uprising against the Romans in 168 B.C. Copies were discovered with the Dead Sea Scrolls at Qumran, and certainly the books were known to Christ. Some sections were written as late as the second century A.D.

The second Book of Enoch, called the Slavonic Book, dates from about the seventh century, though it rests upon an older Jewish work written around A.D. 70. It describes visionary journeys, astrological calculations, a highly developed angelology, and personal meetings with divinities along the path to God.

It fell into disfavor because of controversial descriptions of the fallen angels, and most copies were destroyed. In 1773 a Scottish explorer James Bruce, hearing rumors of the lost books, travelled to Ethiopia and found three copies. In 1821 they were translated into English by Dr. Richard Laurence, an Oxford professor of Hebrew, and thus brought to the attention of the modern world.

In the Kabbalah are ten *sefirot,* or angels—fundamental channels of divine energy. They are the ten divine attributes

"Albion's Angel rose"
William Blake. Engraving,
18th century.

that shape and govern the universe, and each unfolds like a rose of light, revealing in its petals a winged figure. As in Zoroastrianism, the names of the *sefirot* are abstractions: Foundation, Splendor, Eternity, Beauty, Power, Grace, Knowledge, Wisdom, Understanding, and Crown.

They stand in a tree. At the foot is the angel Sandalphon, though his height extends up throughout the universe, taller than all "by a journey of five hundred years." Sandalphon is a guardian spirit. Other angels along the way are Samael, the Angel of Evil (also known as Satan or Lucifer), who is blazing with jewels; Zaphkiel, the Angel of Contemplation; Raphael, the Divine Physician; Gabriel, who commands Spiritual Wisdom; and Michael, the Commander of Heavenly Hosts. Another Kabbalistic angel is Phanuel, or "Divine Face."

At the peak is Metatron, surrounded by storm, thunder, whirlwinds, and lightning. He has seventy-two wings and countless fiery eyes. His eyelashes are lightning, his bones are made of embers, his sinews and flesh of flame.

And beyond them all is the mystical contemplation of God, so far removed that no one can imagine what He is. This path of contemplation leads always to a higher and higher ability to love, until it is seen that all life is holy, all life is God and a surrender into love, that everything we do in this exalted state of prayer or contemplation constitutes an act of creation, and that the act itself creates new angels out of God.

The highest of all acts is the *mitzvot,* the study and practice of the Torah, prayer, love, and repentance. Every *mitzvah* that

—When the Lord pleases, the good spirits appear to others, and also to one another as bright stars that sparkle in accordance to the quality of their charity and faith; but evil spirits appear like balls of coal-fire.

—EMANUEL SWEDENBORG
Arcana Coelestia #1527

• • • •

a man does is not only a spiritual act, sacred in itself, but an act of transformation in the material world.

Great rabbis of Palestine and Europe followed these mystical paths, holy men as devout as ever walked the earth; and they profoundly influenced in the eighteenth century the Hasidic social and religious movement that still exists in small pockets today.

We hear only of great prophets and philosophers in history—or of saints and mystics famous enough to be written about.

How many people saw angels or talked with them, and we never hear of them at all?

I have received so many letters. So many confidences. More than one woman wrote of her grief and anguish at the loss of a loved one—husband or child or father or mother—and how in the midst of such suffering comes a mysterious gift: a presence, a ball of light, a wash of utter peace. Or else of seeing the image of the beloved person, smiling in trust and love. One woman wrote of lying in bed, about to go to sleep, when she was awakened by a strong sense of presence and a pair of hands blessing her in prayer; another of a golden light that flooded the bedroom. Always these occurrences come in times of difficulty. The recipient is not necessarily praying, unless grief and despair are a form of prayer. A mother has died, a divorce casts you adrift. And then there comes the light. You see it with your physical eyes, but also with the eyes of the heart, and the utter bliss is indescribable. Outside the window the trees are likewise bathed in light, and in that moment you

—Islam *means "surrender."* Muslim *means "one who surrenders to God."*

• • • •

know that everything is eternal, including you yourself. You are the light, the trees, the love, and you are loved beyond imagining. No angels, merely love.

I have letters about the light coming as a pinprick, growing to the size of a grapefruit and flowing in and through the person. Or of waking in the middle of the night to find a tiny spark hovering at your face . . . and then a kiss! It's gone. What happened? Why the feelings of delight?

Some centuries are richer than others in angelology—the twelfth and thirteenth centuries in theology and literature, the fourteenth and fifteenth in European art. But by the late Renaissance, the interest in angels was on the wane. Martin Luther (1483–1546) referred to his "guides, the holy angels," but Protestants mostly didn't pay much attention to angels. John Calvin (1509–1564) deplored speculation about them as fruitless and unprofitable, for the spiritual was being replaced by an excitement with the New World and scientific discoveries. No longer did serious people believe that the sun or moon were angels, nor that they were guided by angelic forces. Copernicus and Galileo were turning the universe upside down and demonstrating (as had been known to earlier peoples and to other civilizations) that our planet earth revolves around the sun, that we are not the center of the universe, therefore; and meantime new frontiers were opening in America. Suddenly the old world of religion and angels no longer seemed very interesting.

Yet, off in corners, a few mystics and geniuses still saw angels and wrote down what they found. One was Emanuel Swedenborg (1688–1772), son of the bishop of Skara in Sweden. He was a scientist, a member of the House of Nobles, an inventor, writer, civil and mining engineer, who amused himself with bookbinding, clock making, cabinet making, engraving, and lens grinding. He knew nine languages, including Hebrew, Greek, and Latin. He anticipated magnetic theory, the theory of atomic particles, and the invention of the machine gun, submarine, and glider-type aircraft. He was the first to use mercury for the air pump and he pioneered work in metallurgy. He was the father of crystallography, and wrote on mathematics, astronomy, geology, anatomy, on finding the longitude, and on the origins of the visible universe. At forty-six he published a theory that matter is composed of a nonmaterial force and posited four "levels" of particles within the atom. An unusual man, in short.

At twenty-eight he was appointed Assessor Extraordinary to the Swedish Royal Board of Mines, and at age thirty-six he was formally appointed Assessor. Twenty-three years later, in 1747, he resigned to devote himself to studies arising out of his clairvoyant communications with angels. He learned Hebrew in order to further his studies, and he wrote quite matter-of-factly in Latin what he had seen. His numerous books include *Arcana Coelestia* (twelve volumes); *Spiritual Diary* (five volumes) now retitled *Spiritual Experience*; *Heaven and Hell*; *Conjugial Love*; and *Divine Love and Wisdom*. If you search in the Library of Congress, as I have done, you find 198 entries of his works.

Today the Swedenborg Foundation has undertaken a $5 million project of new translations. He influenced (among others) William Blake, Carlyle, Coleridge, the Brownings, Strindberg, Goethe, Emerson, and Helen Keller. His works have been translated into dozens of languages, including Arabic, Burmese, Tamil, Zulu, Lettish, and Icelandic.

Swedenborg gives the year 1743 as the date of the opening of his spiritual sight.

"I am well aware," he wrote in *Arcana Coelestia*, "that many persons will insist it is impossible for anyone to converse with spirits and angels during his life-time in the body; many will say that such intercourse must be mere fancy; some that I have invented such relations in order to gain credit; whilst others will make other objections. For all these, however, I care not, since I have seen, heard and felt."

A spirit or angel, he said, not being composed of material substances, cannot reflect the sun's rays to be visible. Therefore we see angels either because the angel assumes a material body momentarily or because the interior or spiritual eye is opened, the inward eye by which we see. But this unveiling of spiritual worlds is proportioned to the capacity of the person to receive, and this is no greater than the goodness and truth which have become grounded in that being.

The angels told him many things, including that the soul lives in the body not as a bird in a cage but as water in a

—For it has pleased the Lord to manifest Himself to me. He has opened the interiors of my mind or spirit to be in the spiritual world with angels, and at the same time in the natural world with men, and this now for 25 years.

—EMANUEL SWEDENBORG
Conjugial Love #1

• • • •

sponge, every pore fully saturated with it, that after death one's sex remains: a man continues as a man-spirit, a woman remains a woman-spirit, and if they loved on earth, they still continue to conjoin. They told him of heaven, which is an emanation of unbounded love. The divine is not in space, but in love, and they told him how "it is allowed everyone to be in his delight, whether spirits or angels, even the most unclean who delight in adultery, stealing, blasphemy, lying—these are the delights of our nostrils. . . . Everyone whether good or evil is in his own delight—delight of his good, delight of his evil . . . And since that [evil] is our delight we are cast back, and are in torment!"

And he describes the angels at length.

Angels, he tells us, breathe an atmosphere adapted to their angelic lungs. They not only speak but write—though we would not need Swedenborg to tell us this, for did not one of the sisters in the convent of Saint Teresa of Avila (1515–1577) see that saint one day meditating at her desk and the plume dipping itself in ink and writing her memoirs independent of her guiding hand?

But how they speak is wondrous, for they express affection with vowels, Swedenborg says, ideas with consonants, and their total communication with words. They cannot voice, he says, the human language of doubt and ideas, conflict and argument. The reason is simple: angels can utter only what expresses with perfect sincerity the love that lies in them, so that their message is always one of total and unconditional overwhelming love. Is this why mere humans must act sometimes as angelic channels when angels will not do?

Angels, says Swedenborg, have no power of their own. They are agents of God, and if an angel doubted where his power comes from, he would instantly become so weak he could not resist a single evil spirit. (You see, Swedenborg, too, believed in evil spirits, and on several occasions was attacked, as most holy men seem to be, by devils and demons.)

"For this reason," says Swedenborg in *Heaven and Hell,* "angels ascribe no merit whatever to themselves, and are averse to all praise and glory on account of anything they do, ascribing all the praise and glory to the Lord."

Swedenborg's angels stayed with him always, whispering and singing to him. He writes of their communicating spiritually—by thoughts flashing into his mind, and in one of these instructions he learned that angels look on all events as proceeding from God—not as men or evil spirits do, who want everything to come out *their* way and, when it doesn't, give way to doubt or even deny the existence of God, but rather in an outpouring of faith. His angels repeated again and again that we poor beings should not worry about the future but only trust to Providence. For Providence will bring all things that we desire—not necessarily while we desire them, "but yet, if it be for their good, they obtain them afterward, when not thinking of them."

I am reminded of the messages of the Virgin Mary at Medjugorje. Are all spirits trying to tell us the same thing?

—Because He is Love in its essence, that is, Divine Love, [God] appears before the angels in heaven as a sun, and, from that sun heat and light go forth; the heat . . . being in its essence love, and the light . . . wisdom; and so far as the angels are recipients of that spiritual heat and light they are loves and wisdoms; not loves and wisdoms from themselves, but from the Lord.

—EMANUEL SWEDENBORG
Divine Love and Wisdom #5

• • • •

—There appeared to me very beautiful rainbows, as on former occasions, but still more beautiful, with a light of the purest white, in the centre of which was an obscure earthy something; but that most lucid snow-white appearance was beautifully varied by another lucidity, and was thus discriminated as also by little yellowish points like small stars, besides other beautiful variations, and, if I rightly recollect, with flowers of different colors round about, and entering into the most lucid part. This was exhibited before the left eye. On the right were exceedingly beautiful representations, distinguished by the blue and its various related colors, because the right eye represents affections, and they *derive colors not from a white lucidity, but from that which is flamy.*

—EMANUEL SWEDENBORG
Spiritual Diary #3636
Oct. 21, 1748

• • • •

Swedenborg is not always easy reading, although his influence extended beyond the shores of his native Sweden even in his lifetime. His words had particular impact on another philosopher named Rudolf Steiner.

Brilliant and charismatic, Steiner was born in 1861 in German-speaking Czechoslovakia, then part of the Austro-Hungarian Empire, and from the age of eight understood that he could see things clairvoyantly, including other worlds and creatures—things that other people did not. He didn't tell people about his conversations with these disembodied beings until he was around forty, but from then until his death at sixty-five in 1925 he taught and wrote copiously about what he'd seen and understood.

Steiner, like Swedenborg, was trained in many fields, and he ended up working in natural history, mathematics, philosophy, the arts, architecture, medicine, education, and agriculture. He wrote his Ph.D. thesis on "Truth and Knowledge," translated the works of Goethe, and in his late thirties began to teach in the Waldorf Astoria Tobacco Company school in Stuttgart, during which he developed the exceptionally fine system of education that is carried on today worldwide in the Waldorf Schools. He taught with the Theosophical Society ("the wisdom of the gods"), broke with it when director Annie Besant decided that a young Indian, Krishnamurti, was the reincarnated Savior, and formed his own offshoot school of thought called Anthroposophy ("the wisdom of man"). He was brilliant at whatever he turned his hand to—and in the eyes of many was a nut.

He was not a mystic. A mystic goes into himself in contemplation and meditation to find the essential unity of things. Steiner's mission was one of differentiation. Like the medieval alchemists, he sought by investigating the world of physical substance to develop a conscious and discriminating model of a spiritual world. He thought of his work as a scientist, and he felt that we stood at the opening of a new age, where mysteries were no longer to be held in the hands of heirophants and priests of secret societies, but known by anyone.

Steiner described his own hierarchy of angels, different from that of Dionysius and Aquinas, and drawn from Classical Greek as well as Judaic sources; and just to make it more complicated, his angels are tied to earlier cosmic worlds.

In Steiner's system, seraphim, cherubim, and thrones, in that *descending* order, form the first hierarchy. Seraphim receive the ideas and aims of the cosmic system from the Trinity. Cherubim transpose these ideas into workable human plans. The thrones, "figuratively speaking" (he adds), work with humans to put into practice the thoughts received by the seraphim from God and pondered over by the cherubim.

After these come dominions, mights, and powers, followed by archai, archangels, and angels. Angels, or angeloi, are the lowest on the scale. Every human individual, Steiner says, has an angel which guides that person through incarnation after incarnation (because Steiner believed in more than one lifetime, either on this planet or in other planes). At a certain stage you can ask your angel to reveal your former incarnations.

Two Angels. Italian,
14th century.

Angels, the lowest on the scale, stand behind each person, a guiding hand on his or her shoulder, and this influence is strongest in childhood. As the person grows older, the angel retreats in order to permit the human's development of freedom and personal individuality between the ages of twenty-five and forty, when the founding of a family and career are uppermost in his or her consciousness. Later, in the middle years, the person is rejoined by the angelic being, as again he or she turns toward understanding of the spiritual dimension.

Angels are Water Spirits. They rule a sphere from earth to the moon.

Archangels are Fire Spirits, concerned not with individuals but with the evolution of race-souls, folk-souls. They govern the relationship between individual human beings and the whole of a people or a race. Their sphere of influence runs from earth to Mercury.

And rising higher in this last triad, we find archai, or Spirits of Personality, which govern the relationships of the whole human species on earth. These angels live in waves of time, change their spiritual bodies from age to age, and are the "spirit of a time." They rule as far as Venus.

From them come the great beings who descend to earth to lead us. They are the bodhisattvas, yogis, prophets, and saints, who *appear* to be people but aren't, the appearance being *maya,* or illusion, as everything on this earth, including physical matter, is illusion.

The work of Steiner, like the Kabbalah, is too rich to describe in any detail, and it is worth noting only that he based his epistemology on *thinking,* a methodology having nothing in common with the experiential encounters—the cracks in the curtain—that abound in mystical writing. Steiner consorted with nature spirits, was surrounded by angels, but his strict and deliberate Teutonic constructivism is vastly different from the messages of saints or of the present-day sappy and maudlin depictions of fairies, elves, and angels in folklore. He was holding out a scientific plan.

But I revert with grateful relief to the classical mystics, the high and intellectual visionaries, who were graced with seeing God, and who have no interest in choirs of angels or orders, but only with the purity of their souls.

God, of your goodness give me yourself, for you are enough for me, and I can ask for nothing which is less which can pay you full worship. And if I ask anything which is less, always I am in want; but only in you do I have everything.

—JULIAN OF NORWICH
Revelations of Divine Love

PART III

Images & Dreams

. . . .

· CHAPTER 8 ·

Wings of Silence

There's a divinity that shapes our ends,
Rough-hew them how we will.
—WILLIAM SHAKESPEARE
Hamlet, V.ii

· 1 ·

When the gods were young, they created people to play with. Except the people refused to play. They remembered where they had come from and all they wanted to do was to throw themselves back into the bliss of God. So the gods destroyed that batch.

Then the gods sat down together to figure out where they could hide so that humans wouldn't find them and upset the game. They thought and thought. They couldn't come up with a perfect hiding place. If they went to the moon, mankind would build rockets and follow them. If they hid in the bottom of the oceans, people would dive in bathyscaphs. The top of Mount Everest . . . the core of the earth . . . no place was safe from human search.

Then the goddess of wisdom spoke. "Hide in the hearts of men and women," she said. "They'll never think of looking there."

So the gods made a new batch of people and hid inside the heart of every man and woman, and they play like dolls with their children, who, because they cannot ever find God, keep up the game.

*H*ugh Hildesby, former rector of the Church of Heavenly Rest, told me that one of his parishioners was an angel. His name was Phil, and he was a street person—what used to be called a bum. He was also a messenger, said Hugh. A schizophrenic, homeless man, Phil refused to stay in a shelter. He slept in doorways and maintained a careful routine, covering his neighborhood. In the daytime or when the weather was cold, he sat in the church. He was filthy. He was dressed in rags. He never washed, and sometimes he broke out in loud, abusive curses at passersby. "He was offensive and frightening, but he kept us honest."

Once the funeral of a prominent lawyer was in session. Phil sat in a pew in back of the church, dirty, odoriferous, not a pretty sight. The law partner of the deceased came up to Hugh and said with quiet disdain, "Can you get him out of here?"

Hugh said, "I understand completely. Yes, I can get him out. You should know, however, that if he leaves, I'll go with him. He belongs here. He's been a member of this parish for ten years."

The other looked at him, startled: "I think I understand. I'm sorry I asked that."

In that way Phil stands as a beacon of what we're supposed to be.

One night of Christmas week, the church held a Christmas party after a service, and the parishioners were in back with cookies and coffee, when out of the church rose a magnificent voice, singing, "O Holy Night." It was a trained professional voice, radically beautiful, and everyone listened, awestruck, then rushed into the church to see who was there.

"It was Phil and God," said Hugh.

—It can in no sense be said that heaven is outside of any one; it is within . . . and a man also, so far as he receives heaven, is a recipient, a heaven, and an angel.
*—*EMANUEL SWEDENBORG
Arcana Coelestia

• • • •

*I*t is strange to think that so much time and attention was spent by medieval theologians—or even modern Steiners—on working out the rank and place of angels. Angels live no place, as God lives no place. They live in the space of eternity, in the center of our hearts, and sometimes I think we each serve as the channels and angels of God, touched by wings of silence, pushed to angelic acts. I spoke earlier of strangers entering our lives to bring us news we need. But we know when we are being moved as well. It is marked by a sense of anxiety, a nagging nudge that cannot be ignored.

Once when I was living in New York, I was to go to the beach and was busy making the picnic lunch for the children when I was suddenly struck by great anxiety: going to the beach was *wrong.* I *had* to meet my editor for lunch. At incredible inconvenience to four people, not counting my poor kids, I undid all the beach arrangements and raced into Manhattan, not knowing why I felt such compulsion and hating my indecision.

At the table next to us in the restaurant sat a man I had not seen in ten years. We had lost contact, but it was imperative that we meet even briefly and conclude leftover business from all those years before. Had I not met my editor for lunch that day, the man and I would never have been in the same city again.

My daughter Molly had a similar experience some years ago, when she had planned to spend the night in Manhattan with a friend. She was suddenly smitten with that same anxiety—the sense she *had* to return home to Brooklyn. It was 1:00 A.M., but she got to the subway in time to meet and guide to safety an old lady who was, herself, struggling to get back home.

Elizabeth Paige is a writer. Once, while traveling alone in Greece, she went to the island of Páros. She intended to stay only two days and move on to Crete. But on the day of her departure, she began to feel great waves of doubt. Something was nudging her to stay. Yet she had no reason in the world to stay, she scolded herself—she'd seen the island! She checked out of her hotel, bought her ferry ticket, and was moving onto the boat, when her anxiety grew to such a pitch that she suddenly plunged off the ferry, pushing back through the crowd to the dock. Instantly she felt relieved. Puzzled, she returned to her hotel.

Now she had another two days on the island.

That next morning, determined to stay out of the sun, she took a sketch pad to a shady street in the village and spent several hours sketching, thinking of nothing. At lunchtime she found herself wandering past each restaurant and then on out of the village, and up along the road above the cliffs, her feet just moving her.

It was hot. She was alone. It was high noon and the sun beat down on her exactly as she had promised herself she would not permit, but she kept on. Off to her right was the ocean, to her left a hill of desert scrub. Soon she was thirsty. Not even a tree broke the glistening heat; and her feet kept taking her on.

In a few miles she saw a little house down to her right, with a pine tree in front of it. The house, shuttered and closed up, had a sign on it with a telephone number. She stared at it a moment, wondering if the Greek meant "For Rent."

Then, because she was hot and tired and thirsty, she took the five or six stone steps down from the road to the house below and lay down gratefully in the shade of the tree.

She had not rested there five minutes when a motor scooter stopped on the road above. The two women on it looked at

—As soon as you trust yourself you will know how to live.
—JOHANN WOLFGANG
VON GOETHE

• • • •

her curiously, then the older woman got off the scooter and the younger one drove off.

Suddenly Elizabeth guessed it was the owner. She rose to her feet, embarrassed at trespassing, and hesitated, wondering in which of her three languages to speak to the woman. For some reason, she chose her schoolgirl French:

"*Pardon, madame.* I saw the shade of your tree. . . ."

The woman looked at her sharply. It turned out she was French and spoke no English. Insistently she invited Elizabeth inside—would she like some water? And because Elizabeth was thirsty and also curious to see what a Greek house looked like inside, and because she liked the woman's looks she accepted.

The woman, Nicole, was visiting her daughter on Páros. She told Elizabeth why she had been so startled to see her lying under the tree: because the day before, "we saw you on

Angels.
Edith Vonnegut.
20th century.

the beach with your sketchpad, and I said to my daughter, 'That woman, like me, is alone, but she looks so serene and content. I'd like to talk to her.' And then here you are right at my house. It's a miracle."

She had been in the Resistance during the war. She had married a Protestant minister, raised her children, and after thirty years of marriage been left by her husband for a younger woman. Ever since, she had lived in a state of anger, unable to forgive her husband or forget that the other woman had been her friend.

They talked. Elizabeth was surprised to discover how freely she spoke French. She didn't know she knew the language so well.

At a certain moment the woman turned to her: "Tell me— you know this—what is God?"

For some reason Elizabeth was hardly surprised.

"I cannot tell you what God is," she said, "but I can tell you how to find it." They spent the rest of the afternoon talking feverishly about meditation and the spiritual path, about forgiveness and prayer, and suffering, and love, about the writer Kazantzakis, the Buddha, Christ. Elizabeth says that she spoke with a passion that surprised her. She said things in French that she couldn't even say in English, and she listened in astonishment as the words rolled off her tongue, speaking of God.

Before she left, they knelt together and prayed. It was embarrassingly simple—two middle-aged women kneeling on the stone floor, praying for deliverance from pain and for the ability to love and trust again. Praying for knowledge of God. And then Elizabeth walked back to her hotel, marveling at the encounter. Was this why she had not been able to leave the day before? She was swept with humility at the goodness of God that gave her such words in French, that gave her that gift of serving as a channel for His words. For she knew it was not she, Elizabeth, who had been speaking so eloquently that afternoon.

The next day she left for Crete.

A year later a letter arrived from Nicole. It was written in English, dictated from a hospital bed. She was dying of cancer, and she wanted Elizabeth to know how their meeting that afternoon in Greece had changed her life. She thought of it as a miracle, she said, for from that moment she had been released from her anger and had started to make her peace with God. She was dying, but wanted Elizabeth to know.

I once had an angel come as a swan. Or perhaps the swan was an angel. Or perhaps the occurrence is nothing but coincidence distorted: *post hoc, propter hoc.* Which means, because one event preceded another, you decide that the first one caused the second. This is another sailing story, though somewhat silly this time, no lives being in jeopardy.

It was a cold autumn night on Long Island Sound, the night between the last day of September and the first day of October, with a three-quarter moon climbing through the milk of stormy clouds.

David and I had chartered a thirty-foot sloop, left the children with his parents, and had taken off for a two-day holiday by ourselves. Anyone who is familiar with Long Island Sound can retrace our sail.

We set out with a strong running wind that whipped us from Connecticut across the sound to Long Island, landing right on schedule in Port Jefferson. It was late afternoon by then. We thought we would tie up at the dock for the night, eat in a restaurant, perhaps take in a movie, and sail home next day. But when we arrived in Port Jefferson, we found that small-craft warnings were out. We could not tie up at the dock, we were told, with the wind sweeping straight into the mouth of the harbor. We'd be beaten against the dock. And anyway they had no room for us. We'd have to anchor out somewhere.

We went ashore, bought a chicken and a bottle of wine for dinner, and motored out to find a safe shelter for the night.

Off the western end of the main harbor lies a channel like a bent elbow that leads to a deep-water pond or tidal marsh. In the center lies an island of mud and marsh grasses; on the west side of the pond on high bluffs stand large, imposing houses. Nice place to live.

We chugged slowly up this elbow channel, cautiously watching the charts, and dropped anchor for the night. Hardly had we dug in, however, than a man came down on shore and waved.

"You can't anchor there," he called out. "The currents are too strong. You'll be swept ashore."

"Where can we anchor?" we asked. He motioned us forward a hundred yards and said we'd be safe up there. So we hauled up anchor, tired now and annoyed; we chugged forward under motor a fair distance, reset the anchor, and waited to make sure it was firm. By then the flaming sunset was dying behind the houses on the bluff; the light faded into dusk, then dark. The man had gone indoors long before, and only the yellow eyes of houses blinked at us from the hill. For a time we stood on deck, shivering in the cold and wishing the boat had a second anchor to set out at our stern. We would have liked the security of being double-anchored in the marsh. Nevertheless we had dug in deep; we thought we were okay.

We went below, made a delicious dinner of chicken and rice and salad, and ate it in the warm glow of a kerosene lamp. After dinner we fell like stones on our bunks with the exhaustion of those who've done hard work.

At midnight we both woke up. The bow of the boat was pitching around as if bridled at the stern. We pulled on pants, sneakers, sweaters, and raced on deck, into a ghostly night with the moon chasing through shredded clouds and a good wind whistling through the shrouds, the halyards *ping*ing against the mast.

We saw what had happened. The boat had twisted in the night, caught by currents, we supposed, and run around its reins until the anchor line set at the bow had snagged on the propellor. The anchor line was caught beneath the stern, and the boat was bucking on its lead, goosed, as it were, by its own leash. Worse, it had pulled the anchor from the mud. We were being swept ashore.

We stared helplessly. We couldn't turn on the motor and push offshore because with the rope wound around the propeller, we'd likely break the blades.

We couldn't dive underwater and try to untie the anchor line from the prop. The water was pitch-black. We had no gear—no wet suit, no underwater flashlight. Moreover, the water was icy cold. We could die of hypothermia before we managed to grope our way beneath the boat and untie the line.

We couldn't cut the anchor line on deck in hopes it would unwind itself under water from the prop, for even if it did, what would we do then? True, we could turn on the motor and pull away from shore. But we had no other anchor. Once done, we'd have to keep moving out to sea; and how would we manage in the dark to crawl up that narrow, angled channel with the wind smashing at our bow? We weren't equipped for such a cruise.

Meanwhile the boat was being washed aground. A soft bottom perhaps. We'd not be badly hurt unless we hit a rock.

More out of need to act than from any sensible plan, we set to work. We pulled up the anchor line at both the bow and the stern, hauling in every inch of extra rope. We cleated it tightly at either end. The line then ran from the bow cleat, taut as a violin string under the full length of the boat, wound once (or more?) around the prop—no slack—and straight up tight to a cleat at the stern.

All we'd done was ensure that the line was too taut for the current to unwind what it had done.

We stood on deck and watched the black water carry us to shore.

Suddenly, at the side of the boat, I saw a beautiful white swan. I had not noticed it before. It came right up to the boat, eyeing me in profile with its single, hard, black beady eye. I had made some bread for the trip. I went below, cut a chunk, and came back on deck to the swan. (Why not? Had I anything better to do?) I threw the bread on the water. The current was so strong that the bird had to swim backward as fast as it could to reach the bread. I remember that strong backward stroke of its webbed feet, the fine white swing of the long neck as it snapped up the crust. The swan approached again.

"Oh, swan," I said. "I wish that you could dive underwater and release the anchor rope."

It stared unblinking from its eye.

Then: "It's free! It's free!" shouted David.

Immediately I ran below and cut more bread and made two more wishes on the swan, much more important, too, and one so significant that I also made a test. I held the last crust in my hand. "If the swan takes this from my hand, I'll get this wish," I thought, knowing that swans are vicious creatures and that this one might just as likely slice my palm in two. He slipped the bread from my fingers as delicately as the nibble of a cat. All that took less than fifty seconds. I raced back to David and helped haul in lines and turn on the motor. We rejoiced to hear it roar. We swung round the bow just in time to slip us off the shore. We reset the anchor, leaned the boat in reverse to dig the anchor in, and lurched about to ensure our solid hold. All this took time.

When we turned off the motor (stunned by silence), I looked around. The swan had disappeared. I could not see it anywhere.

The running moon shone clear on the water, illuminating land and marsh. Not a glimmer of that luminous white. We went down below wondering what had happened. How could the anchor line unwind from the motor when it had no slack at all? The swan had nothing to do with it, if course; my playing with the swan, making idle wishes—that's just done for fun.

The next morning I looked for a family of swans. There were no swans in the marsh.

· 2 ·

Once I dreamed my husband's dream. I dreamed a man was climbing the stairs toward me, and I could see his face, a hideous mask, all grinning teeth and bloody scars, twisted, contorted. I woke, heart pounding, knowing I had seen the embodiment of *fear!*—and found my husband lying awake in bed beside me, fists clenched, gripped by an anxiety attack. In my sleep I had picked up his emotion.

Scientists have proven that matter—a table, a tree, a truck, which feels pretty solid if it falls on us—is actually composed of atoms whirling about like stones, as far removed from one another, relatively, as the stars of space. Inside the atom the protons and neutrons are bound together in the nucleus by the "strong force," as it is called, in continual interplay with the "weak force." Scientists tell us that if that force were diminished by the most minute percentage, a nano-point, the matrix of the universe would fly apart. Or consider the opposite effect: if the attracting, bonding force were only marginally stronger, the universe would collapse in on itself, protons crushing one another into solid mass. In that case the universe would also be denuded of free protons, which form the nuclei of hydrogen molecules. Without hydrogen there would be no sun or stable stars. Instead it all works. The atoms weave in perfect balance, held by their yearnings, separated by their repulsions and the drag of gravity.

Physicists and mystics are in agreement that we, too, are composed of electrons, neutrons, protons, swirling in the same suspension. Occasionally each of us experiences the melting of the barriers. For a flash we understand things we have no right to know. We read minds, receive insights, reach into the Akashic river of knowledge and pull out pearls, so that we are not even sure if what we see and how we think is something of our own or if it's "in the air," a fragrance everyone else is also breathing at that time.

The literary manager of a theater in Seattle told me once how plays come in cycles. He cannot ignore the phenomenon. For six weeks all he reads will be plays about Hitler. For the next six weeks he will receive only plays about grandmothers, or fathers with strokes, or women being raped, or soldiers in war, or prison tales—as if we were all looking over each other's shoulders, copying out each others' thoughts.

When Charles Darwin was writing *The Origin of Species,* an Australian was working on exactly the same theme and idea. Darwin published first. The Australian charged him with plagiarism, though most people felt it was just coincidence.

Whatever that means.

Carl Jung, the noted psychoanalyst, called it synchronicity.

But some people say that thought is a powerful energy on its own, and they speak of how negative thoughts reflect negative happenings onto the one who thinks them; positive thoughts return only goodness to the thinker, as well as to all those around.

Physicists now study precognition and psychokinesis. They watch psychics move cigarettes around a table or bend nails with their thought. They set up experiments to test the accuracy of prophecies, or events seen from far away—remote viewing, it is called. The question is, Do we merely swim in and out of time? Or do we make things happen with our thoughts?

One day a friend came over to our house for coffee. We were sitting in the kitchen, David, myself, and Joan. I was restless. I like Joan, but she and David were talking business. I wanted to go work and didn't know if it would be accounted rude. David was showing Joan how the kitchen ceiling was composed of large, clear plastic sheets, with fluorescent lights above; he was standing on the kitchen counter, taking out a plastic square, when the thought came to me that it was going

—We are what we think
All that we are arises with our
  thought
With our thoughts we make the
  world.
Speak and act with an impure mind
And trouble will follow you
As the wheel follows the ox that
  draws the cart.

We are what we think
All that we are arises with our
  thought
With our thoughts we make the
  world.
Speak or act with a pure mind
And happiness will follow you
As your shadow, unshakable.

         —THE DHAMMAPADA

    • • • •

to fly out of his hands and hit Joan. I took two steps back to get out of the way just as the plastic shot across the room and hit her in the forehead, drawing blood. She went right home.

I felt terrible about it. Had I willed the accident? Or merely seen it coming? But surely the latter, for never had I wanted to see her hurt!

The search to explain coincidence has occupied physicists as well. It was discovered as early as 1935 that two subatomic particles having once interacted with each other respond to each other's motions light-years apart. It is called the EPR effect—electron paramagnetic resonance. Einstein puzzled over the phenomenon all his life, for it refutes his theory that nothing can go faster than the speed of light. He said it offers science two "entirely unacceptable" alternatives—either objective reality is an illusion or the measurement of one EPR particle violates known laws by "telepathically" influencing the other particle. (This is a very complicated theory, and I can only beg the indulgence of greater minds than mine if my impoverished description offends.)

Once I was struck by lightning. I was driving in a thunderstorm down Reno Road in Washington. An actress, Barbara Callendar, was in the car with me. I suddenly thought, "I'm going to be hit by lightning." It was a preposterous idea, what with all the trees around me. But given the force of the storm—the long peals of thunder and flashes of lightning—it was perfectly possible that lightning might hit a tree and the tree might fall on the car. So as soon as I could, I turned off the low-lying wooded glen and moved uphill toward Wisconsin Avenue, just near the cathedral.

Where the car was struck by lightning.

The lightning must have come straight down out of the sky to hit the car (Volvo, white), bypassing the apartment buildings on both sides, as well as the spires of the cathedral. We were surrounded by blinding light and energy. For a few seconds I knew nothing except the awesome power of the universe, and then the lightning passed, and we were left, Barbara and I, shaking and noodle-legged and alive.

I thought we were spared because of being insulated by four rubber tires. It turns out that the car acts as a Faraday cage, its metal encasement transferring the energy of the lightning down and around us swiftly to the ground. Afterward I felt like a figure in a fairy tale, warned by the fairy godmother that she will prick her finger at age fifteen, who, in trying to avoid the action, brings it on. Does that mean we can't avoid our fate? And why would such useless information be given anyway? Or is it just to let us know that destiny exists?

Conventional thinking does not admit that we affect the future with our thoughts. Most psychiatrists consider that people who believe in thought control may be suffering from an obsessive-compulsive disorder, one mark of which is compulsive neatness and a desire to control and another a propensity for what they call magical thinking. This includes the belief that thoughts create events.

Once David went on a ten-day trip to the West Coast. I

spent all week in solitude and silence, meditating by myself. My children were in school and nearly grown by then, the youngest being twelve. So I had time to myself—and wanted it. I had much on my mind. Our marriage was strained, David depressed and I confused.

The day before he returned, I went for a long walk with the dog, up into Rock Creek Park and deep into the woods. I remember I was so happy I thought my body would break. I have on other occasions been so unhappy I hurt all over, but only rarely have I felt such exquisite happiness that my bones ached, and only after such prolonged periods of silent meditation. That's what I was feeling then.

Walking along, I had a vision. I saw a small plane. David was inside, and suddenly the left wing of the plane was dipping down. It was about to hit the mountainside. For one moment the thought flashed through my mind: *Ah, that would solve everything.* And simultaneously in my mind's eye I cupped my hands under the plane protectively. *Let him live,* I thought, or *Give him life.* There is no way to translate the swift clarity of pure thought, or what enormous meaning was intended by that verb *to live.* Instantly it was over.

I whistled for the dog and continued home, wondering what it meant.

The next day I picked up David at Dulles Airport. He said, "You know the strangest thing happened to me yesterday. I was coming into Seattle in a private plane from Richland. We were landing, when suddenly the wing dipped down. It came within inches of the tarmac. If it had hit, we'd have flipped

The Meeting of a
Family in Heaven.
William Blake. Engraving,
18th century.

over. I was right behind the pilot. He yelled, 'Sonuvabitch.' He was pulling on the stick, and it didn't respond. Then for no reason at all the plane suddenly righted itself and we landed. I talked to the pilot afterward. He said we were caught in the backdraft of a jet, when the stick jammed. He thought we were dead for sure."

I reeled. "What *time* did this happen?"

My vision had occurred several hours *before* the actual event, even accounting for the difference in time. But what exactly had happened? Had I foreseen the event? Or actually affected the accident? More to the point, if in my vision I had batted down the plane, would it have crashed?

*D*reams and images. This is a difficult section to write, for now we are out of the path of ghosts and angels and demons and saints and into sheer perception. Or is perception angels too? Saint Gregory said, "In this visible world, all dispositions are executed through invisible creatures." Are our senses guided by angelic thought? The important thing to note is that all these things represent ways of receiving information that transcend the routine levels—analysis, reasoning, logic—which we are taught to trust. These means of receiving information are not open to us all the time, and some people have more access to these routes than others; whether by practice or by accident they become conduits, somehow, through which the information may be passed. It is my belief that the information is passed through an electrical energy and that this energy has something to do with love and also with the suspension, even momentarily, of doubt.

I believe it is like a river, a flowing that we hook into at times to receive transcendent information. We do not know where it is coming from, but we know how it comes—surrounded by light, crashing over us with total conviction—that it is different from our egotistical thoughts, from mere desire, or the tug of fear. It must always be tested against reality, but when it has passed the tests, you must always act upon it, even if other people say it cannot be true.

Western peoples in the last century have given angels and demons new meaning, remythologized into a trinity of super-ego, ego, and id. But I have seen light pouring off the hands and skin of people. This may seem odd, given what I have written of the darkness of the human soul. Once I had an operation. I was two weeks in Massachusetts General Hospital in Boston, and when I was recovering, I had an epiphany. I have often wondered if it was induced by drugs, but in that case would not everyone have such moments in a hospital? I saw with extraordinary clarity. I marveled at it: *This is the way artists see,* I thought, humbled by the miracle of a towel rack, the fold of a sheet. A tree outside the window, the children playing football on the grass reduced me to tears. I was reading Dostoyevsky's *The Brothers Karamazov* at the time and could take in only a few paragraphs without putting it down, it so affected me. One day standing at the window, looking at sky and clouds, I was smitten by the order of the universe. I could hear the singing of the planets, the low, deep roar of

—Do not believe me simply because I have seen Heaven & Hell, have discoursed with angels . . . Believe me because I tell you what your consciousness and intuitions will tell you if you listen closely to their voice.

—EMANUEL SWEDENBORG
Divine Love and Wisdom

•   •   •   •

stones and rocks. I understood . . . everything—things that today I don't even have the language to pose questions about, and the beauty of this order was so sharp that tears coursed down my cheeks. And more extraordinary, when I looked out the window, the leaves and trees and grass were flashing with an inner light. I saw light shining from the skin of people, pouring off the hands and faces both of nurses and of fellow patients. (All but one! One patient pacing the hospital corridor for exercise was shrouded in a black, deep cloud: I recoiled, repelled.) The others, however, were haloed with light. Back in Washington in my own garden, I bent in worship at this radiance pouring from the leaves and grass, from every living thing. "Look. Look at the light," I would say. And then realized that other people didn't see it flaming off the vines "like shining from shook foil." For two weeks I could see the earth flaring with this living light, and then it began to fade away. I felt myself losing the capacity to see. I thought, *I would give my soul to keep on seeing that;* and then I realized that I'd just been given it. This was before I saw my mother's ghost.

Only rarely since then have I seen light shining like that off the skin of people. Once I was in Costa Rica. I was waiting in the shabby airport in San Jose, waiting as all travelers in airports wait; and this time there was no excuse of drugs (as in the hospital), and neither can I trace the event to alcohol or even to fatigue. I sat down, and suddenly I saw ordinary people flaring with light—Indian women with their babies, students, tourists, American businessmen, soldiers, and diplomats. Light poured off their faces, shoulders, hands—wherever they showed bare

Persian peri. Illuminated manuscript.

skin. I sat in that grungy, plastic, South American airport and trembled at the sight; and the tears ran slowly down my cheeks in humility and gratitude. I put on my sunglasses so that no one would see. I was shaking at the *goodness* of people, at the beauty of these luminous beings shining with light.

Once David had a stay in Georgetown Hospital. Mr. Johnson, the man in the bed next to his, was dying of cancer. Soon after he returned home, David was reading in bed. He looked up from his book.

"I think I'll go visit Mr. Johnson today," he said; and at that moment a shock of light passed over him, streaming from his skin.

Who was it who said, "Beauty is reality seen with the eyes of love"?

Since then I have been witness other times to this phenomenon—although I have usually glimpsed it in a veiled or shadowy way, a passing, fleeting, quickening of light flaring in another person and dying down again. It is the light of love.

We speak of sacred things occasionally, but always one-on-one, or at most in twos and threes, and then only when the group is known and the time is intimate and safe. Some things have been shown me that I cannot record here, as everyone has experiences too precious to relate. And what good does it do anyway? To have one of these experiences is like standing on a hillside at night, in the midst of a thunderstorm. All around lies darkness and rolling black clouds; and suddenly the sky is torn open by a sheet of lightning and there exposed before you is the whole valley—trees, pastures, woods, streams, hills. The lightning ends. You are plunged again into darkness. But now you know what's there, and no one in the world can persuade you that you made up what you saw. Let us say that a friend is standing with you on the hillside in the dark storm, back turned when the flash of lightning comes. "Oh, wow," you say, "Lookit *that*!" But when he turns, the light is gone. Is he wrong to say there's nothing there? To him, the night is black. Both people operate on their individual perceptions of reality, and both are correct, for all we can do is to trust our own experience.

What force governs? Looking back and seeing the pattern, I understand that that has been the question at every moment of my life—differently phrased at times and answered differently at different times. It keeps being redefined. My answer at the moment is that there are two worlds, visible and invisible. They tangle with each other in increasingly perceptible ways . . . if we have the courage to see. I begin to think now that this blending is perhaps so complete that we cannot separate the butter from the batter, the physical from the spiritual. It's all one thread, the wild, mad, beautiful, and ever-changing creation of the dreams of Brahma sitting on his lotus flower. The thing is that the dream can be dreamed by us as well, dream and participant and dreamer being all the same.

The connection between these worlds can be developed, it seems, by thought or spiritual exercise. Sometimes it simply comes, like wind.

I was found by those who sought me not.
I became manifest to those who did not ask for me.

—ROM. 10:20

I don't know if it can be lost, but when the perception comes, it often brings with it heightened energy and power, as if an invisible force were flowing through us. It is my experience that three rules make this work for us, and they are the same rules that operate in prayer. We have to

Ask
Notice
Respond

—Everything we call a trial, a sorrow, or a duty;
Believe me, that Angel's hand is there.

—FRA GIOVANNI

• • • •

And then give it away again.

The forces of the universe have a wondrous way of bringing us to heel. Eventually everyone is forced to his knees, her knees, in total, forced surrender. Forced to ask. A person can be content, complacent, satisfied with his money and career, marriage, kids, the steady, constant life; and sure as the sun comes up, some damage will be done—the back of the hand to you, sir—until he's lying clobbered in the street; and then if he knows what's good for him, he'll *ask*. And if not, sure as night follows day, he'll get hatcheted by life until he does.

Then she or he must kneel in humble submission, for until you bow down before this force of the universe, until you are brought right to your knees by pain and despair, you still withhold yourself and your prayer has less effect.

And this is why we cannot even determine after a while

what's good, what's bad. What we thought a blessing has such thorns, we can hardly hold it in our hands, while what we thought was terrible turns out to wear a crown.

All God's angels come to us disguised;
Sorrow and sickness, poverty and death,
One after another lift their frowning masks,
And we behold the Seraph's face beneath,
All radiant with the glory and the calm
Of having looked upon the front of God.

—JAMES RUSSELL LOWELL

So loving is the universe, so joyful, so determined to give us everything we need and to love us and show us the way to live, too, that we are beaten to the ground, boiled by God's waves, as we play in the surf. We are toyed with, played with, socked down, in order that this loving force may pick us up in Her arms and carry us to safety up the beach and wrap us in warm towels and let us rest in His most maternal motherly embrace. Goethe knew it.

The Gods, the Eternal Ones, give all things to their Darlings. All joys, all sorrows. To their Darlings, everything.

I have written about prayer at length in *The Path of Prayer,* but let me give a nod to it here, for prayer is what draws angelic help to us.

Many people don't believe in prayer, but prayer is nothing

more than thought. It is a yearning of the heart. It is a concentrated thought, gathered and sent out from us, and if by thought we create our world, then surely by the concentrated thought of prayer we create it as well. The problem is that we aren't taught how to make a prayer that can be heard, that can be answered when we ask, and therefore when we don't receive the answer—or don't receive it in the fashion we expect, or in the time frame we set up—we think it wasn't heard, that prayer is ineffectual or some other cosmic joke.

But prayer is a law of the universe, like gravity. You don't even have to believe in God to ask, but you must follow the rules. Imagine there is a giant radio station out in space, beyond the stars, a receiving station, and all you have to do is to beam your thought, your longing to that station, and *if it is received clearly,* without static, the answer comes pouring down upon you immediately—instantly, with an abundance of delight; for it is the pleasure of the universe to give us what we need.

The question is, how do we send our thought in such a way that it can be received?

—Therefore, I say unto you, if ye have faith and doubt not . . . whatsoever ye shall ask in prayer, believing, ye shall receive.

—MATT. 21:21, 22

• • • •

• HOW TO PRAY •

Asking

1. First, you must use the present tense. The universe does not understand the future or the past, for it has no concept of time: all things happen simultaneously once we are beyond the boundaries of our little world. ("Time is God's way of seeing that everything doesn't happen at once.") Therefore, It cannot cope with past-tense thoughts or projections into the future. It knows only NOW.

2. Next you must phrase your prayer in a positive sense. For, again, the universe does not understand the concept of "not." There is no absence or negative in the universe, and therefore It deletes all but the active voice and positive words.

Many people do not know this. So the mother may be on her knees in supplication, praying, with all the yearning in her heart: "Don't let my baby die." But there are two negatives in her prayer—the "not" of *don't* and the word *die.* Better for her to say in words what her heart is longing for: "Let my baby live!" Or even better, in gratitude, since the universe has no concept of time: "Thank you that my baby lives." It is imperative that we guard the language in which we form our thoughts, for if we say, "Don't let my baby die," we are, against our very will, imagining our loss, grieving and mourning it already, so that it becomes, through our thoughts and fear, the more possible. This is what Christ meant when he spoke of having faith.

Still, even as she prays, "Don't let my baby die," the mother's heart is speaking its own silent language—that her baby live! What is received by that radio station, therefore, out at the fringes of space may be only static: the clatter created by the clash between heart and fear. If only static is received, the universe cannot respond. Or it may receive her heartfelt prayer, her desire having overpowered doubt.

—Do not fear, only believe.
— MARK 5:36

• • • •

—Put me to the test, says the Lord of hosts, if I will not open the windows of heaven for you and pour down for you an overflowing blessing.

—MAL. 3:10

. . . .

—Fear not, little flock, for it is your Father's good pleasure to give you the kingdom.

—LUKE 12:32

. . . .

3. Some people pray correctly, on their knees in submission, and with the correct language, careful to articulate (in gratitude) the desire for (having had fulfilled) the wishes of their hearts—and then are swept by doubt. *What am I doing?* they interrupt themselves. *I don't even believe in God. Prayers aren't answered, and thank God, no one can see me here, on my knees. This is absurd.*

What is received at the station is, again, static—the fervent prayer followed by the negation of the same, expressed in "I disbelieve. Prayers aren't answered." To which thought must It respond? If the negation and doubt are louder than the concentrated thought, the universe will respond with that—with what the person wanted, so loving is this deity, so willing to give us everything we want, even pain and doubt and despair and isolation and alienation and fear, if that is what we want. . . .

4. After holding in one's attention even for a few seconds the *idea* of the completed, answered prayer, then submit to the universe again: "Thy will by done." For Providence knows more of what is best for us than we ourselves. It is for this reason that people say to be careful what you pray for—because you'll get it. " 'Take what you want,' said God, 'And pay for it,' " is an Arabic saying.

Noticing

The second requirement of prayer is to notice when the answer comes, and again many people pray and receive the answers to their prayers but ignore them—or deny them, because the answers didn't come in the expected form. We're like children when the Good Humor truck comes by, ringing its bell, and we run inside to our mother, saying, "Mom, Mom, can I have an ice cream?"

She says, "Not now, it's almost dinnertime. You can have one after dinner."

"*No!*" the child responds. "I want it *now.*"

Or she says, "Yes, but that one's too expensive. I have a quart in the freezer. Have some of that."

"*No!*" says the child. "I want the ice cream from the *truck*!"

Or she says, "Yes, here's a dollar."

In each case she gave her child an ice cream, but the child believes she gave it only once.

That's how it is with prayer. Many times we refuse to see the answer. I think that this is the step—recognition—that seems to elude extreme rationalists, those who admit the existence of nothing beyond the material world, and perhaps to frighten them as well, challenging that voice in all of us of skepticism, scorn, rebellion, fear, the side that clings to the flotsam of a physical world in our desperate attempt to keep control. The alternative, after all, is terrifying: What if we're not in com-

—For whatever you ask in my name, I will do it . . . if you ask anything in my name, I will do it.
—John 14:13, 14

• • • •

—*Until one is committed there is hesitancy, the chance to draw back, always ineffectiveness. Concerning all acts of initiative (and creation), there is one elementary truth, the ignorance of which kills countless ideas and splendid plans: That the moment one definitely commits oneself, then Providence moves too. All sorts of things occur to help one that would never otherwise have occurred. A whole stream of events issue from the decision, raising in one's favor all manner of unforeseen incidents and meetings and material assistance, which no man could have dreamt would have come his way.*

—W. H. MURRAY
*The Scottish Himalayan
Expedition*

• • • •

mand? Most of us, however, as we get older do pretty soon come to the realization that there's more out there than we can readily explain. And I have yet to meet an atheist who at a moment of peril has not, against his will, cried out, "Oh, help!"

Responding

Once we have noticed that the answer has been given, then the third step comes naturally. We can only accept the gifts with awe and wonderment and then, in gratitude, we are obliged to say, "Thank you." And try to pass the gift along.

CHAPTER 9

My Black Angel & Other Friendly Spirits

· 1 ·

*T*he angel came first. It happened long before the ghost appeared in Brooklyn, and long before I had real questions about the reality of God. Contact with angels consisted of nothing more real than my mother's voice asking that my sister "be an angel and take the garbage out." Or listening to odd Bible stories that we heard in church (of all places!). In those stories angels appear as common as grapes, as do archangels and seraphim and cherubim and other spiritual soldiers of the Lord. They blow trumpets or hold lilies and often appear to women (Sarah, Elizabeth, Mary) to announce news that every other woman gets by morning sickness or tender breasts or the absence of her monthly cycle.

We listened to the stories. We never talked about them. An angel appeared to Abraham to tell him not to kill his child. Another marked the houses of the Jews in Egypt to save the firstborn sons. Angels wrestled with Jacob or came for Elijah. At Christmas we listened like stunned steers, eyes glazed, while the minister retold the story of the birth according to Luke. I liked it. It was comforting, and I didn't for a minute believe it was myth; that is, one part of me that likes a good story is always willing to suspend disbelief for a while and quiver as the wicked stepmother hands Snow White the apple, or as Paris sets in motion a generation of war, shipwreck, and devastation by giving the golden apple to Aphrodite in return for love.

In the Christmas story, three wise men track down a baby in a stable to do worship, though they might as well have stayed home and considered their own wives and children, one would think, showering them with some of that gratitude and grace. Or were they just tired after their long journey, so that finally at the inn they agreed to give up their wandering, and hearing a new baby had been born said, "Enough! Let's give him something and get on home"? In that same story shepherds abandoned their flocks to walk into town, led by angels who appeared for no other reason than to tell them not to worry. And when they got to the big city, crammed with people (no room in any inns), the shepherds, to hear this story, were in no way disappointed to discover nothing more inter-

—Have no anxiety about anything; but in everything by prayer and supplication with thanksgiving let your requests be made known to God.

*—*PHIL. 4:6

. . . .

Joachim and the Angel.
Albrecht Dürer. Woodcut,
16th century.

esting than a wet, red, newborn baby boy. Which they, too, knelt down and worshipped, as if they didn't all have children of their own, and brothers and nephews and nieces and baby sisters and dozens of cousins back at home.

We turned our white-moon faces up to the minister every Christmas and listened to this story without a shred of contempt—not a guffaw in the church, not a shrug of wonderment, possibly not a single thought. The communicants were waiting for the swallow of wine that would wash the paper-thin wafer off the roofs of their mouths; and we children were trying not to squirm or kick the pews and earn our mother's displeased looks. That took up our attention.

Yet no one in my presence questioned why such a panoply of gifts and glory was given out that day, in contrast to the abysmal neglect when He died miserably a few decades later, hung up on the Cross. Not a single angel in sight then to recognize his death. And so far as I know, no one of my family or acquaintances ever wondered out loud about the curious absence of angels and the heavenly host in our own day, though they could all come trumpeting out unnecessarily for one birth.

So where are the angels? Do they avoid the unpleasant, where they might have a chance at doing good?

We need the angels now.

When I saw the angel, I didn't go to church, and neither do I remember praying very much. I was twenty-eight. My husband was a writer for *The CBS Evening News* and we lived in Greenwich Village, in a fifth-floor walk-up, struggling. I had left a career to follow David to New York. We had just had our first baby, and suddenly I found myself trapped in an apartment with an infant entirely dependent on me, who could not talk or give back either emotional or physical help. How did I manage? There were days when I could easily imagine picking up the baby by the heels and smashing her head against the bare brick wall. . . . I wept a lot. During the day I dared not leave her alone. At night, when David came home, the streets were said to be too dangerous for me to go out walking all alone. I was a prisoner.

I found part-time work. I wrote. The baby grew bigger. I grew stronger. My attention was hardly directed to the mysterious, therefore. I was struggling with practical realities—doubt, confusion, suffering.

One day a friend telephoned asking if David and I would join a party of his friends for a week of skiing in Val d'Isère in France. We agreed. We left the baby, ten months old, with my mother (bless her!), and found a charter flight to France.

We were both good skiers. We had spent time learning it with the discipline and concentration that we brought to most of the things we did. In addition I found in skiing something so pure and fine it lifted me beyond myself. Riding a single chairlift, swinging in the silence of the winds, and blinking against the ice-encrusted trees, prisms glittering against a hard blue sky, my body taut and fit; I thought that nothing could match the crack of such sensations. Fast and

—One of life's most fulfilling moments occurs in that split-second when the familiar is suddenly transformed into the dazzling aura of the profoundly new.

*—*EDWARD B. LINDAMAN
Thinking in the Future Tense

• • • •

fearless, I shot downhill, fell, rose, and plunged on in that cold white air.

Just once when skiing I had seen something else.

When we were newly married, we'd gone skiing in Austria. We joined a class and were toiling across a difficult slope on a long uphill traverse, when I looked up and saw the sky flaming with color.

"Look! Look at the sky!" I pointed, dumbfounded by the shimmering pinks and greens, colors I had never seen in sky before. Our guide and David and the class looked up and then away, as if it were of no significance. Didn't they see it? Or was I sun-dazzled—overworked perhaps—so that I only imagined this effect?

"Yes, we often have interesting phenomena in the mountains," said the instructor, and continued with his class. Continue the lesson! I was riveted to that blazing sky.

I did not remember that sky again until I saw it for a second time, in Val d'Isère.

At Val d'Isère you feel you're standing at the top of the world. High above the treeline lie white fields of snow. Sometimes you ski in clouds. Sometimes the air is clear as the stratosphere. You ski on tracks, or *pistes.* These are marked by an occasional red flag stuck in the snow. But mostly you know where to go by the tracks of other skiers, and you do not leave the paths. There are two reasons. First, you can plunge off a cliff, and second, you can start an avalanche. There is no ski patrol at Val d'Isère to sweep every trail at night for injured skiers as there are in low-lying mountains like Stowe, Vermont, or Aspen, Colorado. At least there wasn't a ski patrol then.

One day our party skied to Tignes. It is a full day's trip, up the funicular to a high peak, then one long run that takes most of the morning and ends in the nearby town. In the afternoon you ski at Tignes and take a bus back home.

It had not snowed for weeks. The track was packed hard as a toboggan slide. I came fast around one curve and just at the edge of the path, I fell, and found myself sliding on my back, head first, downhill. When you fall skiing, you're supposed to twist your skis around to the downhill side, dig into the snow, and brake to a stop. No matter how I tried, I could not make that twist. The ground was hard and somewhat pebbly. It acted like a billion ball bearings, carrying me along. I remember thinking it was ludicrous, sledding on my back, headfirst, battered against small stones. I was not afraid, though I knew I was off the *piste*. After two or three attempts, however, to flip my skis, I decided it didn't matter, that soon I would hit a tree—no, I meant a rock—and stop.

For my attention was captured by the sky. The sky! It wasn't just blue sky. It radiated blue, green, yellow, pink; and my heart was wrenched out of my body with rapture as if it recognized something—*Home!* I was barreling downhill at thirty or forty miles an hour, bumping over stones, yet filled with joy. I saw the perfection of all things, including this mad, headfirst slide. What did it matter if I died right then? I thought irrationally. That, too, was welcome. Wondrous.

Angel Traveler. Gustave Moreau.
19th century.

Suddenly a blur of black—and I piled into another skier's legs.

David, at the top of the slope, saw what happened as he stood there wondering what to do. He told me later how a man shot past him, "out of nowhere," as he said, skiing like crazy. He tore down the slope, a bullet winging past me, then turned and dug in his skis. I fell against his legs. It didn't hurt. Neither did he fall with the impact or even apparently stumble and have to catch his weight as one hundred and twenty pounds plowed into him at such high speed.

I stood up. He was dressed completely in black: black hat, black parka, black pants, black skis. This was strange, because no one dressed in black on the ski slopes then, but in vibrant yellows, reds, and blues.

"*Merci beaucoup,*" I said. Then I looked into his eyes. They, too, were black, but full of such light I could not move.

"*Merci,*" I said again. I wanted to hear him speak. I don't remember any voice. He turned and started up the hill, herringboning, but at such speed! He had the strength of giants. Each of his steps counted for two or three of mine, though I could keep up with any skier I'd ever met before. I clambered after him, hurrying, pushing myself. I wanted to look into his eyes again. I wanted to ask him who he was and hear his voice, though these were not developed thoughts, but merely the propelling force. At the top he took off immediately, ignoring David, who reached out likewise to thank him. He zoomed away. A minute later I reached the top. David caught me.

"Are you all right?"

But I pushed away. "Yes, yes," I called as I raced down the track after the man in black, who had already disappeared around the curve of the hill.

The path here was wide and steep. It plunged downhill, curved to the left around an outcropping of rocks, and opened to a vista of the whole valley below—mile upon mile of open space.

No one was in sight.

I came past the rocks, casting right and left, looking for a pocket in which he could have disappeared. The only people in sight were tiny specks far down the valley in Tignes, black dots. It was inconceivable that he could have shot the valley walls that fast. Yet he had disappeared.

I skied on. Partway down the mountain my stomach dropped. To my left rose a cliff. It was at the top of this that I had fallen. Had I not been stopped, I would have fallen off the cliff to a rubble of rocks below. Only that skier had stopped me from being killed.

We skied to the valley floor, David and I, stopped for refreshments, and took small runs on the T-bars and Poma lifts until it was time to take the bus back to Val d'Isère. Everywhere I went I looked for that man, so easily identifiable in black. I told myself it was only because I wanted to thank him properly, but on the bus ride back to Val d'Isère I stared out the black window at the darkened countryside, lost in the memory of those eyes.

For the next week I looked for him. I never saw him again.

The Annunciation.
Gustave Doré.
Engraving, 19th century.

. . .

At first I did not permit myself to think about it—the man in black, that ringing sky. Years have passed and I have never again seen sky like that, although I'm sure it was what Tiepolo was trying his best to paint. But I could not stop wondering what it meant. I was caught by the terror that life is more meaningful than I was prepared to accept. My life was saved, by man or miracle I could not know. But why? I had done nothing to deserve it. My life was—is—quite useless in the scheme of things. I was frightened by the responsibility implied. I used two tricks of mind. On the one hand I decided that perhaps my life had been saved for my children, one of whom was not yet even born. I passed the buck, then, to the kids. On the other hand I pushed such thoughts aside. Insane! As if our lives were predestined! I did not believe that. With defiant passion I disbelieved. I disbelieved in an outside force, a God that meddled in the everyday affairs of men. My savior was merely human.

But then I could not forget that melting sky, or my sense of joy! If an angel could come save me, then why not a troop of angels, to save our world? Why did spiritual beings not sweep over us to save mothers from bombs and napalm burns, or babies from dying of starvation or disease? Why do not angels lift up planes shot down in war and hold them in their winged hands as a mother would in setting her baby in a crib? But, no, planes are shot down, men are scalded, dismembered on battlefields, women imprisoned, babies thrown under the wheels of cars. If angels are present, why don't they intervene to prevent things that matter, not save one useless woman on a frivolous ski trip in France?

Blood splatters on our earth.

Blood fertilizes it.

Blood of mankind shed by man. Is that why angels cannot interfere? They did not stop the Crucifixion. Are angels helpless against our rage?

*N*othing changed. I went away and brooded over the meaning of the skier in black. But nothing came out clear. It would be nice to imagine the end of all questioning, all doubts, anger, depression, despair, loneliness, insecurity, fear. Yet these persist, as does physical pain. They have a way of crashing in on you, often from behind, the hand of the mugger clapped to your throat too fast to pull free. Surprise leaves you vulnerable to pain.

What good are angels when they can't ward off the ghosts of the past or the spirits of the inner judging voice? What good is a glimpse of the divine when your own doubting mind will talk you into the position that it represents no more than a chemical malfunction, or an electrical disturbance, a blown-out fuse that might produce a temporary vision until the circuits got repaired?

Ten days ago I wrote this account of my trip to Val d'Isère and immediately spiraled into a depression. For more than a

—Look homeward, Angel, now, and melt with ruth.

—JOHN MILTON
Lycidas

• • • •

week I have cried. I hurt all over, and my soul howls in the darkness, a blind worm crawling at the empty edge of hell.

Loss and emptiness. For a week I have been grieving the separation and loss of people close to me—my divorce, my father's death, professional failures, the separation from a man I love, and these clouds pile up in the sky of my being to towering dimensions, until they reach the one true emptiness. That sky. Those eyes. Writing of Val d'Isère has reminded me how I've pushed the event away. I am filled with a sense of darkness. Failure. Again and again I have been given gifts—a feast spread out before me—and not only have I done nothing to deserve them, but made nothing worthy of them. Other people, shown such things as I have seen, have founded religious orders, organized nursing orders of women, built hospitals and churches and shelters for the derelict and poor.

I am sick with guilt.

Better not even to entertain the idea of angels than to undergo the torment of such responsibility. It was a man, that's all, looking out of place in black. Probably he'd just arrived in Val d'Isère and didn't know that black had been out of fashion for ten years. Perhaps he skied down to Tignes and went straight into a ski shop and bought himself some proper clothes—and that explains why I never saw him again that week. Or perhaps it was the last run of his vacation, and he was hurrying to make his train, when he paused to block my body from hurtling off a cliff. He didn't even have time to stop and talk a little, make chitchat. Instead he skied down to

—It is in rugged crises, in unweariable endurance, and in aims which put sympathy out of the question, that the angel is shown.
—RALPH WALDO EMERSON

• • • •

the town, unstrapped his skis, and took the bus back to Paris or Lyons, to his cashier's cage.

• 2 •

*M*y last story differs from the others in that it did not happen physically, with accompanying tangible physical proofs. It came in a dream of sorts.

A friend had offered to take me on a past-life experience. I didn't believe in reincarnation, saw no reason to trust such images, which are more likely composed of the debris of a lifetime's trashy reading than of memories stored in our cells before conception. But it sounded fun. I also distrusted my ability to imagine shooting out of my body, as the directions call for, and hovering five hundred feet above the house and then taking off looking for pinpricks of light. Still, I'm game for any play.

I lay down on a couch. Mark sat on a chair beside me. We spent considerable time hooking up a tape recorder for the session, and then he talked me into a quiet, meditative state. Throughout the two hours of this mental journey, he directed me, asked questions, guided the event. He asked me first to imagine myself rising straight upward, through the roof of the house.

"What do you see?" he asked, and I described the streets and view of Georgetown, but with a curl of derision, knowing my description could be constructed by anyone with the imagination to take a bird's-eye view. The fact that I could de-

—For a good angel will go with him, his journey will be successful, and he will come home safe and sound

—Tob. 5:21

scribe it in no way convinced me this was real. Then he had me take off in a certain direction. I chose the river and was traveling happily toward it.

"If you see a prick of light," he said, "go toward it." Even as he spoke, the light appeared. "Tell me when you're there."

"Oh no," I answered. "You're going to tell me to go down that hole, aren't you?" Because the light had turned into the mouth of a tunnel. He laughed, and sent me down the hole.

The sides were smooth. I was falling rapidly.

"Tell me when you hit the bottom," he said. But he needn't have asked, because I hit so hard that my legs twitched on the sofa from the impact. (So much for being out of body, as they say.)

Once standing, I was instructed to look down at my feet and describe what I saw, and then to move my eyes up my legs and see my clothes. Once you establish your new sense of self, you look around. A scene develops, peopled by others, and you walk through the streets of this dream imagery; you may have changed sex and social class, be a totally different person than the one you are in this life; things happen to you; time passes. It is quite fascinating.

It is not my intention to explain how to take a past-life journey. After he had led me through a number of "lives," Mark asked, "Do you want to see what the next one will be like?"

"You mean a future life?" I laughed. "Sure, yes."

Again I was sailing through the darkness, looking for a light. Again I saw a light-hole, again slid down it. . . . Dreams and images. I make no claims that what occurred is true, any more than I would claim some factual basis for the past-life in-carnations (as they're called). Lying on the couch, the dream occurred. Since this one happened to a future personage, let the pronoun change.

"Tell me when you land," Mark murmured as before. But she did not land.

"Have you landed?"

"Well, I'm here," she answered, aware that she was nowhere, in clouds of hazy brown.

"Look at your feet. Tell me what you see."

"Oh, feet. You want *feet*?" She dissolved in giggles. Imagine *feet*! The very concept was absurd, but if he wanted feet, then she'd give him them; and feet appeared, brown and bare. Following the next directions, she moved her gaze up her an-kles and calves. He wanted clothes? And clothes appeared, some brown, rough garment hanging at her knees. It was ab-surd. She could not stop giggling; whatever this state con-sisted of, it was hilarious. She felt wonderful, and the next moment she was corkscrewing through the air, horizontally, feet first, brrrrrrr; just playing. She could stop and go, slow down, speed up. The whirling corkscrew motion was terrific, cutting the atmosphere. Or she could flip over on her head; laughter rippled from her throat. The giggling would not stop.

"What are you doing?" he asked, confused.

She choked trying to explain, but it was almost useless, since he couldn't move that way or imagine how it was done.

"What gleams for joy!"
William Blake. Engraving for
Night Thoughts, 18th century.

"Are you a being from another planet?" he asked.

"No, no. I'm here." She was sure of that. "I'm just learning how to fly." Meaning that she didn't have her footing yet. She was new at this. The others knew what they could do.

"Do you have wings?"

"No." Wings? She hadn't thought it necessary, but if he wanted wings, then wings he could have; and wings sprouted from her shoulders, huge feathered ones, quite clumsy, and perfectly useless given her ability to move fluidly through this medium of timeless space. But *fluidly* is not the word, implying as it does substantialness, whereas she could have substance or not, depending on her wish.

"Then stop corkscrewing," he said firmly, "and walk on the ground. Tell me what you see."

Her first reaction was one of panic. "But I'll squash them if I go down there." For she was enormous: she stretched across the sky. And also she felt a quick uncertainty about just how to reduce. But the question was no sooner thought than the answer presented itself.

"Oh, I know how," she said, for she instantly understood how to shrink or expand to any size: so that the next moment she had transmogrified, as he desired, and was standing on the ground among all these little beings, who could not see her, but who moved around and through her as if she wasn't there. All the while the watery giggles rippled from her throat (the tape is full of giggling). She was weak with it. She could hear the confusion in his voice when he spoke next.

"What's happening?"

"I'm walking on the bottoms of my feet," she laughed. "You can't imagine! They walk on the bottoms of their feet!" She dissolved, convulsed by laughter. She could feel the ground against her feet, and when she practiced using the bottoms of her feet to propel herself, she could feel the earth touching heels, the middle pads, the toes. It was difficult to hold her buoyant body down, its natural tendency being to bound up into the air, but she determinedly practiced clinging to the ground, on feet, then shot up in the air, hovering overhead.

Now she had an opportunity to observe them and how they lived. This sent her rocketing off into further laughter, though this time at how *dear* they were. They scurried everywhere, hordes of them, scampering in the streets between their structures. And what was equally hilarious, they lived inside dark structures, with little holes that they used to go in and out of, and other holes at higher levels that they used to let in the very air and light they were trying to escape. This struck her as absurd. But everything about these beings was endearing: their preoccupation with problems that weren't problems at all. That's how they spent their time, swarming around, discussing unimportant gossip and getting angry with one another or impatient, or jealous, or being hurt, or caring for one another temporarily, before their short attention span was whipped away by the next emotion or concern. She felt a surge of love for them: how *dear* they were, how sweet in their inability to distinguish what was real. All appetite they were, and good intentions—and the latter going awry because they couldn't keep their minds on anything for long, but liked— they actually enjoyed!—the sensation of being smacked by fear or loss.

How she loved them!

It was difficult to describe all this to the man's voice coming through to her, and much of it she didn't even try, there being so much to see and understand. She knew that she was a Young One, that after she got her powers fully in control, she would be given the task of helping out these little beings, "they" as she called them, not having for them any name. Her task would be to hang around and wait to be of help, though she could not do anything unless one asked for help. She would not be able to interfere, for example, if two of them started a fight or war, since that was what they wanted to do. Then all she could do would be to wait around, in joy, and watch their futile gestures.

"Are there others like you in this place?" came the man's voice.

She answered. "Yes. The Big Ones are over there." Meaning in a middle distance, away from the habitations of these little things. The Big Ones (and she was not Big yet, though that would come in time) were a little frightening in their superiority. She didn't know what their tasks were.

"Go over to them," said the voice. "Go join them."

To do that she had to become a Big One, because otherwise she had no business there, and moving toward their place (if such a word can apply to no place in space or time), she found herself losing her hilarity, laughter, youthful giggliness. She had no interest in playing anymore, but felt instead a quiet stillness settle over her. The Big Ones had wider tasks to do.

Before she arrived, however, in her newfound seriousness (*serenity* might be a better word), the voice again intervened, asking her to go to the final stage. She veered aside from the grown-ups, and moved on. He wanted to know about the Sages, and as she traveled, she felt the stillness, the profundity increase in her. A ringing quiet. She was changing form. She had no form. She sat alone. The voice asked questions. It was difficult to phrase the answers, and she paused for a long, long time before she tried to answer, groping for a way to tell the things she understood in language he could hear. Some of the answers had no translation in his words—even the concept of *being* was different, not to mention the absence of distinctions or differentiation into gender or self.

She was alone, though others existed on this level, separate but the same. She answered slowly through long, weighted pauses, as she tried to do her work, for time has no meaning here. The work of the Compassionate is to sit, in what is neither dark nor light. Pure being. And radiate a silent sound. It sends a vibration throughout everything, a harmonious hum of pure being. There is no time. There is no place. For the Sage there are no lesser beings, although somewhere out there are ones who think they are significant. That is of no concern to the Sage. This nothingness is exquisite beyond description; she is absorbed in harmony, the humming of pure love. It is unfiltered, undefiled; and the Sage is emitting that vibration on which the universe subsists, even as she tries to answer the questions coming from the man, questions that spring from ignorance, irrelevant, off the mark. Compassion includes the man, and so the Sage tries to answer. But the answers come with difficulty. Difficult to find a voice when one had not spoken in many eons now. Difficult to translate the smallness of the questions into the Sage's own real terms, and after that difficult to translate back the immensity of what she knows into this strangulated language, which lacks the words to grasp the necessary truth.

Difficult mostly because whether the Sage answers or not is

Angel Musician. Melozzo di Forli. 16th century.

of no importance. It is the love that matters, the silent, emanating sound.

"Are you God?" the man asks.

The question has no meaning in the Sage's terms. The pause extends so long that the man repeats the question: "Are you God?" At which the answer comes, in a low, deep voice:

"No." It is not completely true. In a moment the Sage will be able to go on and inform the voice that he could as easily have answered yes. (Or she.) He answers no because she takes the question as it's asked. He responds at the level at which this voice interprets God. In that way, certainly he's not God, for God does not exist as the entity this man believes. It is much more complex than a single God. But, yes, because all things are made by God. Godness in all things. There is the whole, one center; and also, yes, there's God in the source that fashioned all of this, which could be explained, if the man is patient . . . since it had no beginning and never will it end.

"No," she answered, for there is something greater, which he'd call the Source. But yes for Godness lay everywhere, including in himself, whose task is to release the silent sound, compassion, which is God, into the spheres of God to fall as God on all else that is God, transmuting into God.

"No, I'm not God," the Sage begins, and paused to breathe out harmony for one eternity. But the man's voice could not wait.

"What will happen after this life? Will you die?"

Eons had the Sage been there, and eons more would pass before she drifted on, leaving space for others to do his work.

Saturn. Gustave Doré.
Engraving, 19th century.

In his knowledge she saw himself tilt over the edge in total blackness at the end of all. It, too, was perfect in its nothingness. He caught the word.

"After this life there is nothing." And started to consider how to describe that pitching of formlessness into void, and how it was correct, of no import, no matter for either congratulation or regret, but simply so, without an end. . . . Meanwhile the harmonious hum was all he knew.

"You must come back," said the man's voice. "It's time to come back now. Move forward until you see the hole."

Slowly, weighted against all worlds, the Sage considered. "To go back, I have to go through all the prior forms. I can't go forward now into that sphere."

"Then return through all the forms," directed the man, and slowly (sorrowfully) the Sage departed from that state of loving silence. Moved back to the Big Ones, picking up speed as she passed, and eons flashing by; until she was giggling and looping through space, convulsed with hilarity again, and exclaiming with delight at the light, the radiance, the people whom she tended and whom she found so enchanting in their ignorance.

"They're darling!" she exclaimed, overcome with loving kindness for their kind; they scurried in and out of their holes. And then she was being sucked up the tunnel backward, disoriented by the whirling speed . . . and landed on the couch.

It took a few moments to recover, to open her eyes, and dazedly wake up.

. . .

*T*his is all that I know about angels. I don't pretend to understand any of it. Other people have their own experiences, and some of these may conflict with or contradict my own. But I think of the words of the French philosopher and priest Teilhard de Chardin:

> Someday, after we have mastered the winds, the waves, the tides, and gravity, we will harness for God the energies of Love: and then, for the second time in the history of the world, man will have discovered FIRE!

Then I am embarrassed at everything set down here. What if people laugh at me. Like Yeats,

> I have spread my dreams under your feet;
> Tread softly because you tread on my dreams.

PART IV

Letters on Angels

. . . .

During the course of my research for this book, many people wrote me of their encounters with angels or the Divine. Some angels came as voices, dreams, or whisperings, others as balls of energy or light, and a few angels appeared in the flesh, so to speak, to carry messages or to save their lives. I set some stories down here in hopes they may inspire you, as they have me.

When my first son was born in Minnesota, he had a hole in his heart. It came from an overdose of medicine to his mother, and he came out blue with a leaking heart. We were very concerned. At the time neither we nor the doctor knew what had caused the hole. The heart was shunting blood, and we thought he was going to die.

That same night my father in Buffalo, New York, woke up with the window shade slapping lightly against the window, and he heard a voice: "Don't worry. John will be all right." He didn't know what it meant. The only John he knew was his brother, and he was dead. My father stayed up to ponder this.

I can't ever tell this without getting teary. . . .

He was still up when I called. "John has been born," I told him, "but he has a hole in his heart. He's hooked up to an oxygen machine."

"Don't worry," my father said. "He's going to be all right." He was choked up, and said he couldn't explain just now how he knew—but not to worry. Then he got on the phone and called a doctor who got the premier heart doctor at the University of Minnesota to come to the hospital, first thing in the morning, with his golf shoes on. He examined John, checked the medical records, and discovered the double dose of sedative that had been given during the delivery. The doctor said, "Don't worry. Your son's going to be all right." There's a special little valve in babies' hearts just for that purpose to keep the baby alive, and after six weeks that special valve disappears. The valve kept the blood going through his heart and brain, although the rest of his body wasn't getting much.

And the baby was fine.

—MARSH WARD
Washington, D.C.

*T*his happened to my great-great uncle, Calvin Jones, and it was instrumental in making me choose the ministry, because we've always been close, and I think I'm the only person he told this story to.

Calvin will be ninety-six this year, 1989. He's always lived in Boswell, in Izard County, Arkansas, in the northern Ozarks. It's the most remote inhabited place in the United States, without even a road into his farm. He has river frontage but no road frontage. So he has lived there in isolation and great stability, with no radio and no TV, unpoisoned by what's going on in this country, and as a result, he trusts in what he sees and hears. His experience is limited to his own experience. He's lived alone since his wife died ten years ago. They were married in 1912. That isolation affects everything. He's always been a faithful Christian. But mountain people never have community worship; it's not a community-oriented religion.

The Voices happened from late fall to early spring of

Angel Weathervane.
American, 19th century.

1984–85, from first frost to first thaw, the nonworking time. And I heard about it in the summer of '85. Calvin began hearing songs, music playing. There were the voices of women, men, and children, singing both sacred and secular songs, but when he started listing the songs, Calvin remembered only a few. One was "The Little Rosewood Casket" and another "After the Ball"—parlor songs; and then some gospel, like "Whispering Hope." The singing was repeated daily every dawn, always with the same characters, so he came to recognize their voices, and "one of the men," he said, "had the coarsest voice I ever heard."

He never saw anything, but he heard it: a Singing Procession in the sky, about thirty-five degrees above the horizon and moving from south to west—not with the voices moving, but *extending,* actually, like the mercury in a thermometer, until it filled the whole southwestern horizon.

He lives in a hollow, ringed by mountains, so the procession followed round a ridge, at the front of the house, window to window, following the path of the White River.

He was never self-conscious about angels. He never interpreted them as such, never said, "Oh, boy! I'm hearing angels!" He reached instead for natural explanations, and without revealing what he'd heard, he would ask questions of people: "It's awful cold. Are there campers nearby with radios?" Was it water that he heard? But he never asked, "Was it supernatural?"

One day he was visited by a university professor doing an oral-history project with a tape recorder. He thought, "Here's my chance," because he has great respect for a university education. The Voices began to sing. Calvin said, "Can you hear them?"

"No," answered the historian.

"Turn on the tape recorder, then," said Calvin.

"You sing along with them," said the professor, and Calvin began to sing "After the Ball."

After the choir faded and stopped, they turned on the tape recorder and to Calvin's astonishment he heard only himself. He was mystified. To his ears the whole of creation was singing, and on the tape it was one old man.

He found he enjoyed singing with them.

At no point did he go looking for these people or address them. Neither did he assume he was crazy. People spared the twentieth century never think they're crazy. And to him nature is so wondrous that it's no miracle nature would sing.

One day as the weather warmed enough to open a window, and when it was still dark, for the first time ever Calvin used his voice.

"Who are you?" he asked. He hadn't thought to ask it before.

The man with the coarse voice answered, and in Calvin's own Ozark dialect: "This yer's from heaven. Cain't everbudy hear it."

That satisfied him. The voices continued to sing off and on, but not as frequently. And now that it was satisfactorily explained, Calvin took it for granted. He noticed it now and again but didn't dwell on it.

But it changed my life.

"There are seven countries in heaven," Calvin told me. "We know all kinds of history. We know the history of America, and we know the history of Arkansas. And these angels tell you the history of heaven." Then he said farewell: "If I don't see you in this world, I'll try to see you in the next one."

—MARK LEWIS
Washington, D.C.

One evening in Holland, I had to be at my brother's at 6:30 P.M. I walked, had no watch on, and wondered about the time. All of the sudden I looked upward and saw a big clock hanging in the sky showing twenty past six. No clocks at all in the neighborhood.

During the war (in Holland) one evening, it was dark, I rode on my bicycle. I went very fast and all of a sudden I heard a voice from the sky very loud: "STOP." I stopped immediately, and if I had gone on for another meter, I would have plunged to certain death. There was a bridge, which had been blown up by the Germans, which I did not know. The bridge was over concrete at least thirty feet below.

—Mrs. S. Van der Elst
Nelspruit, South Africa

One Friday, near the end of my sophomore year at Indiana University in Bloomington, Indiana (the latter part of April), my girlfriend and I piled as much of my personal stuff as we could get into my old Dodge Charger and drove fifty miles to my mother's house in Indianapolis.

When we got to the house, it was late afternoon going into evening. We removed everything from inside the car and said we'd get the stuff in the trunk later.

We ate dinner and then I took my girlfriend home. Monday morning I saw my mother off to work. An hour later I was walking toward the car but did not walk through the short patch of grass to the driver's side like I usually do. Instead, I walked past the passenger's side and around the back of the car. Looking closely, I thought I saw the trunk of the car *slowly lifting,* just a couple of inches. I just stood there looking, and then I slowly opened the trunk and there was everything I could possibly jam into this trunk on Friday afternoon still in there Monday morning.

I would have driven all the way back to school with a stuffed trunk had it not been for the kind soul watching and swaying my body from one side of the car to the other to make me see my oversight. . . . There has always been a little voice that says, "Look, the door is open to you. Go now!" But never have I seen a real door opening with my own eyes until that Monday morning.

I believe everyone has angels, good spirits, teachers, and guides looking over us, and if we live life just the right way, when we do hear voices, have funny feelings, and get warning signs—if we stop and think of what the message means—we can determine for ourselves if it is good help coming from a good source and use that help to make our lives a little easier.

—BETSY KENNEDY
Indianapolis, Indiana

I am thirty-two years old now. When I was a little girl, my mother and father would take my three brothers and myself to Sacramento to visit my mom's sister, Aunt Marie. Marie and her husband, Uncle Johnny, had a large family and they were very poor. When we were children, we did not understand the conditions under which they lived. My brothers and I would always get together with John and Marie's chil-

Balinese Angel-mermaid.
Wood, modern.

dren and run through the fields and get eggs from the chicks
and chase the goats. When I was twelve, my parents di-
vorced. It was about one or two years later that Aunt Marie
died an alcoholic. Up to then we had always kept in touch
with Marie and the kids. Cliff was the oldest, and in his early
teens he started getting in trouble with the law. We used to
visit him at the Nelles Home for Boys in Whittier, California,
because he was too young to be in jail. As he got older, he
did eventually end up in prison. I used to write him when he

was in Soledad and Folsom prisons in California. His crimes
were for bad checks, stealing, etc. But after Marie died, we
lost touch with the entire family.

The years passed, and in 1978 I went to work for a Christian radio station in Pomona, California. It had been ten years
since I had had any contact with my cousins. I went on vacation up to Sacramento and was visiting my aunt one day,
when I decided to just go out for a drive; I told her I'd return before nightfall. It was summer, so I had a long day. I
started on the freeway and decided just to explore. As I
neared the mountains, I came to an exit sign that said Folsom Dam, and I thought I'd drive around the reservoir—
when out of the blue I heard a voice as clear as if it had come
from someone sitting next to me in the car: "You have a
cousin in prison." I suddenly remembered my cousin Cliff. I
hadn't heard from him or written to him in so many
years. . . . I couldn't even remember his last name. The voice
came to me again; "You have a cousin in prison." Okay, I
thought to myself, I have a cousin in prison. Could he be in
this prison? No way! I had to really think hard to remember
Cliff's last name. I knew I had to check it out. I didn't know
why and it seemed like the craziest thing to do. If I went to
that prison, they'd think I was nuts looking for my cousin.
There was absolutely no way he could be in that prison. But
the *voice* wouldn't leave me alone and I knew I had to check
it out. Then Cliff's last name came to me.

I followed the exit sign off the freeway and followed the
signs that pointed the way to Folsom Prison. It wasn't all

that far. But I remember that when I got to the prison, I felt my heart in my throat. When I saw the guard towers and the stone walls and the wire along the walls, I did a U-turn and got out of there! I drove to the nearest pay phone, which was at a gas station. It was early afternoon and I decided I would just call the prison and see if Cliff was there. It sounds stupid, so ridiculous. Even if by some stretch of the imagination he was in that prison, one can't just call a prison and ask, "May I speak to so-and-so?" It's not like calling someone's home. I had to keep obeying the voice I heard; it was with me always now and I no longer had any question in my mind of how my day was going to be spent.

I got out of my car and went into the phone booth. I remember it was so warm in there on this summer day.

I called information for the number to the prison, then called the prison, and when the operator answered, I explained to her my situation. I simply told her that I was on a trip, saw the prison sign, remembered I might have a cousin in prison and was he there? I gave her his name and by God . . . he was in that Folsom Prison!

I asked her if I could speak with him and she said she would connect me with a counselor. I spoke with a wonderful man and once again explained my situation. The counselor said Cliff was working in the kitchen that afternoon, and he would try and find him and call me back at the phone booth. He said it might take an hour or more. I said I would wait if there was any chance I could really speak to him after all these years.

I gave him the number of the phone booth and went back to my car, sitting there in a daze. After all these years I had found Cliff. I had my Bible with me in the car, so I decided since I had to wait so long, I'd read. Only ten minutes passed at the most and the phone rang! I jumped out of the car and ran back into the phone booth. When I picked up the phone, it was Cliff! What a reunion! It is too hard to describe that feeling of actually talking to your cousin after so many years, and he couldn't believe how I'd found him! Less than two hours before, I was visiting with my aunt, and now I felt as though I had driven to the corner of the earth that no one else had known about. I was overwhelmed. We had a short but wonderful visit over the phone and exchanged addresses. I knew my mother would be so happy to know that I had found Cliff. She always felt close to Marie's kids, and ever since her death she had worried about where the kids were.

I said good-bye to my cousin, told him to thank that counselor I spoke with, and we promised to write.

As I turned to walk out of the phone booth, I caught a glimpse of something to my right out of the corner of my eye. It looked like a piece of paper or a flyer that was taped to the outside of the phone booth. Funny, but it wasn't there when I went in to use the booth either time. As I walked out of the booth, I turned to read the paper that was now blowing slightly in the afternoon breeze. As I read the sign, I was overcome with goosebumps and stood there and stared. The sign read, "Out of Order."

That phone booth was never out of order for me! There was no sign when I drove up. If there had been, why would I have gone in to use that phone? No one would do that if they knew that the phone was out of order. I used that phone twice and *twice there was no sign.* I was the only person around those phones the whole time, so no one put the sign up while I was there. If that sign *was* there, someone or something caused me not to see it for the purpose of using the phone for a miraculous phone call.

—JILLAYNE BREWER
Azusa, California

I rarely tell my incident to other people for two reasons: The first is that the memory of it is so precious that I find myself hoarding it in a corner of my mind the way a child hoards a special toy under his or her bed. The second reason is that the intensity and power of that moment was so tremendous that it is difficult for me to convey its impact to other people. I generally end up speechless, babbling repeatedly, "You just can't imagine! You just can't imagine!"

I do, however, nurture it and turn it over many times in my mind for fear that I may in time forget one tiny detail and some of the wonder of the moment will be lost forever. Also, when my day has been particularly stressful, this memory, along with a peaceful stroll through my flower garden, gives me much serenity. . . .

It happened six years ago when my daughter, Jenny, was seven years old. It was about two o'clock in the afternoon. Jenny and I were driving downtown to the bank. We were on a familiar street waiting for a red light to turn green. It was a four-lane street, and I was in the third lane. Nobody was on my right, but there was a white Cadillac in the second lane and a truck like the type that delivers furniture for stores in the far left lane. We were all in a row at the light, with no cars behind us.

As the light flicked orange, a sudden, heavy, dark "cloud" zapped my brain. It was not heavy as in weight or dark as in color; but rather it was like a foreboding and a direct warning, and yet the message was clear—Warning! Then a more direct message came into my mind, and although I heard no words, it said, "Don't move!" This took about two seconds before the third and last message occurred. In my mind, a car came from the right into the intersection, ran the red light (for my light was green by now), and went on.

I must have sat there for a while after all this, because my daughter, who apparently received no warning, said, "Mom, you can go now. Why don't you go?" I answered her, "Oh, I think I'll wait." At that moment a Volkswagen driven by a mother with her two sons in the back roared from the right into the intersection, going around the cars that had stopped. She tore through the intersection heedless of all stop lights and cars. If she had hit us, she would have hit my car first on the right passenger side, where my daughter was sitting. Considering the tremendous speed she was traveling, the accident would have been horrendous. I noticed that the two cars to the left of me also never moved. Did they receive the same warning I did? I can't help but think they did, or they would have pulled into the intersection when the light changed. Instead, we all sat at the green light for a good ten to fifteen seconds after it had changed to "go." I wish I had their names so I could ask them.

I feel among the lucky ones to have experienced such an incident—not only because it saved my daughter's and my life—but also, I don't believe such a wonderful thing hap-

Bugaku Dancers (detail). Hanabusa Itcho. 18th century.

pens very often to people. I do not fool myself into thinking that this sort of thing happened to me because I am one of the "chosen ones" who leads a pure and holy life. On the contrary my life is an active one—full of movement and life with no time for traditional religious orthodoxy. No, I am certain the reason why I was singled out was simply the message that came through clearly in the warning: "This must not happen: it is not time!" This message leads me now to believe that most major events are laid out for us and that any monkey wrenches that may accidentally be tossed into the preordained mechanisms of life must be diverted if at all possible.

—CARLENE ANDERSON
Rockford, Illinois

*A*bout one year ago I "dreamed" I was suddenly in a place and I was looking at a large group of people exiting a doorway—rather like a group of people leaving a movie theater or something. I looked up at a man, a largish man, in his forties, with a beard, and who bore no resemblance to anyone I know. I hugged him and said, "Please don't make me go back, I've missed you so much!" He laughed and I felt my soul slam back into my body and I woke up. I have waited to go there again, but if I have, I don't remember it.

—MARY E. FREEMAN
Albuquerque, New Mexico

I recall one time when I was under particular stress. I'd just gone through a divorce; my children went to live with their father; my parents were blaming me for the episodes in my life that caused *them* shame, and in the midst of despair, I stood at the kitchen sink with a knife in my hand, and one part of me—I will say it was an idea, a vocal thought in my mind that said, "Do it! Cut your wrist, it's better on the Other Side. . . ." My hand would not *move!* It wouldn't obey the idea. Then came another vocal thought: It said, "Don't do it. You might fail. . . . Then you'll end up in the hospital, you'll have more bills, more problems, you'll look more ridiculous than ever, and, *believe me, if you kill yourself you will not have peace or freedom; you will have pain—just what you're trying to escape.*"

I put down the knife and cried. That was in 1979. I was thirty-six years old. Three months later I moved to Israel to live. I write this in hopes anyone in distress [will realize that] suicide won't solve your problem.

Shortly after, I had another, far more incredible experience. I was a sad, searching woman, and one night, about 5:00 P.M., I headed out the door of my apartment. I was angry. I'd done everything I was told to do in my church. I thought I was a "good person," and why . . . why had such problems befallen me?! As I left the apartment, I heard music coming from someone's room. The song, in part, ran, "Broken dreams, (something) schemes . . . give them all to Jesus. . . ."

I was so angry at the idea that I'd followed a dream of Christian "goodness" and been burned that I stated out loud: "I won't, it's not real: He can do nothing, He's not God."

I felt a force inside and outside of me, and it moved me back into my apartment. Again, I stood crying in despair, deep, wailing, all-is-lost despair.

Then I got the most incredible—"healing" is the only word I can use. It was like a tap on the head, but there was no one present. There was instant PEACE inside my mind, it felt like lamb's wool, it was so soft inside of me. It was a warm rush of Peace. In a flash my mind visualized the motives of myself and the others I associated with. I saw myself wanting to win approval. Listening to others and not trusting in myself. I *blamed God for everything.* I saw that very clearly.

Then a voice, a crystal-clear voice, said, *"Feel me. I'm as gentle as a lamb and I don't hurt."* I saw myself with an image of a punishing God, and everything that went wrong in my life, I blamed Him.

Then I saw—I guess Heaven. It was/is and always will be IMMENSE. It was higher than the sky and broader than will ever be seen. I was shown that This Spirit, or This Immense, Creative Being was literally in everything. There was so much love and care in everything that it cannot be expressed in words. It's beyond the walls of towns, countries, nations; it's larger than any rabbi, priest, saint. I saw that humans want others to follow a single interpretation, but that this

Spirit of Love knows absolutely No Bounds. It loves Buddhists, Taoists, Christians, Jews, Moslems, on and on and on with incredible Love. It has no End. It has No Beginning. It is not limited. Man limits his love and calls it "God's Will." Man wants to "own God," and says that God sees only one group as great and everyone else as wrong. This Spirit I met that night is limitless in His Love. . . . I saw what This Spirit sees—how people shoot up dope and abuse themselves. If they only knew what real, deep, penetrating, loving care was, there would be no use for abuse. No need to compete, destroy, be disillusioned. Just total contentment, pleased with self, with others, the environment. . . .

I could go on, but it may be enough just to say that it's a reality. It's free. It's a state of mind, and it costs nothing.

The ghost or Spirit that I've come to know is honest, reliable, chastizing when necessary, thought-provoking, listening, caring, inspiring, creative . . . and I could go on. I guess the most important thing I could say about it is that how one thinks directs one's path and one's path directs him or her forever, and while one can change the path, he or she only has so much time to do so, and that is what one doesn't know.

—SUSAN CALLAS
Reno, Nevada

On November 1, 1971, a very dear and lifelong friend left this world on earth to cross into the dimensions of the afterlife that so many doubt or question. I was devastated by this loss, as it was impossible to understand the reasoning behind it all. My friend was shot during a disturbance on a college campus in which he was not involved, just after returning from abroad after serving in the armed services.

Afterwards, I could feel his presence all around the house. I was constantly looking over my shoulder. Then I heard my name being called in a soft voice. I went into the room where his mother and sister were to see if they had called me. The answer was no. I assumed it was my imagination.

A week after the funeral I was playing a favorite album of his and lying on the bed. He came to me in what I thought was a dream. He told me I should not mourn his departure, because he was happy and at peace. I was told that we would meet again in his new world and to be patient, that our love would never die. The last thing I remember was he wanted me to listen to a special song of ours on the album I had been playing before lying down. When I awoke, I felt at peace. I didn't realize it was *not* a dream until I noticed the record was playing on the opposite side, which had our special song. I began to cry, realizing he had really been with me.

This experience awakened me mentally and spiritually, and since then I've had two others. Twice I have awakened from sleep to see something mystical. I sat up in bed to convince myself I was not dreaming.

To the right of me, hovering about five feet from the floor, was a bright mass of energy, a yellow and orange ball about six inches in diameter. I closed my eyes and reopened them.

I even pinched myself to make sure I was really seeing what was before my eyes, and there it remained until I fell asleep again.

I was frightened. About a year later, the same thing happened under the same circumstances. However, this time I asked questions subconsciously and they were answered. They were all in reference to my friend who had left this world. And the overall summation was, I was not to fear or worry, because I was being watched over. His protection, caring, and love were continuing, though his physical being was gone.

The latest occurrence was in July 1984, when I was attending a family reunion and many photos were taken. In one, I noticed a circular mass of particles over my shoulder. It startled me at first, because I wondered if it was a flaw in the film development. Now I accept the fact that I've been blessed to be able to view the dimensions of the other side.

—TERRI L. BEELER
Louisville, Kentucky

On November 1, 1977, my mother telephoned, saying one of my dad's co-workers had called telling her my dad had had some sort of attack and he was being treated by paramedics in an ambulance. I hurriedly left work to pick up my mother so we could both go to the hospital. Driving to her house, I had the feeling this was very serious and if he were still alive when we reached the hospital, my father would probably not live very long. However, I didn't have time to dwell on this; I had to concentrate on my driving. There were two large freeways to enter and exit, and, in addition, the weather had turned nasty—cold and rainy. I was within one mile of my mother's house and shaking from cold and fear when I came to a curve in the road. I physically felt something (energy?) around my shoulders; then came a wonderful, peaceful, happy feeling. I knew at that moment my father had died and there was no reason to grieve, because he was free and happy. There were no witnesses and I saw nothing.

After my mother and I arrived at the hospital, we were told he had died in the ambulance. I've thought about that moment many times in the years since it happened. What was that feeling? An angel trying to prepare me for what was to come? Or perhaps my father saying "good-bye" and trying to transfer what he felt at the time of death—peace and calm.

I wish I could say I could recapture that feeling now at will, but it's not true. However, just the memory of it gives me strength. It's as if I got to "peek" at the next world.

—JOYCE SLATER
Dallas, Texas

I have always thought that life after death made sense, but for the past year and a half I have absolutely no doubt what-

soever that there is life after death. It all began when I
started to get interested in reincarnation. I was reading on
the subject and from there I began to get in touch not only
with my own soul but with my spirits or guides (whatever
you choose to call them) as well. They have proven to me
that they are real. They appear like constantly moving electricity, almost like shadows. They've only been visible to me
in the dark, but I feel their presence every day and night.
When they appear, it's not only the vision but it's the incredible electricity in the air. Their connection with me is one of
love, comfort, and security. On three different occasions I
have actually felt them all hug me, not as we know hugging,
with arms, but an embrace with their whole being; and I feel
tingly and a surge of pure electrical love runs throughout my
whole body.

The most recent experience happened around May 10,
1985, at 2 A.M. while I was lying in bed with all the lights off.
I had just gone to bed and wasn't at all sleepy. I saw at the
far end of my room a gray form that was in no particular
shape but it almost looked like millions of little molecules all
constantly moving. I felt its presence immediately. It then
started to move closer to me; as it approached me, it got
lighter. While it came across my room toward me, it almost
danced happily across my room in the air, making its way
joyfully toward me. I watched it intently, feeling almost familiar with this playful presence that I had never seen before.
Finally it was a bright white color that grew larger, because I

could feel it right in my face. Not only could I see it an inch from my face but I could feel it. It started to make me a bit uncomfortable, because that's not even a comfortable distance for humans to be. So I brushed my face and said, "Don't." The second after I spoke I felt an electrical charge on my lips, only lasting a second. I didn't feel it anywhere but on my lips. Then the bright whiteness of it backed away and turned a lighter gray, finally returning to the original gray color and smaller size until it disappeared. The experience didn't frighten me at all. It made me excited that I should experience such things.

—TERRI PAGE
Ramona, California

*H*i, my name is Vicki Israel. My mom saw your letter and suggested I write to you. This is what happened. The summer that I turned six we had a Fresh Air child come live with us for two weeks. It was one night when me and Shonta were sleeping. I woke up and saw two angels standing in front of my closet. I didn't really feel scared but of what I remember they didn't have wings, like what we think of angels. They were two men, tall men, and they were talking softly. I will always remember that beautiful night.

—VICKI ISRAEL
Somerset, New Jersey

I cannot be very specific as to dates and witnesses, but I still remember the details well. It is only recently that I have been able to speak of this.

In 1947, when I was barely three years old, I caught the measles. My temperature got dangerously high and was nearly 107° Fahrenheit when my parents took me to the hospital. I remember nurses and the doctor moving quickly and getting me wrapped up in icy-cold wet blankets on the hospital bed. My mother told me that prior to this I had been delirious, but suddenly I started speaking clearly. I was saying the Nicene Creed and repeating the liturgy from our (Lutheran) worship service. She said it frightened her because she wasn't aware I knew the words, and I was saying them perfectly. Then I started talking about the angels, and how beautiful they were. I have a very clear recollection of floating up in the corner of the hospital room, with an angel on either side, watching the nurses and doctors work on the body (my body) on the bed. To this day, I can close my eyes and hear the music, which cannot be described, and see these two beings, in white, with a golden aura around them. There was an opening in the ceiling with a long, lighted path, all golden, and the music was getting louder. They asked if I wanted to stay or come with them. I clearly remember saying I wanted my mother—and I was back in the hospital bed, and they were gone.

I guess the most profound effect this experience had on

me is that it took away all fear of death. I *know* there is life after death—because I have seen it.

Mother told me that after I started talking about the angels, I lost consciousness, and they were very concerned because all my vital signs were going down rapidly. While I did not clinically die, I came very close to it—and then all at once the fever started dropping and I started to get better. When I was nearly well, she asked me about the "beautiful angels" I'd mentioned, and I wouldn't talk about them—but I have never forgotten. I was so pleased to see your letter and request—there are very few people I have told this to, and most are skeptical.

—MARY L. HUEMOELLER BURNS
Waterloo, Iowa

When my mother, Sally, was a young girl in 1905, in Calquit County, Georgia, an angel appeared to her in a bright light and said, "There will be eighty-two in all." She wondered all her life what it meant. She was a very busy woman with her large family and charity work unlimited, but she never forgot this and often talked of it. She described it in detail to a granddaughter who did a painting that hangs on my wall.

As she grew older, we began to think that it meant her allotted years, but she went into her eighty-third year and

Angels Take the Soul to Heaven.
Illuminated manuscript,
15th century.

began to count everything, including descendants. But alas! there were already eighty-three of these and two more on the way. Shortly before her eighty-third birthday we talked of her angel, and she said, "I guess He's waiting to tell me when I join Him."

Two weeks before her eighty-third birthday my first grand-child was born. She was carried to visit on a Sunday after Mama turned eighty-three. Mama died the next Tuesday. Since I am the one who keeps the family records, I made the list of survivors for the paper and was struck like a ton of bricks—two grandchildren were adopted! My granddaughter was the eighty-second and the last one Mama saw!

I said to my sister that I hoped Mama knows.

"Who do you think told you?" she replied.

Mama indeed had it revealed to her and told me, but I missed seeing her. Dad died seventeen months later, and his last words were, "I see Sally."

Thank you for letting me share this with you. She was Sally Tayler, married to Thomas Gandy.

—JANE OGLESBY
Sylvester, Georgia

*M*y name is Bozena Kalinic, aged twenty-seven. White female living in South Africa but Yugoslavian by birth.

At the time, I was thirteen, living with my father and younger sister; my sister and I slept in the same room. It hap-

pened one night at about 11:00 P.M. or so. I was awakened
by some force, and I sat up in my bed; and there was the figure on my dressing table. It was truly a beautiful sight, although at the time I was frightened. I saw a man in the flesh.
There he stood on the table surrounded by a magnificent
light. He was about six feet tall. His hair was brown and
wavy and reached just below his shoulders. He was wearing
a blue and white robe. Above his head was something
strange. Possibly it looked like a gold rock, hanging. He had
a smile on his face and his arms were outstretched. I saw him
in full color and light, "hovering" on my table. Only I never
saw his feet. I was utterly stunned by this vision, and, as any
child would, I hid under my blankets. A few seconds later I
peeped from under my blankets and to my relief he was
gone.

My sister never stirred that night. I told everyone close of
my "angel," but no one believed me. The family said it must
have been a childish figment of my imagination. I still wonder, what did that visit mean and why me?

—B. KALINIC
Boksburg, South Africa

I, too, have had a few extraordinary experiences. Naturally
one is reluctant to recount the stories for fear of being
branded cuckoo, and few people have heard about my own
special angel or an unusual perfume of roses, a posy of vio-

lets, and how, at the age of seventeen, I had a most overwhelming premonition of the sudden death of my father.

I was reared and educated in a Roman Catholic home and
convent with all the (to me) attendant fearful tenets of mortal sins. I read books on apparitions of the Saints and the
Virgin Mary and was usually appalled by the way in which
the visionaries were quizzed, punished, or even tortured. As
for spiritualism—or interest in what happens after death—
well! that was the devil himself!

My first marriage was a disastrous revelation of a man's alcoholic abuse, but remembering my vows I stuck it through
till Death Did Us Part, sixteen years later. Toward the end of
this period I became, for want of a better title, a "free
thinker."

By the time I was halfway through my miserable first marriage and praying for guidance, help, in my unhappy state, I
began to think of a special sweet saint to whom I turned for
intercession one afternoon. The garden gate squeaked and
my husband staggered toward the house. I shot up from this
"meditation" in the bedroom and rushed down the passage
with the idea of putting on the kettle in the kitchen. Suddenly I stopped, for behind me was the Presence of Someone! And I knew that, had I turned back, I would most
certainly have seen "Her." All at once I felt enshrouded or
cloaked by the most overwhelming perfume of roses. It
burned into my very nostrils, so strong that I had to hold my
nose to stop the pungency. It seemed we were encapsulated
in time itself. Then the doorbell rang, and the magic was

gone. How long this took, I cannot say, but for months afterward I would push my face into a bouquet of roses and yet could never recapture that essence of roses again, nor have I since! When I mentioned this to a Catholic priest, his patronizing words were, "You've been particularly blessed!" And that was it, end of conversation! I was a real "kook" and, once more, I felt no one would believe me.

And then, years later—after I had remarried—came the most wonderful experience of all. To this day, I have no idea what prompted it, nor can I say I was even worthy of it. It happened in 1978, a Tuesday evening in November. (Here in South Africa, at that time of year, it is summer.) It was a warm, still, and moonless night.

My mother, who lived with us, had gone to bed, as had my husband. I had been writing letters and then retired myself and went to sleep. I was awakened by the gentle breeze of the flapping sheet against my cheek and, as I roused to wakefulness, I—once again!—experienced that Essence, that Presence of Someone in the room.

I did everything to avoid looking in one direction! I turned my head and clearly saw the lamp, an ashtray, and even the cracks in the white paint of the bedside pedestal. I turned my head in the other direction and saw, clearly, the quiet, recumbent, sleeping body of my husband (his back toward me). I saw all this in a beautiful, diffused sort of light. Remember, there was no moon and no wind either.

Then, not being able to hold out any longer, my eyes strayed and were finally drawn toward one spot in front of the large white dressing table in the room. And there She was! As real a person as the very flesh of your body as you read this.

She stood perfectly still while I took in every detail of her appearance and attire. The name Bernadette came into my mind. I got the impression that she was (or had been) deaf and dumb!

She was short, girlish, seventeen years old perhaps, with a most beautiful head of coppery-blond hair, thick, arranged in a pageboy style with a wide green bandeau across her lovely crown; not a hair out of place!

She wore a brown, flared, pinafore-type dress with a cream-colored blouse (seemed like silk) underneath; Peter Pan collar with tiny pearl buttons down the front, and leg-o'mutton sleeves, the same pearl buttons running along the outside of the wide cuffs. Her stockings were brown (woolen was my impression), and on her feet were the shiniest pair of little brown brogues I had ever seen, with the laces tied neatly on top.

Her expression was sweet, but she was not smiling.

I lay looking at her a long time, and then, to my astonishment, she moved toward the bed, knelt down beside me, and asked me (it seemed telepathically) to give her my hand!

By this time my heart was thumping, mostly through sheer fright at the oddness of it all; but I pulled my arm from under the covers and laid it along the edge of the bed. In her kneeling position, she placed both hands over my arm and I looked down to see a most perfect pair of hands with the most perfect set of manicured nails. She raised her face up as if in prayer and I was thus able, at this close range, to study the beauty of her rounded face.

Her skin was flawless except for a few freckles that dotted her short nose, and her hazel eyes, beneath neat, fair eyebrows, revealed those little dark specks that one sometimes sees in such light-colored eyes. Her beautiful mouth, quite red, it seemed from natural color, was full, almost a cupid's bow, but not quite.

I dared not speak until she got to her feet and moved away from me toward the wall, to the side (this time) of the dressing table; and somehow, I knew she was about to leave.

"Will I ever see you again?" I asked, almost begging her not to go.

"No," she replied, with that beautiful, angelic expression. "But I've come to tell you that, one day, I will come to fetch your mother." And then it seemed she was standing behind a plate-glass window, down the front of which water was pouring. She blurred and was gone! And then, believe it or not, the room was once more in total darkness! I was left blinking, wide awake, not able to return to sleep. I could not bring myself to tell my family about this, but she haunted me the next day to the extent that I tried, time and again, to draw her. But nothing matched her beautiful radiance. Even now, my description is purely the mere use of human words.

There is a sequel to the story. On the Thursday of that same week I was invited to a spiritual meeting. No sooner had the usual prayers been said than one of the medium's guides addressed me. (Remember, at this point, I had spoken to no one about this apparition, thinking it had been only a dream.)

"Patricia," the guide said. "You got a big fright the other night?"

Taken aback, I replied. "Oh, yes, I did."

"Not to worry," he answered promptly. "Only good people come to you!"

"But who was she?" I asked.

"A French girl," he said. "Bernadette, one of God's working angels."

We moved from Pretoria to Jeffrey's Bay shortly after that, and my husband died. But I still have to get confirmation of Bernadette's promise to me—if she really did come to fetch my mother, who followed my husband within a few short months.

—PATRICIA STEPHENSON
Jeffrey's Bay, South Africa

I am an arthritic grandmother now, but if you are interested, I'd like to tell of some of the angels and ghosts I have known.

I called my mother back from the dead when I was eight. We were in a nursing home together, I for tonsillectomy, she for a big "op." She died and, being in a private ward together, I heard the doctor say so. They covered her face with the sheet and turned away. I *screamed,* "Mummy! Come back!" The nurses held me down, and my mother sat up. She said she had left her body but had to return when I cried out.

When I was twenty-three, the spirit of my beloved young husband who had died two days before in Libya (1941)—and we had not yet had news of this—came to the window of the room where my sister and I were talking, knocked on the glass, and blew a kiss to me. We both ran out, calling gladly, but he was not there. He appeared later quite a few times when I was distressed and brought me great comfort and was the proof to me that life goes on after death.

My mother died at age eighty-six, in my sister's home. We both nursed my mother with the help of Lucy's wonderful husband. Lucy was very sad, hoping Ma would recover, but her husband and I knew this was not going to happen. One evening I felt I almost had to push my way through the thronging spiritual beings in her room. I said nothing, but when B——, Lucy's husband came in, he said, "Can you feel all the spirits here tonight?" Lucy could not, but I could. Mother lay quietly for another two days, and then a simply enormous angel in brilliant vermillion and orange and gold clothing came with cohorts of smaller ones. They simply made nonsense of the brick walls and curtains. They towered into the sky, and B—— and I both saw them. It was night. Mother had "gone" by morning, but her body kept on "living" for another three or four days, when it died. Those angels had come to fetch her soul. She had no disease or pain. She died as gently and beautifully as an autumn leaf dropping off a tree.

—ELIZABETH ROWLAND
East London, South Africa

*I*t was the week before Christmas, December 1918, when my grandfather died. I was five years old and the youngest of six children. The funeral arrangements were being made. I couldn't comprehend the true meaning of death. I kept begging Mother to take me to Grandpa, or else go and bring Grandpa home.

On the evening before the funeral, I remember taking my cousin by the hand. "Let's go into Grandpa's bedroom, maybe he is there." We opened the door. There in the middle of the room, in dazzling brilliance, stood an angel. It had long golden hair that hung down its back, a flowing white gown that reached to the floor. It had lovely, gossamery wings somewhat outstretched. It did not move or turn toward us as we gazed at it in awe and bewilderment. Its beauty is indescribable.

We ran to tell mother to come see the angel in Grandpa's room. She came, most likely unbelieving, I don't know. There was nothing to be seen anymore, neither to her nor to us.

—HELEN RUFF
La Moure, North Dakota

I have had many experiences during my entire lifetime. But a recent one meant so much to me. August 3, 1985, I was trying to complete planting wildflowers in the ditch fronting the road by my land, and a friend came to offer a ride. In rushing to accept the ride, I forgot to remove two deeply cherished pieces of gold jewelry I was wearing on a fine chain. We drove to the field of wildflowers, and I began digging the plants. It was very hot and sunny. I finished getting the plants and we drove back and began unloading and transplanting them before they were shocked by the heat. I then, tiredly, went to roll up the plastic sheet that had protected the car, when I realized my two precious golden items were gone; the chain, broken in two places, was glued to my sweaty neck. A genuine sense of loss flooded me. I searched futilely for them on the driveway, lawn, planting area, and all through the car. . . . I wept as I told my friend they were gone; and outside I had been powerfully, silently praying they would be found.

Feeling totally desolate, I sat down, weeping, and just gave up. Then I prayed out loud. And a friend from another level appeared and I "saw" him. He motioned to me to be still and then he very powerfully impressed on my mind: "Go back to where you were digging. Go back to the field. Have faith. I'll help." I told my friend and she willingly drove me back to the field. True to his word, as he had always been, he went with us. When we got out of the car, he impressed on my mind exactly where I should walk and then said, "Have faith, Joretta," and told me to take five steps to my left. I did. He then stopped sending his impressions. I stood a minute and then looked down at my feet.

There was my little Star of David with its royal blue trim! And a few inches from it was my handmade tiny gold ankh. I felt my spirit guide leave as my body trembled. I couldn't move. These two pieces symbolized a graduation for me after years of spiritual study. I went back to the car and sat. I couldn't speak. I was bursting with an unspeakable joy. It was too enormous for tears. My friend said, "Well . . . ?" Head bent, reverent beyond anything I ever felt, I could only open my hand. Blushing, she could only say—"Ooooh!" We drove home in silence. I rushed into my bedroom and placed the tokens in their little box and vowed I would never risk them doing work again.

Suddenly my powerful spirit friend appeared, and very gently, he told me, "Tokens are fine. Your love is what really

counts. This is for *you,* Joretta, so it will never be the last."
He made a motion of his hand. Late that night I had a vision.
His hand moved again over my face. And he said, "It's living
it that counts." And over my heart, in royal blue, was a huge
Star of David. Etched into my cells, on the inside, where it
counts.

Angels are Light and Love. I've met two kinds. Those that
are perfected by their own work; and I see them with a form,
of sorts, and with helpers. Then . . . there are the Great
Minds of the past, and they are "mind" and pure light, with
no form. . . .

When one of the angels comes at a moment of danger, the
"stopping" of all physical sensation is total; but the subconscious still takes in the horrors, and after the angel has left,
there is a "release," a physical reaction throughout the body
and sometimes the mind. Also, it takes a well-fed, healthy
body to be the receiving set. This is of utmost importance!
Also a happy subconscious that gets its little rewards and
treats of life. Also . . . one must be childlike to see and talk to
angels. Childlike means trusting, *believing.* Most adults are
destroyed—all programmed by school, family, church,
friends, life. There is an "opening" to the other realms, and
even I get knocked down by a cynic who snarls, "Who are
you kidding?" or worse, "You're crazy."

The only time I ever remember losing my angels is when my love for people caused me to soften and I began putting others' feelings ahead of their direction. They "left" and I really know I would have died had they not shortened the lesson and let me return to mutual Love and Peace.

— "JORETA"
Grayslate, Illinois

Musical Angel with Lute. Melozzo da Forli (1438–1494). Pinacoteca, Vatican Museums, Vatican.

*A*bout ten years ago I came to New Mexico to see if it was the right place for me to live. I was with my son (then twenty-six) and his girlfriend, driving from a remote retreat east of San Cristobal back to Taos, where they lived. It was February, cold and muddy. I wasn't particularly unhappy— concerned, perhaps, about where my husband and I would live, if we moved from the Hamptons in New York—but mostly I was concentrating on the muddy, winding road with no guardrails. I was driving slowly toward the village of San Cristobal when I noticed up ahead a lone figure standing on the left-hand side of the road. With his blond hair, he looked like a model. As I drew closer, I saw he was dressed in full cowboy regalia. He might have been dressed by Ralph Lauren or some other designer: perfect jeans, boots, shirt—not a speck of dirt despite the mud everywhere. As though someone had said, "This is how you dress when you go to cowboy country."

I remember thinking, *Why is he standing there? Where is his truck or horse? Does he need a lift? He's looking at me with such love.*

There were no roads or paths near him, no vehicles, nor was there a horse, car, bike or any other means of transportation. As I drove past he just stood looking at me with incredible love out of gorgeous, penetrating blue eyes.

I thought later I should have stopped and asked him who he was. But with that glance I felt so loved, watched over and protected that I didn't feel I had to check him out.

I slowed, however, and turned to look back over my shoulder. He had gone: no one there. My son said, "Mom, I think that was your guardian angel." His girlfriend saw him, too.

The reason my son knew about my angel is that I had told him of a visitation I'd had years before in a lucid dream, when he was kneeling on the floor at the right side of my bed. I had looked directly into his eyes, and afterwards I had consciously "channeled" him a few times, for that was a period of great spiritual awakening, grace, elation, joy as I opened to states I hadn't believed in before. In the dream he was dressed differently.

I think he came as a cowboy as a confirmation that the area was where we were to be, to say: *I'm with you, I love you.* It's been fifteen years since I saw him by the road, but I know he's with me still.

—PINTKI MURRAY
Taos, New Mexico

I was traveling alone on the Ventura Freeway in California in my little VW Bug. I had just left my Science of Mind Sunday service in Westlake, and stopped at a health-food store with a snack bar to buy a very tall and thick date-shake, and now I was driving home along the freeway. To exit, I swung onto my off-ramp, which lay at the top of a rather steep hill. On the right was an open area, allowing me to see down to the next intersection on the right—but on the left a solid ten-foot wall completely blocked my vision of oncoming traffic.

As I proceeded to exit at probably 40 miles-an-hour, I heard a voice right behind me coming from the backseat of the car. It shouted *at the top of its lungs*—STOP! I looked up in a state of shock and in the rearview mirror saw someone sitting in my backseat. This "being" was angelic-looking, complete with long, light hair, big, piercing eyes, and some type of white flowing garment, and it was yelling STOP!

I stomped on the brakes as hard as I could.

Needless to say, the date-shake flew everywhere around the car and of course on my head. The car stopped on the ramp just a few feet from the main road. The light was green for me, but I knew I should not move. The being was still there.

I was frozen.

Within milliseconds, a very large older American car came speeding past from the left, at eighty or ninety miles an hour. *Needless to say, I would never have seen that car until I was out on the major road, right in its path of destruction.* There was a car sitting at the red light on the far side of the road; the driver and I both watched the speeding car hit a bump at the next intersection, fly into the air and crash at a Kentucky Fried Kitchen. There were many people to help. We were both stunned. We rolled down our windows, to say, "Oh my God. Look at what happened!" We both agreed that if that car had hit my little VW, it would have killed me. My memory of the driver was of an unkempt individual with light hair.

After watching this spectacle in horror, I looked in the backseat—but the being was gone. I drove home and searched the car for any signs left by the being, and there were none: only the image seared into my mind of that being sent to my backseat by God so that there would be no mistaking the audible order to stop!

As for the date-shake, I spent days picking its remnants out of the interior of my car.

The writer continues with a story similar to Pintki's in New Mexico, except that her "cowboy angel" did nothing but love her, while this one delivered a message of help.

*I*n January 1996 I moved from Lost Angeles to the East Coast. At a friend's recommendation, I sold most of my furniture to cut down moving costs and kept a small load of boxes. I shipped my car to my brother's in New York, and took myself, my dog, and as many suitcases as I could carry by plane to New York. Then on New Year's Day, I drove eight hours in ice and snow from New York City to the Washington, D.C., suburbs in Virginia: dog in the car, suitcases, stuff in the trunk.

Before I left New York City I had made a hotel reservation near the new apartment. By the time I arrived in the Washington area, however, I was lost. I couldn't find the hotel. I was in tears, screaming and driving frantically around the Beltway (no cell phone in those days), searching for my way. I slowed near an off-ramp, hoping to get my bearings, and then saw someone standing by the road, waving dramatically for me to get off. He was dressed in a hat and small jacket, and there was no car near him. I felt strongly compelled to exit. As I drove off I looked in my rearview mirror, but could not see the man any longer.

At the top of the off-ramp was a huge hotel. I drove in. The hotel clerk said they had only one more room available, due to a last-minute cancellation. Needless to say, I took it, thanking God profusely, and that magical figure.

In the morning I found that I was not far from the apartment I had rented.

But there is more.

The apartment did not suit, I won't bother explaining why. The management agreed to let me out of my lease under one condition. I had to move all my possessions out by midnight on the last day of the month or I would have to pay another month's rent. No exceptions.

That gave me only a few weeks to find a new place, pack everything up again, and move. I had only a part-time job and really no money to put down on an apartment. I found a small condo where I did not even have to give the security deposit. I started moving my thirty-plus boxes and other possessions in my car. The car was small, and I couldn't take much on each trip. Moreover, with my job I could only move on the cold and snowy evenings.

By 8:00 P.M. on the last day, my arms ached. I was delirious with pain. I sat down in the snow on the steps to the building and began to cry. I had no one to help. Even my family, for whom I had moved east, could not help me.

As I sat in the falling snow, a tall, slender, dark-haired gentleman walked up the path toward me. He was carrying a small exercise bench and nothing else. He was wearing shoes, no boots, no hat or gloves. I looked beyond him and saw a "U-Haul $19/day" van parked at the curb behind my car. It had not been there a few minutes earlier, so I assumed that he had just driven up in it.

I asked, was he moving in? He said yes, he was moving into the unit on the second floor and wanted to bring by a few things. I knew they were in the middle of renovating that unit, so I couldn't imagine why he was moving now, in the snow. Also I couldn't help but notice that his exercise bench was too small for me, much less a guy six feet four.

What's he doing with that? I thought, but he was soft-spoken and kind and very tall and slender. I told him my story, how I was trying to move out, and was so exhausted I could no longer lift and carry boxes.

I asked if I could pay him twenty dollars cash for his van and use it to move the rest of my things. He said of course, but that the van would have to be returned to the U-Haul depot no later than 8:55 P.M. or he would have to keep it overnight and pay an extra day's rental fee. The depot was only two blocks from my new apartment. I knew it closed at 9:00 P.M.

He walked back to the van, I presume to put the exercise bench back in it. I never saw it again—nor any of his other possessions, for that matter. Two Hispanic men jumped out of the front seat and followed him toward me. The three of them went to my apartment, lined up in relay style from my door to the van, and with my help began moving the last fifteen boxes. It took no time! (Suspicious as I am—former New Yorker—it never occurred to me that they would steal my stuff.)

The man followed me the few miles to my new place. We quickly unloaded everything at the back door into grocery carts (available for the residents). I thanked him, gave him the cash, and he left, while a few nearby neighbors kindly helped me move my boxes upstairs. It was only 8:45. The entire operation had taken no more than half an hour.

Curiously, the two Hispanic men never spoke a word during all this time, either to me or to each other.

Something told me I should go to the U-Haul depot and thank him again. I jumped into my car, leaving the rest of the boxes at the back door, and drove to the depot, where I expected to find him checking out at the counter—or at least find the van, if I had missed him. I approached the desk. The owner was closing down the office. I asked if someone had just returned a van to his depot. He said no; that no one had come in to rent or drop off any vans for days, let alone in the last half hour.

I then asked if the man could possibly have taken it to another depot. He said the next nearest one was miles away and they all closed down at 9:00 P.M. I then wondered if my savior had decided to keep the van for another day, but the owner said no one had rented a van out of this depot for quite some time, and moreover no vans were available in the whole area: and he would know, because they were in high demand. The man and van had simply disappeared.

It took many months for my arms and hands to heal from the strain they received in moving boxes. I rarely ask for help: I've been disappointed too many times. Now I believe that this "gentleman" and his two Hispanic helpers were angels, sent by God to help me in what was one of the most traumatic and sorrowful times of my life. It was also a lesson for me to learn to ask for help.

By the way, the "gentleman" never moved into the second-floor unit of my former apartment building.

—ROSEMARY FICAMORA
Virginia

I am forty-two years old, married with two sons, Tristan, sixteen years old, and Johannes Alexander, three and a half. I'm still studying at the university to become a teacher for handicapped children.

I'd like to tell you about one event that happened two years ago. At that time I was nervous and afraid whenever one of the family left the house.

At the time my husband had to leave for work very early in the morning—almost still night. One such night I heard his footsteps leaving, the door shut, and then his car driving away. Before he left I had felt him kiss my cheek, as he always did, and right after I heard the car drive off, I closed my eyes for some seconds. Suddenly, I felt another kiss. I know I was awake. I felt a touch on my shoulder. I thought it was my husband returning, perhaps because he'd forgotten something. I turned, expecting to see him, but there was nobody there! But I had really felt a kiss.

Again I closed my eyes, when after some minutes I felt a caress on my arm. I didn't dare open my eyes, but I knew

there were no bad persons around me. Then I heard an unknown male voice right in my ear: "Elke, we're going now."

That was all the voice said. I opened my eyes and turned
to look. No one was there.

I was afraid only about the strangeness of the situation,
but I was not afraid of these unknown people. Deep inside I
knew that "they" had come to comfort me.

—ELKE WATTJES-BECKER
Recklinghausen, Germany

*I*t all took place in a place called Macdonald, West Virginia,
a very, very tiny suburb outside of my home town, which is
Mount Hope. My aunt, Alicia Porter, was about five years
old when it occurred. She's really my cousin, but I call her
my aunt, as they do in the South. This was sometime in 1901,
I think, because Alicia was born in 1896 and married in
about 1920.

Her father was president of the New River coal mine, and
Alicia was ill. The doctor came to the house (as they did in
those days) and told them she had scarlet fever. There was
no cure; she couldn't live. They told her mother to prepare
for her death. Also, it's a contagious disease; the whole family was quarantined, which meant that Mr. Porter had to stay
home from his office in Mt. Hope. They built a tiny coffin
for her and prepared her shroud.

One day, while the child lay dying, a man came to the office looking for Mr. Porter, and the secretary said he was at home, quarantined with his family, because his daughter was dying of scarlet fever. The man said, "It's very important; I'll go to the house."

The secretary said, "They won't let you in, but you can try."

So he goes to the Porter house and maid answers the door, and he asks for Mr. Porter.

She says, "No, you can't see him. His daughter is dying of scarlet fever, and everyone is quarantined. They aren't allowed to see anyone."

"Yes I know," he said. "Have you tried everything?"

"We've tried everything anyone can think of, but there's no medicine for scarlet fever. Nothing you can do."

"I have a suggestion," he said. "Would you be willing to try it?"

"I don't know."

"Do you have chickens? A rooster?" Well, everyone had chickens in those days. "Do you have red flannel in the house? Well, boil water. Cut the red flannel into long strips about six inches wide. Go out back and find a rooster, pluck the cleanest tail feather that you can get out. Then dip the flannel in boiling water, and wrap it 'round the child's throat, as hot as the child can stand it. While doing that, swab out her throat with the feather, and keep on doing this. Can you do this? Try it."

With this disease, you choke to death, drown on the phlegm in your throat. Today we have penicillin. The red flannel heats the phlegm up and pushes it up the throat. The feather pulls it out.

They did this, and Alicia was cured. And she lived to eighty-seven.

Mr. Porter spent the rest of his life trying to find the man. He hadn't left his name either with the secretary at his office or with the maid at the house, where he was so insistent on going. And that's strange. He turned up, a total stranger, and then simply vanished.

After she got well, Alicia wore her shroud one day to Sunday school. It was made out of white lace, quite lovely. But that will show how close she was to death. They had made a shroud for the little five-year-old, saved by a stranger at the door.

—NAN SNYDER MUNTZING
Potomac, Maryland

*T*his is just a little story—a lost glove. It's so trivial, it's like it was an experiment, to show me that asking for help works. I was on a ski vacation in Keystone, Colorado, with my husband and our two-year-old son. I had been reading a book about angels that said to ask for an angel's help in any difficulty, whether the need is important or not. If you ask, they will help you, the book said.

We were at the slopes, renting equipment and trudging about, when my son began to get fussy. It was his naptime, and I was taking him to the bus to go to the hotel, when I discovered I'd lost my leather glove. I decided to ask for an angel's help. "Please guide me to where I dropped my glove," I was praying; but my little boy was getting increasingly fussy, and I realized I didn't have time to look for the glove. "Okay, angels," I said, "I cancel the request. It's not important."

We got to the hotel, and a few hours later after skiing, my husband met us there. We had an errand to run. We went to the car, and there was my glove in the passenger seat.

I thought I'd just left it there, but my husband said, "Oh no, there's a special story about the glove. When I came down from skiing and went to the parking lot, I found an elderly couple standing at our car with your glove in their hand. They said, 'We knew this belonged to someone in your car, and we wanted to get it back to you. It dropped out on the passenger side. We were afraid you wouldn't see it. We've been waiting for you.' "

I know this isn't a big event—except it was like a sign. Imagine that old couple waiting in the lot to return the glove to me. After that I'm not afraid to ask.

—DR. ADRIANA P.
North Bethesda, Maryland

I was thirty-three years old and the mother of four children. My marriage was on the rocks, and I had been in deep depression for about a year. I was being treated by my family doctor and a clinical psychologist. The family was seriously considering having me committed to an institution for treatment.

I had gotten up one morning after the children had left for school and my husband had gone to work. I had planned to take my life that morning. The house, which was in the country, in a small town in the Midwest, was quiet. I laid out my Valium. I poured my glass of vodka. I went and took my shower, washed my hair, put on my best nightgown, and did my nails. I was ready! I sat on the edge of the bed, contemplating.

All at once I was on my knees at the side of my bed. My head was in a lap, hands were on my head, and a feeling of love, peace, and hope was overwhelming to me. I didn't want to move. I wanted to remain there forever.

I never saw the "angel," but I knew it was one, and I knew that I was, at that moment, well.

—TRUDY BLEDSOE
Keene, New Hampshire

I am a recovering alcoholic and compulsive overeater. I spent fifty years trying to master my disorders—of being constitutionally unable to stop drinking or eating once I started. My life was hell. I finally found Alcoholics Anonymous and two years later its sister program, Overeaters Anonymous, which addresses food addiction.

Now, as long as I'm careful not to put any of the addictive substances in my mouth and as long as I work the twelve spiritual "steps" of the program, I am happy, free. Gone are the violent mood swings, cravings, fear, loneliness, and depression. I truly believe it can't be done without the help of God. But I have to tell you what happened in the beginning.

After six months of effortless abstinence in Overeaters Anonymous, I got lazy. I had shed many pounds, but little by little I found it harder to say no. Or rather, I had to say no by teeth-clenched use of my own willpower rather than finding the freedom and ease that had been mine earlier.

One morning I had a business appointment, and planned to follow it with a noon AA meeting. On my way to the appointment I stopped to buy two breakfast bagels, and instead bought four. Two for breakfast, I told myself, two for lunch.

However, as soon as I bit into the second breakfast bagel, the urge to wolf down the third and fourth became overwhelming. I was holding myself back by sheer willpower, and knew if I ate that third I'd be back in the old pattern of binge eating and dieting. (I didn't yet know at the time that white flour and sugar trigger this chemical response in the brain—an inability to signal when I've had enough.)

Driving along, all serenity was gone. I was filled with fear and self-pity: business was bad, my family relationships worse. I wanted to eat. Somewhere amidst my confusion, prayers started popping into my head: old, rote prayers from my youth, new ones, and in desperation just plain "Help!"

Then something happened.

As I pulled out onto the highway a homeless vagrant stood beside the road, hitching a ride. Intellect said, "Picking him up is stupid and dangerous, drive on." Intuition urged: "Do it. It's okay. You're safe."

I found myself pulling over and offering him a lift.

He was a black man about my age, fifty, with salt-and-pepper hair, and two or three days' growth of beard, white against his dark skin. There was a quiet dignity about him, with neither the sickly subservience nor haughty arrogance so often associated with street people. His clothes were tattered and dirty, as if he'd slept in them for months. He wore an old tweed coat, neatly buttoned, a dark sweatshirt, dark blue cotton work pants and black, heavy workshoes. Under his right arm he carried a bedroll—a small, soft, snow-white baby's blanket!

As he climbed into the car I tried to catch his eye, but he seemed preoccupied. I extended my hand in greeting. "Hi, my name is Bill." For a brief second he paused, then held out his own. As I took it, I saw that his palm was young and clean, like that of a child, yet the back of his hand was old and bony with leathery skin. My body began to tingle.

I asked where he was going. "Denver," he replied. Two thousand miles away? I thought, *how strange.*

Unconsciously my hand reached into the brown bag and I heard myself offering him the bagel that had obsessed me only moments before. As I did I kept glancing over, trying to catch his eye. At first I noticed that while the three-day growth of beard looked like it was there, it really wasn't. He had no facial hair—only the coloring and a raised texture. Then I noticed the hair on his head. It was impeccable and perfectly groomed. As I stared at his profile I saw he was both much older than I and much younger. The tingling grew stronger, mixed with a heightened sense of awareness. He was beautiful. He was radiant. If I were a sculptor I would have wanted him as a model.

He took the bagel and as I concentrated on the road, he mumbled something.

"What did you say?" I asked.

He replied in a sure, natural voice: "I'm saying my blessings."

I felt a rush and in that moment the compulsion that had consumed me only minutes before was gone, replaced by peace and joy.

The next minute the car filled with a powerful but somehow not unpleasant smell of unwashed body odor. I cautiously asked him to roll down the window, hoping not to interrupt the moment. As he complied, he said, "It's time for me to leave now. Could you please stop?"

I did, though we had traveled less than a mile of the ten I was going in his direction.

But I realized as he got out that yes, it was time: his job was done. It was not I who had picked him up, but he who had picked up me. He, who had nothing, said his blessings over that humble bagel, while I, who had so much, had been obsessing over it. I think he was my guardian angel, coming in answer to my cry for help. He had taught me what to do.

The sense of wonder and awe stayed with me for days. Two things puzzled me for a long while: why the small, soft, white baby's blanket, and second why the overpowering smell of body odor at the end?

But a friend reminded me that when I first started in terror and despair to go to the Alcoholics Anonymous meetings I'd felt I had been caught in a wonderful, white safety net of light, enveloping me in love. Was the baby blanket a symbol of that tenderness?

As for the odor, I think it was a reminder that, unusual as the experience seemed, it was not a product of my imagination. It was real.

—BILL B.
Rockville, Maryland

A story I love to tell is one where I was walking through a parking lot near home one night and suddenly had one of those moments. I felt a tingling and got some sort of pleasing message: "I really like this parking lot," I thought.

Afterwards, I felt an odd mix of very emotional and a little embarrassed and confused. It's just a parking lot. Until I looked down and saw a twenty-dollar bill on the ground next to me.

Then I understood.

Just a little thing, but so nice.

—MARGIE LIDOFF
Washington, D.C.

*M*y father was suffering from stage four brain cancer and participating in some experimental treatments at Brigham and Women's Hospital in Boston. Periodically, I would fly from my home in Washington, D.C., to my parents' house in St. Louis, pick up my dad, and take him to Boston for his treatment. He was in a wheelchair, as balance was a problem for him. The cancer had also affected his ability to communicate: he could not read or write, and though he could speak, his brain functions were such that he could not get out the words he wanted. Communication through words was often difficult. I learned a lot about how meaningful other forms of communication are during the two years he was ill, and the time we spent together on these trips was precious to me. At the same time, the trips were exhausting, first dealing with both of our emotional states and then physically challenging me as I struggled to maneuver the wheelchair.

Brigham and Women's is situated on a steep hill. One of his treatments had been scheduled on a particularly windy and icy winter's day. We came out of the hospital and started down the hill. I slipped on a patch of ice and lost my grip on the wheelchair. I watched in horror as it careened down the hill with my helpless dad, gathering momentum, and heading straight toward a busy intersection full of traffic.

I looked for help and saw no one. I began to run as fast as possible in a fruitless attempt to catch up. I will never forget the panic that rose in me at the wheelchair crashing into the traffic.

Suddenly two well-dressed gentlemen appeared and effortlessly, as in a dream, stopped the wheelchair right at the corner. One on either side. There was no sign that this required any strength. The wheelchair was bounding forward and then it wasn't. I had not seen the men coming or I would have called to them for help. In a second I caught up and first leaned down to my dad, who I am sure had just had a terrifying experience. "Are you all right?"

When I looked up to thank the two men, they had disappeared. There was no one there. A few pedestrians. No one had gathered to watch this incident or help. The men had not vanished into a crowd. One moment they were there to help us and the next they were gone.

At the time it seemed incomprehensible. Where had they come from? Where had they gone to so quickly? Any pedestrian who had stopped to help would surely have seen that my father was ill and I myself in a panic and would have stayed to make sure we were okay. It was clear we had just come from the hospital. The men did not even stay long enough to receive our thanks. Very shortly afterward I happened to pick up Sophy Burnham's *Book of Angels,* and then I knew without a doubt—these men were our angels.

—SACHA MILLSTONE
Boulder, Colorado

When I was a young girl of seven or eight, a film came out called *King of Kings.* It was the first time the face of Jesus was to be shown in the movies. I went alone. At the point of the crucifixion, I began crying and couldn't stop for *days.* I stayed in my room, I loved Him so much and couldn't believe what people had done to Him.

Years later, when I was around sixteen or seventeen, I decided religion was a hoax, a way for the rich and powerful to control the poor. I became an atheist. During my freshman year in college I was lying in bed, studying for a biology exam. It was dark, and I was reviewing fern reproduction as I stared out the window.

Suddenly, a warm cloud began to move through my body until it filled me. A million things flashed through my head. A "male" voice interrupted, asking, "Why have you forsaken me?" I immediately apologized in my head and began crying. He is with me always. Many times I have experienced divine intervention, but none so dramatic as the angel visit below.

Three years ago I was in deep despair, despite all the blessings given me. I was at a point of true decision, lying in the
dark of my bedroom in Atlanta. Suddenly an incredibly
bright light, about the size of a pea, came before my closed
eyes, and it spoke to me. "Keep your eyes closed, for it is
true that we can blind you."

It moved closer and closer, and the Light was unbeliev-
able. Even with my eyes closed as tightly as I could, I wanted
extra lids, because the light hurt my eyes. Finally it wrapped
its wings around me and completely enclosed me in its embrace. I felt absolute peace, love, and protection.

Now I could "see" my angel through closed eyes. It wasn't
either male or female, it had wings. It told me the Mother
had sent him/her to let me know I am watched after. I felt so
bad, because I was raised Episcopalian and we didn't spend
much prayer or interest on the Mother. She guided me out of
the dark and into my new life here in New Mexico. Since
I've been here, many new spiritual doors have opened to me.

As you note, these experiences don't preclude life's trials,
but somehow they give strength and peace.

—GWEN SCOTT
Albuquerque, New Mexico

A few years ago my father died. I was pacing the floor one
night, in tears, missing him horribly. Suddenly I was directly

guided to open a Bible in the bookcase. In it was an old letter that my dad had written to me a few years before he died.
It stated that he had found peace with God. The reading of
the letter gave me a wonderful sense of peace, and I felt very
close to my father.

—MTZ
Washington

*I*t happened on a cold night before Thanksgiving several
years ago. We had retired for the night. Around 11:00
o'clock the barking of a dog awakened me from sound sleep.
I tried to return to sleep, but the barking continued.

I lay there, wondering whose dog it was. We lived on a
main thoroughfare in our small town, and the only dogs in
the neighborhood were house dogs.

Finally I got up to look out. There was a full moon.
And when I stepped out on the porch, I saw this big German shepherd standing between our big oak tree and the
highway. It was such a handsome dog! And when it spotted
me, its barking quieted down into a softer, more gentle
sound.

It was then I saw the baby. She had nothing on except an
ankle-length gown, and she was crying and shivering from
the cold and fear. She had curly blonde hair. She was beautiful. And she was two years old.

When I lifted her in my arms, the dog stopped barking, watched till I opened the door, then slowly trotted away. I brought her into the house, put scuffies on her feet, wrapped her in a blanket, and woke my husband. After a cup of hot chocolate, she explained where she lived down the block from us.

Within the hour mother and daughter were reunited. The mother had planned to spend Thanksgiving with her in-laws, where her husband was working 100 miles from our home town. She had put her two-year-old, who was asleep, in the backseat of the car and gone back in the house for the other two children. The child awoke and got out of the car before the mother returned with the other children. She'd put them in the front seat and driven off. Thirty miles up the road she'd stopped for gas and panicked when she saw the baby wasn't with them.

For several days after this incident, my husband and I searched the neighborhood and made inquiries about the beautiful dog. It had never been seen before and was never seen again, and no one knew anything about the dog.

—Patsy Craig
Herrin, Illinois

The next writer always refers to himself in the first person plural, the "we" connecting us, he says, "to other aspects of a being that doesn't manifest in this physical body at this time."

We have two stories to share with you.

A few weeks into the academically challenging sophomore year of engineering at Lafayette College, we became severely depressed: for example, the formulas for impact velocity learned in physics were being applied to how hard we'd hit the ground after jumping from a third-floor window.

One evening we somehow managed to crash one of the freshman social mixers, where an extraordinary beauty astonished us by being pleasant toward—even attracted to—us. We corresponded thereafter and we termed Janie our "angel." Of course, this one was alive, and the term was used figuratively.

But was it merely figurative? Had the universe not loaned this gentle and caring being to us in our time of crisis? To this day, we owe our presence on earth to a few months that brought an angel into our life, then went her way. But the other story involves no human appearance or intervention.

With a friend, we were road-testing our six-month-old Camaro before the warranty ran out. We got on a still-unopened stretch of I-81 and pressed the accelerator until we hit 115 miles-per-hour. Suddenly in the dim light of dusk, a line of trees appeared in front of the ribbon of concrete, which we'd been told continued for miles. (Obviously faulty information.) The pavement dropped out from under us, and we were sailing at 115 miles-per-hour on wet gravel. The tree line was *near* and approaching *fast*!

Knowing the geography of the area, we knew we'd soon

fly over the edge of a hundred-foot cliff, at the bottom of which flowed the Conodoquinet Creek.

Two thoughts entered our mind: 1) Don't turn the wheel or the car will cartwheel, and 2) Our wallet's gonna get wet (it's true, that was the thought!) once we hit the creek.

The next thing we knew, we were lifting our face off the steering wheel. The engine was hissing. The transmission was stuck up between the bucket seats. Never thinking to question our own survival, we called to see if our friend was alive. To our relief, he answered.

We both clambered out the passenger door, the driver's door being wedged against a tree. We stood on the slope of the cliff.

What saved us both? We give the seat belts some credit (one of the few times we'd ever buckled up). Credit also goes to the incredible odds of each headlamp of the car striking a sapling simultaneously, causing the Camaro to be stopped in mid-flight beyond the cliff's edge and dropped onto the steep slope. Hitting one tree would have rolled the car end-over-end and side-over-side as it fell, surely a fatal combination.

Credit finally a miracle that brought these factors together and allowed us to walk away with nothing more than bruises and a cut lip. If one ever needed a hint that one's time to die had not yet come, that life still expected something of us, this episode qualified.

—Larry E. Arnold
ParaScience International
Harrisburg, PA

I won't bore you with details defining my "normal human being" status. Suffice it to say I am not easily swayed.

I was twenty-seven years old, married with two small children. I was going through an agonizing break-up of my nine-year marriage, and one evening after a particularly heated argument with my husband, I sought solace in the arms of a mutual friend, a man. Please bear with me. This sounds like a confessional, but the background is necessary to explain my spirit or angel.

I was awakened the following morning with a piercing cold-hot electric jab on my right shoulder. (I was sleeping on my stomach.) I pushed up and automatically turned to my right to see who was poking me. It was early morning, the room was filled with light, and in the corner of the room was a darkly shrouded figure watching me. I don't know the time frame, but it seemed a minute went by. I turned to see if my friend was playing games with me, but he was sound asleep.

I turned back as the figure faced me. But now I received a message. It was clear, concise, and very much a warning.

I was told to dress immediately and find my children, because my husband knew about my assignation and was going to take the children away from me. Sure enough, my kids were not at home. I found them finally at a friend's. She told me my husband was furious.

During the divorce that eventually followed, he did indeed try to take the children, but without success. I look back on this experience and remember in detail that strange morning and the angel that came to warn me.

Name withheld by request

I said earlier that angels can change all the physical laws of the universe. I don't know why they should do it so often in relation to cars, but the next two stories tell of cars that dematerialize. Did they really go through each other?

I was driving on a narrow, two-lane country road, when a car suddenly pulled out from the road on my right to make a left turn. It was directly in my path. I was going to hit it broadside! Coming from the opposite direction, a large SUV had stopped (facing me) to allow the car to pull out, and I remember the driver looking in my direction with horror as the next events occurred.

I swerved to the left to avoid the oncoming car, then around it to the right—congratulating myself on my driving skills. And then I had passed, and we had not hit. But after my pulse slowed down and I had a chance to reflect on the incident, I realized that going left around the turning car, I should have hit the waiting SUV head on. There wasn't room to go around him. One moment we were about to collide,

and the next I was on the other side. I have no idea what
happened.

—HL
Baltimore, Maryland

And this from Michigan.

*I*t was a sunny fall afternoon. My wife, Carol, and I weren't
doing anything special, just running errands. Then something extraordinary happened to us. It defies logical explanation, but we both came to the same conclusion: the hand of
God had intervened.

Carol was about to turn left onto a busy five-lane street. A
van was slowing to turn right beside us onto our road. We
moved across the first of the five lanes, but as we cleared the
van, we saw a car swooping down the second lane. It had
been hidden by the van. Carol hit the brakes. We were already in the middle of the second lane, and the car was bearing down on us at about 45 miles-per-hour. The car didn't
swerve—there wasn't time. Carol's door was directly in its
path . . . but the car never touched us. The people inside
didn't honk their horn; they didn't even brake. One moment
they were on one side of us and the next on the other side,
continuing on their way as if they had never seen us.

The car did not pass in front of our car (by moving into

the third or middle lane) and the van was blocking the lane behind us. It seemed they went *through* us.

I was stunned that we had not been hit. I have no memory of what the passengers looked like or how many people were in the car.

—ROBERT NAVARRE
Lansing, Michigan

*I*t was a clear, cold Sunday and I was under a blanket reading your book on angels, when I began to wonder if an angel would come to me, if I asked. I closed my eyes and began to meditate, holding the vision of a large, loving angel in my mind, but after a time, though I felt a quiet sense of peace, I was disappointed that an angel hadn't appeared to me.

Meanwhile the sun would be setting soon, and I hadn't taken my dogs for a walk, so I laced up my boots, put on my coat, hat, and gloves and headed out into the woods with the dogs.

We live on a large family property surrounded by acres of woodland. At a certain point, I saw my husband's uncle Joe riding on his tractor. I didn't want to stop and talk just then. I wanted to be alone. We waved, but I was glad when he turned down another road.

A few days later my uncle and I met at a family birthday party. "Who was that big man you were walking with the other day?" he asked.

"Who? I wasn't walking with anyone."

"No, that really big guy. He was over six feet tall, maybe close to seven feet. Who was he?"

But I'd been walking alone. I could only think it must have been an angel, and a chill ran through my entire body. I'm not alone.

—TONIANNE ROBINO
Junction City, Ohio

When I was seventeen years old, I was a member of the Holy Trinity Church choir in Lowell, Massachusetts.

One night, I had a call from a choir member. She asked me to wait for her at the corner of the street where I lived. She did not know where the house was located. As I stood there at the corner, under a lamp post, for about twenty minutes, I saw two men coming forward on the other side of the street. One was a young man, and the other a middle-aged man. They passed me and then, all of a sudden, they turned and started coming toward me. I was naive then, but I had a feeling that they were up to no good.

I was frightened and started to pray to the Blessed Virgin. I didn't know what to do. I couldn't run because the street was dark with only that one lamp post, and the houses had no lights shining through to the street. I prayed hard. All of a sudden, seven little children, around the age of five, came running out of an alley to my left, carrying large sticks. They

walked around me and started to chant "ah, ah, ah . . ."
Their eyes were wide and dark, like those in the Keene
paintings. I asked them what they were doing out so late—it
was nine o'clock—but they didn't answer and didn't even
look at me. They just kept walking around me making the
"ah" sound.

Suddenly, frightened, I remembered the men and turned
to see where they were. There was no one in sight. The night
was quiet, and no one was around. I turned back to the children and saw the heel of the last child disappearing into the
alley. I was puzzled and went to see where the children had
gone. To my amazement the alley had no exit. It was a dead
end.

—MARY KOSTOROS
San Francisco, CA

*I*t was the day before Thanksgiving, 1951, and we children
had spent much of the day helping our mother prepare for
the big feast. In mid-afternoon, all that could be done had
been done, and we were sent out to play.

Earlier that day, as we returned from a trip to the grocery
store, my eight-year-old sister, Kathleen, my four-year-old
brother, John, and I (aged six) had seen great mounds of autumn leaves raked to high-peaked perfection at the corner of
our street. We could hardly wait to bury ourselves in the
crisp leaves. But as we neared the corner where we had seen

the leaves, we discovered that the collection crew had already finished clearing the east side of the street near our home. On the west side, great piles awaited collection at some future date. Although we weren't allowed to cross the street, we decided to bend the rules and import leaves from the west side to our side. We'd walk across empty-handed, and return with great billowing armloads.

After several trips across, we had the leaf pile of our dreams. Just as we were about to jump, I realized that I had dropped my handerchief in the middle of the street. The last thing I remember was turning to retrieve it.

I'm told that a speeding Cadillac hit me, tossed me into the air, threw me down the street in a wide arc, and hit me again before driving away.

Kathleen and John ran to the spot where I landed and tried to help me, but couldn't get me to breathe. After half an hour or so of wandering around in shock, they told a neighbor what had happened. An ambulance was called and, when it arrived, I was pronounced dead. Kathleen was told to go and get our mother.

Mom had just stepped out of the shower when she heard the news. She raced down the street—pulling on her clothes as she ran—and was horrified to see me lying lifeless on a stretcher in the center of the large crowd of onlookers. Mom often told me that a man with a radiant face approached her and asked whether she would allow him to pray with her. She thanked him and said she would be honored.

As the story goes, Mom ripped away the tarpaulin that

had covered me, and—as she held me up in the air—cried out, "Give me back my child." At that moment, everyone could see that I was alive.

Later, my mother asked people if they knew the man who had offered to pray with her. One of our neighbors said she thought he was a priest assigned to the Episcopal church near our home. When I was out of danger, my parents went to that church to thank the priest with the radiant face. No one there had ever heard of him.

—ELLEN PERKINS
Washington, D.C.

When I was a little girl in Michigan, I got double pneumonia. I was in the third grade—eight years old, I suppose. They thought I was going to die. I remember hearing Dr. Engle outside the door saying I wouldn't live through the night. Then an angel appeared beside my bed. She was so beautiful! Her face was so beautiful. Even all these years later, I can still see her beauty. I get emotional just thinking of it. She had long golden hair. And her wings—every feather was distinct and differentiated, and they were opalescent—were all colors. Radiant. She stood by my bed and with her arm, or her beautiful wing, she swept up the whole length of my body, from my toes to my head. I felt myself moving upward, not in an out-of-body experience, but detached somehow. I will never forget it. She was so beautiful.

Afterwards I went to sleep. The fever broke, and the next day I seemed completely well. I was made to stay in bed a few days, but I was ready to get up anyway. I sat on the side of the bed even though I wasn't supposed to, and within a few days, I was out and playing again.

I will never forget her.

The same angel came again when I moved to Virginia. I'd made a horrible mistake of marrying a man who turned out to abuse my little daughter. He was a respected man of position. I was married to him only for one year. I knew there were problems, but I didn't know what. One night when he was in New York, I opened the door to my daughter's room, and I heard his voice so clearly, saying out loud what he intended to do to her! I was startled. I think it was the spirit world recreating his voice to warn me.

But I looked in her room and there was a shaft of light over her in bed. Light filled the room. All shadow disappeared. I looked up and at the top of the shaft I saw the same angel that had come to me before. Oh, I will never forget her! Her beautiful face, her long golden hair. No words can describe it. She was dressed all in white, the whitest white, and her wings radiating all the colors of the rainbow.

I knew I had to make changes in my life. Fortunately the warning came in time to avert real harm to my little girl.

—ANNE GEHMAN
Springfield, Virginia

About the Author

SOPHY BURNHAM is an award-winning playwright, novelist, and nonfiction writer. Three of her books have appeared on the *New York Times* bestseller list. Her works have been translated into twenty-two languages. Her articles and essays have been published worldwide in such publications as *Esquire, New York, The New York Times Magazine, Town & Country,* and *Reader's Digest.* As executive director of the Kennedy Center Fund for New American Plays, she worked closely with famed producer Roger Stevens, awarding money to theaters to produce new plays and to playwrights to write them. An international speaker, she has appeared frequently on television and radio programs around the country, including *Oprah, Larry King Live, To Tell the Truth, Good Morning America, The Today Show,* and *CBS Morning News.* In addition to her theater interests, she is a psychic, or intuitive, a healer, and a spiritual director. She lives in Washington, D.C.

Grateful acknowledgment is made to the following for permission to reprint previously published material:

GUIDEPOSTS MAGAZINE: "The Day We Saw Angels" by Dr. Ralph S. Harlow is reprinted with permission from *Guideposts* magazine. Copyright © 1963 by Guideposts, www.guideposts.org. All rights reserved.

PENGUIN: "The Delicate, Plummeting Bodies," copyright © 1980 by Stephen Dobyns, from *Velocities* by Stephen Dobyns. Originally appeared in *The New Yorker*. Used by permission of Penguin, a division of Penguin Group (USA) Inc.

RANDOM HOUSE: "The Ninth Elegy," "The First Elegy," "The Second Elegy," "The Tenth Elegy," translated by Stephen Mitchell, copyright © 1982 by Stephen Mitchell, from *The Selected Poetry of Ranier Maria Rilke* by Ranier Maria Rilke, translated by Stephen Mitchell, translation copyright © 1980, 1981, 1982 by Stephen Mitchell. Used by permission of Random House, Inc.

ALFRED A. KNOPF: Excerpt from *The Dhammapada: The Sayings of the Buddha* translated by Thomas Byron. Copyright © 1976 by Thomas Byron. Reprinted by permission of Alfred A. Knopf.

PENGUIN: "Verse 21," from *Tao Te Ching: The Definitive Edition* by Lao Tzu, translated by Jonathan Star, copyright © 2001 by Johnathan Star. Used by permission of Jeremy P. Tarcher, an imprint of Penguin Group (USA) Inc.

The excerpt from "He Wishes for the Cloths of Heaven" is from *The Poems of W. B. Yeats: A New Edition* edited by Richard J. Finneran (New York: Macmillan, 1983).

ILLUSTRATION CREDITS AND SOURCES

Page 10. Scala/Ministero per i Beni e le Attività Culturali/Art Resource, NY; *20.* Courtesy Library of Congress; *30.* Scala, Art Resource, NY; *38.* Courtesy Library of Congress; *46.* Scala/Ministero per i Beni e le Attività Culturali/Art Resource, NY; *58.* Courtesy Edith Vonnegut; *71.* Granger Collection, NY; *87.* Courtesy Library of Congress; *89.* Collection of the Library of Congress; *92.* Erich Lessing, Art Resource, NY; *95.* Scala/Ministero per i Beni e le Attività Culturali/Art Resource, NY; *96.* Courtesy Library of Congress; *103.* The British Library Board; *105.* Courtesy Board of Trustees, National Gallery of Art, Washington; *107.* Arthur M. Sackler Gallery, Smithsonian Institution, Washington, D.C.; *109.* The Metro-politan Museum of Art, Gift of the Humanities Fund, Inc. 1972 (1972.145.15); *115.* John G. Neihardt Papers, c. 1858–1974, Western Historical Manuscript Collection; *120.* The Metropolitan Museum of Art, Gift of John D. Rockefeller Jr., 1932 (32.143.14); *126.* Collection of Susan and John B. Magee; *128.* The Metropolitan Museum of Art, Rogers Fund 1938 (38.158.2a–g); *130.* Réunion des Musées Nationaux/Art Resource, NY; *133.* The Metropolitan Museum of Art, Bequest of William Christian Paul, 1930 (30.75.34); *136.* Courtesy Library of Congress; *139.* Arthur M. Sackler Gallery, Smithsonian Institution, Washington, D.C.; *143.* Courtesy Library of Congress; *168.* Courtesy of the Collection of Herbert Friedman; *172.* Courtesy Library of Congress; *194.* The Metropolitan Museum of Art/Art Resource, NY; *195.* The Metropolitan Museum of Art/Art Resource, NY; *204.* Courtesy Edith Vonnegut; *221.* Freer Gallery of Art, Smithsonian Institution, Washington, D.C.; *233.* Courtesy Library of Congress; *238.* Bridgeman Art Library, Musée Gustave Moreau, Paris; *252.* Scala/Art Resource, NY; *261.* Courtesy Board of Trustees, National Gallery of Art, Washington; *266.* Author's collection. Photo: Rand Hendrix/Richard Basch Studio; *272.* The Metropolitan Museum of Art, Seymour Fund, 1957 (57.52.1); *284.* Courtesy Library of Congress; *297.* Scala/Art Resource, NY.